Beyond These Walls

Beyond These Walls: The True Story of a Lost Child's Journey to a Whole Life

Rachel Gunner
Hanna Gabriele

Forward by Bernie Siegel

Author of *Love, Medicine & Miracles* and
365 Prescriptions for the Soul

Beyond These Walls: The True Story of a Lost Child's Journey to a Whole Life
Copyright © 2006 Rachel Gunner and Hanna Gabriele
Published by Argun Books Third printing revised
 All rights reserved. No part of this book may be reproduced (except for inclusion in reviews), disseminated or utilized in any form or by any means, electronic or mechanical, including photocopying, recording, or in any information storage and retrieval system, or on the Internet/World Wide Web without written permission from the author or publisher.
 "Authors' note: All events described in this book happened as remembered. Names have been changed to respect Ms.Gabriele's privacy."

Cover design by:
Powell Sheperd

Printed in the United States

1. Title 2. Author 3. Dissociative disorders – Treatment and Multiple Personality

Library of Congress Control Number: 2006921298
ISBN: 0-9777691-0-0

www.argunbooks.com

Dedication

For all lost children.
May there always be Hope.

Foreword

I believe we are all multiple personalities and when they, and all their needs are acknowledged, life becomes easier and ultimately more enjoyable through an understanding of one's life experience. And when one understands, one can forgive, love and be healed.

As I think about it, I literally ask myself WWLD whenever I am in a difficult situation. My inner personality then helps me to survive. Who is it? Lassie. The question is, *What Would Lassie Do?* He is one of my personalities and helps me to make wise decisions in stressful situations.

The unloved and abused can survive their past and their pain by finding the divine child that dwells within each of us. I see the effects upon the bodies of those whose pain is stored within their organs. We know this is true, because the donor's memories go with the organ when it is transplanted into the new recipient.

The role of personality we choose to play in life affects our health. An actor's blood chemistry and immune functions are altered by the role they play. It is amazing what one personality will experience and be afflicted by medically, that others have no problem with. So, the personality you become affects your emotional and physical well-being.

The loved have a lot of joyful children within, who experience themselves in the moment as a child or animal does, and make life interesting and creative. You can re-parent yourself and become the person you want to be. In so doing, you save your life by letting the untrue self and the things which are killing you, be eliminated from your life.

Hanna's children helped her survive their pain. Once hated, they found love, the weapon that kills with kindness, and life changed. When I asked anthropologist, Ashley Montagu for help, he said to me, "If you want to be more loving, behave as if you are." What we all need to do is to learn to love ourselves and then, practice and rehearse our loving, multiple personalities until we become the personality we want to be.

It is not about guilt, shame and blame, but about inspiration and the desire and intention that lives within us and our personalities.

Bernie Siegel, MD
  author of *Love, Medicine & Miracles* and *365 Prescriptions for the Soul.*

Rachel: Prologue

> *"We are all faced with a series of great opportunities brilliantly disguised as impossible situations."*
> **—C. Swindoll**

Why is this story different? Hanna says it's because of me—that I care; that I don't get angry if "they" call me late at night, that I'm honest and kind, make a real effort at understanding, and am pathologically optimistic. I say it's because Hanna is different. She has an intensity to learn, a yearning to heal, a survival instinct beyond natural strength. Of course, she's often thought that was a weakness and that she was a coward because she just didn't "get it over with" and die.

This is our story—our journey through hours, days, months and years of learning together, challenging each other, understanding one another, being scared, feeling hopeless, breaking down barriers and roadblocks, feeling hopeful and above all, discovering how love for, and faith in, another human being is the most powerful healer.

We write this book as a testimonial for a truly honest, helping relationship between a therapist and client. We hope that it will compel each mental health professional to examine his/her belief systems, ethics, reasons for being in the profession of healing, and interventions used in dealing with the difficult, resistant and desperate individual. It is not enough to know theories. I believe therapists have an obligation to search for and reach the core of a human being.

We hope everyone can learn from our mission: that love triumphs over abuse, determination over frustration, and life over death. Our words may bring tears to your eyes—tears of great pain for the loss of a childhood, and tears of great joy for a young woman's rebirth. We hope our honesty will help both professionals and laypersons grow to be better human beings. *Rachel Gunner*

Hanna: Prologue

"Imagination is the beginning of creation. We imagine what we desire; we will what we imagine; and at last, we create what we will."

—**George Bernard Shaw**

When Rachel asked me to write this book with her, I was floored to say the least. We had not been working together that long - about four and one-half weeks, and I had just tried to fire her so that I could kill myself with a clear conscience. She was not willing to let me go quietly. After talking to many of my personalities, she had just accepted that I had what is called, Dissociative Identity Disorder (DID). I was unaware of them, not willing to accept this diagnosis and be called crazy. I thought that Rachel was crazy. She had asked me to come to her office so that we could discuss my decision face-to-face. Of course, I did not see any reason for me to change my mind; I had no hope that anyone was capable of helping me.

We had been talking about our first impressions of each other when out of the blue, she made this suggestion for us to write a book together. My first thought was, "*WHAT*—*has this woman gone mad?"* But she was very serious and seemed excited by the idea, so I decided to give it serious consideration.

While she was trying to convince me to write this book with her, all I could think was: *"This is a woman that I have great respect for and she is asking **me** to do this with her. And after all that I have put her through."* So I said yes, if she learned how to play cribbage. She was shocked and elated.

I would not be writing this book if I did not have a deep and true respect for Rachel Gunner, the therapist and human being. Nor would I be writing this book if it were just for the two of us. It is for someone else, someone who is going through a private hell called DID; someone who is working with a person who has DID; someone who knows someone who is suffering from DID.

What makes this story different is that it is not only about the horrors that someone like me has lived through, it is more importantly about the process of *healing*. It is a dialogue between Rachel, as therapist and myself, the client. It is about finding that special place inside oneself and then learning to share it. It is about relearning life's most basic lessons so that one can grow. It is about learning the healing power of simple respect and love for oneself and another human being. It is about sharing hope and learning to live when what you want nothing more than anything, is to die. Above all, it is about learning to find joy in life.

May this book give you hope. *Hanna Gabriele*

List of Personalities in the "system" of Hanna Gabriele

(in alphabetical order)

1. Alfred (age unknown) (Male)—Chairman of the committee. He controlled my access to the children.
2. Andrea—(five years old) (Female) - Street kid who thought burning and cutting were good to do. She and Copula seemed to have had similar experiences.
3. Brian—(five years old) (Male) - Tigger's protector and interpreter.
4. Catherine Webber (twenty-eight years old) (Female) - Christian name of client.
5. Chrissy—(under five years old) (Female) - Believed the children were responsible for Mom's death.

6. Cobalt—(five years old) (Female) - The gang leader (under ten years old).
7. Copula—(age unknown) (Asexual) - Had unusual speech pattern where she didn't use verbs.
8. Death (fourteen years old) (Female)—Wrote poetry which described the pain of the abuse. She too, would burn the body. Suicide was her mission. As therapy progressed, I changed her name to Hanna to symbolize a new life.
9. Gabriele—(fourteen years old) (Female) - Created to act sane to the outside world. She was lonely and Randy was created to be her playmate.
10. Little Catherine—(four years old) (Female) - Had flashbacks of people (including Mom) dancing and cutting.
11. Mathew (fourteen years old) (Male)—Acted like a tough guy and also protected the children.
12. Mikhail (eighteen years old) (Male)—The one who read and took care of the family.
13. QED (age unknown) (Female)—The historian of the system. She rarely came out into the outside world.
14. Randy (eight years old) (Male)—Child alter. Acted as a spy for the "system."
15. Sandy—(five years old) (Female) - Was described by the others as the crazy one. She would try to fly by jumping out of windows.
16. Snotty-nose-brat—(under five years old) (Male) - Would wipe his nose on his shirtsleeve. He would stay up all night for fear of the mom coming to punish him.
17. Stephana—(fourteen years old) (Female) - Called herself a "bull dyke." Could fix anything, heal the

body, and became my right-hand man, telling me how the children were doing.
18. Storm (fourteen years old) (Female)—She was a mother figure who took care of the children in the "system."
19. Stupid—(under five years old) (Male) - Stuttered. He and others were scared of buildings.
20. TBF (seven years old) (Female)—Trial by Fire—She was always scared and would try to burn herself.
21. Tigger (two years old) (Female)—The firstborn and core of the system who could not speak. She screamed and would bite her arm. Death was created to rescue her.
22. TOB (fourteen years old) (Male)—The obnoxious bastard—he would cut the body.
23. William (fourteen years old) (Male)—His role was to protect the outside world from "them." He was a member of an internal committee which censored information given to me.

The Killers (Little is known about these children):

24. Cryin—(five years old) (Male) - An elective mute. Would write backwards to communicate.
25. Stephan (Male)
26. Oliver (Male)

Other Characters

1. The mom—Died when Catherine was a child.
2. Stuart—Mom's husband who abused Catherine (Gabriele, et al).

3. Jeffrey—A little boy that died in what appears to have been a satanic ritual in which Gabriele, et al, were involved.
4. Tom—Uncle who was abusive.
5. Lynn—Cousin.

Rachel: Chapter 1

Journey into the Unknown

"Could a greater miracle take place than for us to look through each other's eyes for an instant?"
—Henry David Thoreau

May 26, 1998, was a routine day at my office—a private psychotherapy practice. I had scheduled eight clients and had seen six already that day, when the call came into my answering machine with a simple message. "This is Catherine Weber. I'd like to talk to you about counseling. I work at DCC and have insurance." There was something about her voice that made me want to return her call immediately: a sense of desperation and fear. I wrote down the telephone number and called, feeling an urgency to respond to the fear. The message on the machine didn't indicate that a Catherine lived there and this upset me. Had I copied down the number wrong? I have a tendency to switch numbers and have often wondered if I were mildly dyslexic. I left a message anyway, and was reassured when she did call back and again left a message on my machine. She cleared up the confusion. Catherine was her Christian name, but

Gabriele was her chosen name, the name she wanted me to call her. Telephone tag can be very frustrating, especially in a clinical practice. She said to call her in the morning, because she was off to work on a night shift and wouldn't be home until late.

I pondered at why I hoped that we'd connect the next day. Again, something in her voice intrigued me; it was a combination of softness, yet strength. There was something unspoken that was more important than her actual words. I trust my intuitive sense, which often has no basis in logic. Indeed, it would become a major tool in the amazing journey that began at 8:30 the next morning.

A groggy voice answered, but when she heard who was calling, she seemed to awaken instantaneously. She began asking me some very pointed questions, something I respect in prospective clients. After all, each client needs to take charge of the therapeutic process in which he/she is engaging. She asked if I had my life together. I found that question most unusual, but again was impressed. Why should a client entrust his life, his inner most being, to just anyone? Having a degree doesn't ensure emotional togetherness, maturity, confidence, and the ability to explore issues without counter-transference and identification. I felt very comfortable in answering "yes." I shared a personal vignette about how when I was at a Family Therapy Symposium and how, when the presenter asked how many people came from "functional" families, I was the only therapist in the room who raised her hand. My family was an average, middle-class one of Orthodox Jewish background. This meant we followed many familial rituals and practices that kept our family bound by tradition.

My mother is a loving, nurturing woman who stopped work to raise her three children. I am the middle of three daughters. Because we were so different, my older sister and I weren't as close as I wished. School was very difficult for her, and expectations were lower for her to succeed. I don't think expectations were overtly expressed, but I always felt I needed to be perfect, which was "a curse," I tell my clients. My younger sister and I are similar in nature; I loved to dress like her when we were children. She too, is a therapist.

Dad was a hard-working man. We knew he was the disciplinarian, because Mom would tell us that Dad would deal with us when he got home. I only saw him lose his temper one time. In his discipline, he spoke to us firmly and with a tone of disappointment that was enough punishment for us to ensure we didn't break the rules again. He was a man of honor and integrity. We didn't learn to fear him, rather to respect him, and he taught me to respect others. Mom taught me the importance of being emotionally available and present. I believe that all these values my parents instilled in me have helped me as I practice my therapy. I have always known psychotherapy to be an art and a science. The science is the particular skills and techniques we learn: the ability to assess, diagnose, and create a treatment plan, the ability to set boundaries between client and therapist.

The art is the use of oneself combining the intuitive sense; the naturalness in expressing comfort and caring; the ability to relate to all people, no matter what their past includes; and the comfort in self-disclosure while knowing that boundaries are still operating from the science side.

Gabriele asked if I shocked easily. I wondered what was behind that question. What could she possibly tell me about herself that I haven't heard or dealt with in my twenty-five years as a therapist? Did she look strange? My background in rehabilitative medicine, working with disabled persons, has helped desensitize me to physical appearance. I don't shock easily.

She asked me if I worked with other women who were depressed. "Yes, many," I said. And she asked if I worked with child abuse issues. Again, I answered "yes," and added that in my experience, there was a correlation between women who have been abused as children and who are depressed as adults. The two questions that followed told me a great deal about her need to work with someone who was open and honest. I made an assumption (something that later she would always call me on), that she must have had some negative experiences with other mental health professionals. In this instance, it proved to be right. She asked me if I knew everything and could I admit it if I was wrong. I told her I definitely didn't know everything and that's what I loved about this profession. I am constantly growing and learning from each new client and new experience. I am very comfortable in being confronted by a client, and in admitting my own shortcomings or misunderstandings. I believe it takes a person of integrity and inner strength to continually reflect and re-examine one's actions, words and thoughts. I hope all my clients can learn that being open to one's vulnerabilities can help us grow.

And she wanted to know if I was comfortable working with lesbians. I replied honestly, "Yes, I have clients and friends who are gay, lesbian or bi-sexual; I do not judge them or differentiate between them. After all, we are all human beings." Although the teachings of Orthodox Jewry oppose my beliefs, I cannot accept that any human is less because of different sexual paths.

I knew I had passed her test when she asked if I was taking on any new clients. Her employee assistance counselor told her that she needed to see someone immediately or be put in the hospital. As luck would have it, I had just had a cancellation for the noon appointment that day. After thinking for a few seconds, she said she'd take it. I was pleased.

That afternoon I entered my waiting room to see a large, heavyset woman, short hair hidden beneath a baseball cap, wearing a loose shirt over baggy jeans. She looked anxious as many do awaiting their first meeting with "the therapist." I stretched my hand out to welcome her and introduce myself. Grease covered her hands; her car had broken down on route to my office. She didn't think that she would make the appointment. No matter how chaotic her life would get, Gabriele always tried to be on time.

She removed her cap and I glanced into her eyes. There was an almost angelic quality to them. They were quite a contrast to the rest of her physical appearance. Contradictions and polarities were to become themes I would need to explore. I kept this thought in the back of my mind. I asked her why she had come to counseling. She told me she had been feeling very depressed for the last five weeks. She wasn't eating and she laughed nervously when she said she'd actually lost thirty pounds. She wasn't sleeping and she was feeling suicidal. Her arms told a painful story. They were covered with healed and open wounds from cuts and burns. She was having a hard time concentrating at work. She was responsible for dealing with large equipment in a computer manufacturing plant, and was scared of hurting herself or others because of her present physical and emotional states.

The immediate problem, as she described it, was in not dealing well with the breakup of her relationship. "Not dealing" was too mild a description. Rather, she had become severely depressed, angry, unfocused at work, and even suicidal. She felt very confused, causing her to lose sight of things, of thoughts. She was afraid that she was going crazy. I listened intently. I didn't want to intervene and break her chain of thought, but I knew that I would need to return to her depression, confusion, memory lapses, and suicidal thoughts.

My strategy, in initial interviews, is to ask only general questions concerning a client's past. I believe that throughout the course of therapy, more will unfold to help me complete a more detailed map of his/her life. Also, it is important to stay more in the present, and to give a client the attention and understanding for any current discomfort that brought them to my office. I want each person to feel that they have been heard, and that there is a plan to help mitigate their pain or confusion.

The history that Gabriele shared was expressed matter-of-factly, as if she had rehearsed it and played it back many times for many people. There was no affect, no change in tone or expression, as the following information was laid out for me: She was a "civil servant's brat," having lived in a number of foreign countries and several states within the United States, arriving in Texas in the early 1980s, and for the most part, living here ever since. *I wondered how all these moves affected her. Was she able to have close friends?* Her mother had married seven times by the time that she died when Gabriele was a young child. *How did so many different men affect her concept of commitment and love?* She and her husbands had been physically and sexually abusive. *I know this history of abuse had to cause deep wounds. What did she do, and from whom did she receive comfort?* Her mother died in an accident near her home that Gabriele saw from her bedroom window. *How awful for her—or was it?* She never did see the body in the casket. This information would help explain the suspicion that she could still be alive. Gabriele never knew her biological dad. He had deserted the family when she was two years old. When her mother died, Gabriele was sent to live with relatives, who were also very abusive. *How much more could a child take?* She was in their home for two years until the Texas Department of Child Protective Services (CPS) took her away. *Why did they wait so long?* She lived in twenty-two foster homes in four years, as well as several residential treatment centers. She was very angry, often out of control. *How could she not be angry? What kind of life did she have? It was certainly not one of stability, security, or nurturance.* She had been in and out of outpatient and inpatient treatment, including state hospitals. She made it clear that she didn't trust therapists. *I couldn't blame her.* She needed to know what I would do if I knew she was going to hurt herself. She did not want to be hospitalized.

I respect my clients. I told her I did not have the power to stop her. She was an adult. It would be her decision, her choice, but I would feel sad if she chose that route. I did ask her if we could make a contract that she would not hurt herself while engaging in treatment with me. She could not agree to that, but said she would fire me first before following through on her suicide mission. It is very difficult for therapists not to feel that perhaps we had missed something that might have prevented a client's decision to die. Gabriele was trying to make it easier for me not to feel this pain; after all, she would no longer be my client. But I don't differentiate between client and person. Should suicide be her final destination, I would be deeply saddened, but I accepted her compromise. At least her firing me would be a warning of her decision. It would still give me a chance to convince her otherwise. Realistically, I knew that I might have little power to influence her choice, but I had never lost a client to suicide, and I had to believe I could stop that final act.

She proceeded to tell me that she had previously received a diagnosis of Dissociative Identity Disorder (DID), also known as multiple personality disorder (MPD), but didn't believe it. She wanted to know what I thought. I don't like to label clients and until I see evidence for any diagnosis, I make very tentative assessments. They are, however, subject to change as the therapeutic process unfolds. What I did not pick up on was the fact that she was testing my initial reaction to her disclosure of this very serious mental disability. I consciously chose to shift to another subject, leaving DID to be stored in my memory bank and my thoughts. Would I be able to handle the complexities of such a disorder? I believed so. I had treated others with multiple personalities. I found them fascinating and challenging rather than frightening, and although difficult and time-consuming, I learned more about the human mind and behavior from these persons than from any other experiences. I also believed in myself and in my ability to handle the unexpected. I was certainly going to be tested for how true this last statement really was.

By the end of our first meeting, I wrote this initial assessment of Gabriele, something clinicians use as the stepping-stone for further therapy.

Gabriele, (her Christian name being Catherine), appears in a deep depression, and not really understanding why. She seems to want to deal with some core issues, but fearful and mistrusting at the same time. She seems to have hidden very deep wounds, and may have protected them through disassociation. She does seem aware of her dominant self. Her past seems to haunt her at night, making sleep difficult. She seems to project an angry, masochistic, macho image, yet deep within lives a scared, lonely, and vulnerable child.

(I was to discover later that I had made a rather erroneous assumption.)

Therapists devise a treatment plan to guide them throughout the process towards the end goal, which is the improvement/diminishment of a client's symptoms and presenting problems. The assessment and plan of action continually change as more information is revealed. Here is what I jotted down as my preliminary short term/long term goals:

1) Build trust *(I did not know at this time how crucial this goal would become.)*

2) Explore past hurts and wounds *(I was unaware of the extensive pain I would uncover.)*

3) Help her heal from this emotional pain *(a question she would continually pose was, do you really think I can heal?)*

4) Stop the self-destructive thoughts and behaviors *(I knew that finding the core of these self-mutilating actions would become a journey unto itself. I was going to learn more than I ever imagined.)*

At the time of this writing, I knew only that this young woman was in deep pain and she was reaching out, somewhat cautiously, to find some way to stop the anguish. I did not know how complex she was, how guarded she really was, and how much more I would be learning in the days, weeks, and months ahead. But, I was ready to embark on this unknown road with her. I wanted to be the one professional that could help her heal. I looked into her eyes once again: so much depth, so much hurt, so needy.

And so a therapeutic relationship began. Over the next week, there were many phone calls from a frightened woman, wanting to burn herself, desperate to stop her mind from remembering horrors. She continued to not eat or sleep. She continued to cut and burn her arms, but was trying to stay alive. I began to feel that those wounds from her abusive past had infected her core, her self-concept. It was as if there was no "self," just a body that was carrying years of torture and punishment. There was no life. This scared me. How could I, one person, give to her a belief in life when every other person in her life seemed to take this away? I was getting bits and pieces of the childhood that was filled with sadness and fears, but it was not until the fourth session that she shared pictures: horrific, pencil drawings of abuse. She could not, and would not, talk about them. Although I tried to discover what was behind these graphic symbols, I didn't push. I knew that when the time was right, I would learn more, an avalanche of painful memories.

She did tell me how she had wished her mom dead. I told her this was something most children wish for if they are continually hurt. It's a way for the hurt to stop. But when her mom did die, she blamed herself. Could she ever forgive herself for having wished that? Forgiveness would become a major key in unlocking the doors to healing and change.

I knew we had much work to do to get beyond this pain. There was something though that continued to gnaw at me. I was missing a key element in understanding Gabriele. I knew from the literature and my professional experience that sexually abused children often withdraw, and as adults, they build a wall to protect themselves from closeness and potential hurt from others. There did seem to be a wall, a shield, between Gabriele and myself. It manifested itself in the lack of outward emotion as we talked, and in missing pieces of information. Why was she so self-abusive? What was happening late at night that caused such fears that she could not sleep? Why was she not able to digest any food? Why were there so many holes and unknowns?

During all these meetings, I still had seen no signs that anyone else existed but a vulnerable scared woman. I was right about one thing. She was scared and vulnerable, but I was soon to discover that she wasn't just one woman.

Hanna: Chapter 1

Journey into the Unknown

"We gain strength, courage and confidence by every experience in which we really stop to look fear in the face. We must do the things we think we cannot do."

—Eleanor Roosevelt

It is always hard to decide when you need help. Sometimes it can be even harder to ask someone you do not know for help. For three days I agonized over whether or not to call Rachel. I had gotten her name out of my employer's insurance provider book, but had been unable to bring myself to leave the all-important message on her machine. Finally, on May 26th I did, and in doing so, took the first step toward receiving help.

The reasons for my contacting her were fairly simple in my mind: I had been told by my Employee Assistance Program (EAP) counselor that I needed long-term treatment, and that I needed to go into the hospital, or that they were going to have to look into other "options." I knew what that meant: involuntary commitment to a psychiatric hospital on the basis that I was a danger to others and myself. I think I scared them, and their threats were starting to scare me.

On top of that, my manager at work was saying that she could tell that whatever was going on in my life was really starting to wear on me, and she was ready to give me a formal referral to EAP. When she found out that I had already contacted them, she simply said, "Do what you need to do to take care of yourself. You are a good member of my team and I want you here. Okay? If you need to take time off, do so. Just stay in contact with me so that I know what is going on. Your job will be here when you get back, but you need to do something and soon." She said this about a week before I called Rachel. Because of this conversation, I knew that I needed to act, and soon.

When I left that first message, I had already talked to four different therapists. I rejected them all for different reasons. They were not the kind of people that I could find myself working with, or I had a sneaky suspicion they would try to run my life from their office chair. Instead of simply answering my questions honestly and clearly, they would pose more questions or would preach to me: "Why haven't you... I think you should...." This was extremely frustrating and soured me to the whole idea of any form of counseling. But, for some unknown reason, I decided to try one last time, and so Rachel was the last one that I was going to call. I did not expect her to be able to help, and I did not think that I would even be able to work with her.

My life was a living hell, and I was sure that it was only going to get worse and never better. I was ready to go ahead and kill myself and get it over with. *Quit playing games and just do it,* my mind kept telling me. I had started looking into my life insurance policy. I had found out that it would pay out over $47,000 in benefits; twice that if I died "accidentally." So I did feel that some people would be better off money-wise. Not a good sign.

However, my EAP, my boss, and some friends kept telling me that I had to do something or they would. I hate threats. And it was my life. So finally I called and took a leap into the void of the unknown. Looking back, I'm surprised that I ever made that last call.

I have had many bad experiences with therapists, doctors, and hospitals. They would call me a "difficult" patient to treat, telling me that I was playing games and did not want to get better. They would give up on me after a short time. So I had no reason to trust that Rachel would be any different, but at the same time, I hoped that she would be. And, I was scared that she would be.

She called while I was in the shower. I was surprised that she returned my call so quickly. I had assumed that like most professionals, she would wait to return my call at the end of her working day. I was impressed by her responsiveness, so I left another message asking her to call in the morning, and went to work.

At 8:30 the next morning the telephone's ring woke me up. When I reached to answer, I heard, "Hi. This is Rachel Gunner. You asked me to call you." The voice was kind, gentle, and yet somewhat hyper. But there was something I liked about it; there was an undercurrent of strength in it.

Fully awake now, something inside told me to see what she was about. So, I asked a lot of the usual good questions (never go into something like this blind):

"Are you taking new clients?"

"Do you work with many women who are depressed?"

"Do you work with many women who have been abused?"

"What is your fee?

Will you take my insurance?" This is always good to know, because money does matter.

Rachel answered the questions quickly and with confidence, so I asked the other questions that were important to me. "Do you have your own life in order?" I asked, thinking, *I don't want another fucked-up and crazy therapist.* She told me about going to a conference and the presenter asking how many of the people there came from *functional* families. She was the only one to raise her hand. *This is new,* I thought, *most therapists go into the field to fix themselves.* "Do you work with many lesbians, or would this be a problem for you?" I asked next. I was living a lesbian lifestyle at the time and didn't want to work with anyone who was homophobic and believed that they needed to *fix* that part of me. If I was going to change my sexual orientation, I wanted to do so because I wanted it changed, and not because someone else thought that I needed, or had to be, straight.

There was laughter at first, and then Rachel told me that she works with lesbians and no, it was not a problem for her unless it was a problem for me. *Good Answer. Damn. Next question.* I asked her if she had all the answers to everything, or could she admit when she did not know or was wrong. I was thinking, *I hate people who think they know everything and are perfect. Or worse, make assumptions.* No, she did not know everything she replied; she could admit when she was wrong and liked to learn about what she did not know. *Another good answer. Double damn. Now what?*

I had to make a choice about seeing her even once and was thinking, *What have I got to lose? This woman sounds like she has got her shit together, knows her stuff, and is not a band-wagon-jumper. And I almost think I like her. What the hell?* So I asked if she had any appointments that were open, thinking she would probably have something within the next week. She offered me an appointment for noon *th*at day.

Oh God - what am I getting into? And what is this woman's game? my mind screamed. "Okay. I'll take it," I answered instead, in a cold sweat.

I walked into Rachel's office at 11:42 a.m. and wanted to run right back out. *What the hell were you thinking? Leave now. Go get a cold drink and you can always call someone else later—it's no big deal. Better yet, suicide is not that bad. Leave now. Go kill myself - no big loss for the world. Watch this woman turn out to be a nightmare of a therapist. And God, how am I going to explain what the hell is going on when I don't even know?* In addition to arguing with myself, I was trying to figure out how I was going to keep my one 1:00 p.m. appointment with EAP in northwest Austin, which I had been unable to cancel, when I was all the way in south Austin and it was noon.

All of this was racing through my mind and I had just decided to leave when in walked this woman: small, well-dressed, tanned, and with the look of someone with an excessive amount of energy. "You must be Gabriele. I'm Rachel Gunner." Out comes her hand. I don't really like to be touched and I had grease all over my hands (my car decided to break down on the way there and I thought this was a good excuse), so I told her that I did not want to shake her hand. But she seemed unconcerned with the grease and looked like she was determined to shake hands, so I took her hand. It was soft, but firm. Always a good sign. Then she made eye contact: kind, clear, intelligent eyes. Another good sign.

She asked me to fill out some paperwork and the whole time my head was screaming and roaring, *RUN! RUN NOW!* But I stayed.

Sitting on the couch, I wondered what to say and how to explain what was going on so that she could understand, and I could get it out of my head. I answered her questions and then decided that honesty was the best policy. So I told her, "I'm very suicidal and depressed. I'm not eating or sleeping, and my EAP wants me in the stupid hospital. I just broke up with my lover and that is not going very well. I'm concerned about my job and money. Frankly, I don't know what to do. I have not had very good luck with other therapists and by the way, I have this old diagnosis of DID that I think is pure bullshit. What do you think of all that?"

Quiet. Calm. "I make up my own mind and I hate labels," she responded firmly.

I like this woman…maybe, I heard.

She asked me not to hurt myself while in therapy with her. I wanted to think about it and changed the subject, so I ask if she believed in DID. *What the hell are you thinking?*

She did, and was treating someone with it who was doing very well. *Oh, fuck me! Now what? We're in for it now, asshole*, roared in my head. I asked if she was going to give me that label.

"No. Do you think it is true?" Her voice was neutral.

"No. I'm not crazy. Are you going to call the cops on me if I'm going to kill myself?"

"No," she answered firmly.

Yea, right, the roar said.

"Are you going to make me go into the hospital if I don't want to?"

"No, that is your choice, and I don't like hospitals anyway," she said, again with that firm tone of voice.

This woman makes up her own mind. Thank God, my mind screamed. *But, we'll have to see.*

I asked some more questions about what she meant by "hurting myself." I wanted to find out if she was going to freak out, panic, and refuse to work with me if I did hurt myself. She seemed to be more concerned with my actually dying, so I decided that I could make a compromise, but with one condition: "Okay, before I kill myself, I will fire you, as long as you promise you will not try to stop me." *Well, it is a compromise.*

She was quiet for a moment, then said, "I'm not God. Still, I want you to talk to me first. Don't just leave a message on my answering machine and then do something anyway. I want to talk to you before you do *anything*."

"Deal," I responded. *We'll see if you keep your word,* the roaring said. And then I asked, "How often do you think you will need to see me?"

"Once a week," she answered, sounding quite confident.

At the end of that first session, I had many doubts and questions in my mind as I drove like mad to my EAP appointment: *I'm going to get screwed again, I just know it. Why did I have to mention DID to her? And what if something happens and she ends up hating me? How can I even explain that half the time I am not sure what in the world is happening?*

I got to my appointment thirty minutes late. The hopelessness that I was feeling was overwhelming, and I knew that I had decided to give up. I just didn't see any way out of the pain and anguish I was feeling. In this state of mind, I told my EAP counselor that I wasn't sure if I could work with Rachel or anyone else. "I'm not sure that it's worth it," I told her.

Her response was predictable. "You really need to see a therapist for long-term treatment, and moreover, I want you to find a psychiatrist so that you can get started on some form of medication for your depression, or you need to go into the hospital." She gave me the name of another therapist that she thought might be able to work with me. "Call her…today. She is waiting for your call."

I took the name and phone number, but knew that I wouldn't call. What was the point?

I finally arrived at work and decided to leave a message on Rachel's machine that I had changed my mind and thank for her time, but I didn't think I could work with her. But instead, Rachel answered the phone. *Damn. Now what are we going to do?* I heard myself ask her to talk to my EAP. *What the fuck are you saying?*

"I'm surprised that you'd allow two therapists to talk about you and what is going on, since you are into control so much," she responded, after I told her whom to contact.

I was taken aback, not hurt, just surprised at the statement. *How very little you know about control,* a voice said. I decided not to respond.

I told her again that I was not DID. *After all, the voices were not real - right?* I did not want her to explore the issue. I was terrified that she would, and that she'd decide I was crazy.

Rachel told me that she had no intention of doing any digging or pushing, and that anything I talked about was my choice. I didn't believe her.

I hung up. It was time for my shift to start. All during that ten-hour shift, I felt like the world was about to end, with me at ground zero.

Maybe I should give a little history about myself so you can understand my feelings about all this. I had gotten a diagnosis of Dissociative Identity Disorder (DID) back in 1991 when it was called Multiple Personality Disorder (MPD). I did not believe I had MPD, nor did I feel that it was ever fully explained to me why there was reason to believe that I did. The "therapy" for it went very badly, and I felt that the therapists and doctors were telling me how I had been abused in my childhood instead of letting me tell them.

Every time I tried to talk about the things I felt were important, I was told that these issues needed to be dealt with later and that I needed to "stick to the therapeutic program," or have my therapy "terminated." They also threatened to commit me to a state hospital where I would most likely remain indefinitely, because that was where people were sent if they did not "cooperate with the program." I became fearful of standing up for myself. I began to feel completely powerless and became angry, because I felt like I was being treated like an animal. I felt that no one had a vested interest in me as a human being.

In addition, everything I had read on the subject of DID never seemed to fit who I was. I decided to get on with things and let that part of my life stay in the grave, so to speak. I fired my therapist and stopped taking all medications. I also vowed that I would never again allow myself to be hospitalized, nor would I ever see a therapist again. So what if I did not remember everything or if I felt like I lived in two worlds? Everyone has bad days, right?

Then about a month or so before I called Rachel, I started to feel that I was no longer in control of anything. I started to *lose* large chunks of time. I tried to convince myself that time had never meant anything anyway, but I could not continue to explain it away. I was forgetting things that happened, and being told that I had done things I didn't remember doing.

I also felt like there was this you/us mentality in my mind and I was hearing conversations that I never heard before - conversations about me and getting rid of me. There were comments about things that were going on, that were directed toward me, or about how to deal with them. And there was this voice that was saying, "If you don't do it - I will!" The more I tried to keep it quiet, the louder it got.

I started burning myself and could not remember doing it. I had not hurt myself in over two years, so what the hell was going on? On top of that, I wanted to pour gasoline over myself and light it, because I had this belief that I needed to be badly punished because I had done something very wrong, and it would not go away. I had not told anyone about this. I was scared that I would be locked up or told that I was crazy if I said anything.

I was not eating very well and had lost over forty pounds in a few months. I felt like I did not deserve to eat. I was getting only about three hours of sleep a night and it was full of nightmares, but I felt I did not deserve to sleep anyway.

Everything was totally unreal to me. I always had this notion, but now it was getting really bad, to the point that, to me, my life was just a bad dream.

I had to be going crazy - I was sure everyone else saw it too, and they were just being nice and not saying it to my face. I just kept telling myself, *it couldn't possibly get any worse, right*?

My next appointment with Rachel was June 1st, and during the interim week, I had been drawing a lot of pictures about things that I was seeing in my mind whenever I tried to sleep. I asked Rachel if she wanted to see them and she said, "Of course, bring them in." So I did.

I handed her about three sheets of paper with drawings of "flashes," hoping that she would not ask any questions about them. Instead, she started asking what had happened. *Oh hell.*

"They're not that important, they're just stupid pictures." I went to great lengths to avoid making eye contact with Rachel. The good thing about wearing a cap is that you can always hide under it. However, I could hear Rachel turning the pages around, looking at them.

"It would help if I knew what was going on. It looks like someone is torturing you in this one," she commented, referring to one of the drawings.

My mind just started to roar and I felt like I was going to pass out. *What the fuck were we thinking bringing this shit to her? She will never believe us! She is going to fucking run and that will be entirely your fault! I was not supposed to tell. Burn! Burn! Burn!* But, I could not say anything. If I talked, I would die. If I did not talk, I knew I was going to die. I was frozen with fear.

I felt a scream coming up from deep inside me and next thing I knew, the session was ending and she was telling me that she would see me the following week. I got up, feeling like a complete fool, and went home. I just felt like I was lying to Rachel about the things that were going on with me and how I was doing. I did not feel like I was "allowed" to let her into my world. I was becoming more and more frustrated with myself, and I was also becoming more and more hopeless. And I was sick and tired of listening to those damn voices! Why wouldn't they just leave me alone? It was the voices that were enforcing some hidden "rule" about not talking or telling.

My despair was quickly getting the best of me. I could no longer handle what was happening in my inner world, but felt trapped by my own mistrust of Rachel and myself. Death seemed my only option, but in order to be true to my word, I needed to call Rachel, tell her what I was going to do, and fire her. I found myself dialing her number, but I never talked to her.

Rachel: Chapter 2

The Cast of Characters

"Coming together is the beginning. Keeping together is progress. Working together is success."
—**Henry Ford**

On June 6, 1998, I received a crucial call. I was at home, watching my thirteen-year-old daughter and her best friend gleefully playing in the pool. The contrast between their pure joy, their innocence and their freedom, with the anguish of the little boy on the other end of the line, was so apparent. He told me his name was Randy. He was eight years old. He was very worried that I was going to be mad at him because of what he was going to tell me. He then blurted out, "Gabriele hasn't been honest with you. There are 'we' people. We've met, but we don't like each other." I asked for the names of these "people."

He didn't understand why I wanted to know and seemed very hesitant to tell me. I shared with him that I like to address people by name, out of respect, and that if I was going to be able to help each of them, I needed to know to whom I was speaking. I was careful to tune into Randy's chronological age, so I changed my tone and my choice of words, so that he would understand. He seemed scared as he shared more, but told me he would run fast if someone were going to hurt him. Randy told me he was the spy. He also told me that Mikhail was going to be angry with him for telling. At this point, I did not understand why. He continued to say that Mikhail was the smart one. He read a lot and took care of the money. He was the oldest one, eighteen years old. He ran through names of others, but at this time, I became overwhelmed and confused. It took several weeks to sort out who each personality was, and his/her particular pain and way of coping.

As days and weeks progressed, Randy became more courageous in calling and sharing information about Gabriele and the others. He told me about a little girl named TBF. He told me she was the killer. She was only seven years old and used to be a safe personality, until "that psychiatrist" hypnotized her and put her away, alone on a desert island. She was scared and wanted to die. She burned so she could kill Gabriele, and then she would be in control and could die.

TBF stands for Trial by Fire, a significant ritual we were all going to learn about. The mother taught her to burn for screaming. She burned herself now to make "things" stop so she could sleep. TBF still heard the mom's voice. She didn't believe the mom was dead, and if she screamed or cried, she would be hurt. In one of my first sessions with TBF, she drew horrific pictures of what the mom would do to her, including burning in the vaginal area. It was no wonder this child wanted to die, and certainly could not trust an adult.

My intuition, professional experience, and years of being a mother, told me that TBF would require great comfort and nurturing from me, "a big person", as I was to be called by all the children. I needed to reassure her that crying was allowed and she was now safe. The word safe, which should be a basic need that all children have met, was a concept unfamiliar to TBF. Being hurt, rejected, abandoned, and alone were the only experiences she expected to have. I needed to remind myself that what I was offering, a safe haven to unleash extreme emotional pain and heinous occurrences, was not that easy to accept. The unknown can be as scary as the known.

Storm was the one who took care of the "little ones." Because of this fear of the unknown, it was understandable that Storm would need to know who I was. Although only fourteen, she acted like a mother. She made it clear that she didn't like to come out and deal with people on the outside, but needed to know for herself, who I was. She told me she should only be called upon if it was a real emergency, but she would do her best to help out at that time. I thanked her for looking after the children. I knew how important it was that she trusted in me and that she be my ally in this process.

There were many times Storm couldn't watch over everyone, especially Randy. He was always moving in and out, trying to run from danger or trying to keep everyone from killing themselves. Unlike TBF, Randy did not want to die. He was always scared of being beaten up, especially by Mathew, a fourteen-year-old, who sounded like a tough guy. I didn't get to speak to or see Mathew often. What I learned was that although he did seem to enjoy picking on Randy and the other children, he would be the first to protect them against anyone outside the body. I was a person outside the body whom he wasn't sure of. I was told by QED that Mathew was into mind games to figure out what a person was about. I knew he would be difficult to enlist, because of a condescending attitude that I heard in his voice, but I needed his support to ensure that the therapeutic process would move forward.

QED saw herself as the historian of this "system," as she called it. She saw herself as detached from all of them; their mother was not her mother. She made it very clear from the beginning that there was no reason for me to meet her, but that she would come out to help me. And she did. She sent a letter to me (though I did not know who had written it), giving me data on each of the main personalities. This was invaluable in helping me sort them out and understand their distinct selves. Her goal was for the truth to be known, meaning that what went on inside would finally come out. She helped me understand how the use of some words, like "later," had no meaning, because time had no meaning. When I felt lost and powerless in stopping the system's self-destruction, she stood behind me, pushing me to keep reaching until I broke down walls. She was aware that to be real, meant to feel, and as long as they all hid behind walls, feelings would remain hidden. Of course, once feelings did begin to emerge, the system became chaotic for a while, and QED wondered if we were both expecting too much, too soon. I felt confident that as long as feelings were expressed in a safe environment, this track was one I needed to forge on.

On July 3, 1998, at 1:30 a.m., the phone woke me from a deep sleep. I heard painful crying; it was Randy. He was at a gasoline station in a great panic that "she" was going to "kill us." I was about to encounter a significant personality who would join us on our journey.

"She" was called Death. She was very angry. She got on the phone and said, "I warned you. You never had a chance." I wasn't sure what she meant, but wondered if she was testing my willingness to continue therapy, even if it was going to really get tough. I let her speak, all the while responding in a calm voice, trying to reassure her that I was here for her. She told me she didn't think she was real, and didn't understand why I wanted to help. Why did I care? These questions would be reiterated many times during the months ahead of us. She asked me if I knew who had written the poetry, (I had been given some of the most powerful poems I had ever read, by whom I thought was Gabriele, during one of the first sessions). In a timid voice, she told me that it was she who had written them. At that moment, I knew that beneath that façade of wanting to die, was a strong will searching for reasons to live.

She shared with me some of the abuse she had endured from the mom, and stepdads, and how her bed was like a torture chamber. She still heard Mom's voice every night. I later learned that Death wasn't the only one who bore the brunt of the earliest recollections of the torture. My initial assessment of her was that she covered up her tears with anger, that burning was the only way she knew to rid herself of her pain, and that she was petrified of feeling. I knew that one of my greatest challenges would be reaching to the core of her being in hopes of uncovering the secrets hidden inside her for years.

I met with TOB, a nickname for The Obnoxious Bastard, during another one of Randy's calls for help. I initially felt some fear, not only from his gruff voice, but he was steadfast in his belief that no one could stop him from cutting the body. His initial words to me were, "I don't come out to talk to people. I'm not a burner; I slice and dice. Pain goes when blood flows."

I tried not to show him my fear or give him the power to intimidate me. Instead, I asked him where he got his name. He told me, "That woman gave it to me. She was my mother."

I asked him, "How old are you?"

"Fourteen."

In the beginning, I felt that he and I would have power struggles. He refused to let me in. Thankfully, QED helped me learn that beneath the external cover of a tough teen was a self-effacing little boy. To reach him, I would remind myself that his harshness was his protection against great pain. He was understandably mistrusting and would ask me from time to time if I thought he was yanking my chain. I never did think that. I learned from Death that it was TOB that had done a lot of drugs and a few months into our process together, he bought a gun off the streets. I knew that he saw himself as evil and was just living out the self-fulfilling prophecy. He believed that the evil was on the inside and if he cut deep enough, that it would all flow out. He also believed that dying would be good, because then the evil would go away.

My belief system is that each individual has a right to be respected, and I was going to find a way to show TOB that even he could be given respect. I also learned that he was able to detach himself from physical pain. This awareness became most valuable in my understanding of the mind/body disconnection in multiple personalities.

I met William the evening after my first visit with TOB. William did not want to let TOB out for fear that he would hurt me. William's role was to protect the outside world from "them." He told me that he would have to make a deal with "them" first. This concept of a deal was one that was going to help me to build trust with all of them over the coming weeks. I did not have much contact with him for many weeks, that is until some barriers seemed to be blocking my interventions. I learned that there was an internal committee responsible for censoring information given to the outside world, namely, me. William was one of the members of this committee. He didn't particularly like this job, but didn't seem to feel he had a choice whether to belong to the committee or not. Alfred was the chairman, and made it very clear to me that he would make the decision that would give me access to "the little ones." He projected an authoritarian, hostile and defiant image. I knew that he took his role seriously, and strategically decided not to enter a power struggle with him. Instead, I tried to show him I respected his position and would adhere to his rules. It seemed to me that because of this, he backed down and let me meet more of the children.

One of them was the key to unlocking the deepest wounds and the creator of Death. Her name was Tigger. She was the firstborn. I met her by accident one day in my office while working with Death. Suddenly, the young woman in front of me transformed into a little girl who began rocking and biting on her arm. She whispered so quietly that I could barely make out a sound. The others heard her constant screaming. She was the first to be abused by the mother, and only wanted to die. The formidable task in working with her was going to be to help her understand that in the reality of today, the mother was dead. She was two years old and still lived in her world where the mother was still alive and able to hurt her. That was when Death took over. It became clearer to me that they believed the only way to release them from their pain, was to die. Suicide became Death's mission. As therapy would progress, she would ask me, "If I don't die, then what will happen to me?"

Brian was Tigger's protector and interpreter. He would come out after she had surfaced to make sure she was safe, and also to help me understand what she had said.

The other children were not as open with me. I met Little Catherine one evening when Death was having flashbacks of something, but she did not know of what. She kept seeing red. Suddenly, a whispery voice got on the phone. She wasn't sure that she was allowed to talk to me. I asked her if she knew Randy. When she said yes, I encouraged her to ask him if I was someone that she could trust. She did, and after I was given his approval, this seemed to allay her anxiety. She told me about an event that happened one dark night. Her voice became very inaudible as she described the mom and others, dancing, laughing, and cutting each other. She told me how TOB grabbed one of the knives. It seemed that at this moment, the recollection of the incident became overwhelming and she called upon Randy to take her to a safer place. I learned from this interaction that many of the children were very close and protective of the others. I would use this awareness to help me in working with some of the children who were less cooperative. My strategy would be to have all the alters know each other, and work toward a common goal, which was life.

My hope in meeting this goal would be dashed many times, and my strategy tested, because of a group of children known as the "killers." No one wanted me to meet them, because they feared that I would be hurt by them. Perhaps I was naïve, but I never feared that. They did frustrate me, and I made one of my biggest judgment errors that almost destroyed Gabriele. I mentioned to one of the alters that these kids needed to leave and I called them ignorant.

I was the ignorant one. I did not see beyond their actions to the reasons that they existed in the first place, which was to carry out the belief that they were bad. I was only acting as another big person who was putting them down. QED came to my rescue and reminded me that they were just children. I knew that before I could ever enlist their confidence in me, I would need to apologize for my own behavior.

What made it so difficult to see them as young was the great power and influence they seemed to have on the others. I learned that they were carrying out a message that they had received from the mom, being, "You must never tell. No one will believe you anyway. They will think you are crazy." As I got closer to the others, the killers seemed to gain strength and fight my efforts. They seemed to target Gabriele, who was the most vulnerable and the weakest link in the chain. As TOB and Death began to work harder with me, Gabriele became more self-destructive. The killers were giving her the directives. In desperation, I called upon Mathew, who, I had been told by QED, had once been one of these killers. Mathew let me into their world, the world of the secret keepers. He told me that to tell was treason. That is why he would hurt Randy, because he was telling me too much.

Andrea seemed to believe that they killed the mother and therefore, they deserved to die. This belief seemed to stem from the statement that the mother made to them, "If you tell, you will die, or I will die." Death had tried confiding in a teacher and it was soon after that, the mother died in the fatal car crash. My understanding of the child's thinking, that it is literal and concrete, helped me comprehend that in the child's mind, there became a direct correlation and direct consequence: telling equals death. I now was cognizant as to why killing themselves became their only purpose in life. As I would hear many times from many of them, "Rachel, it's about punishment."

Stupid, her nickname given by the mother because she stuttered, told me that they hated buildings. Buildings were where bad things happened. Beds were in buildings and people could be kept in the dark. Again, I was given valuable insights into their deepest horrors, and why sleep was so frightening.

Snotty-Nose-Brat, named because he used his shirtsleeve to wipe his nose, would also stay up all night. Night was when the "mother" would come for him, especially if he had not listened to her. Even when the mother had died, he would see her in the night and hear her telling him, "You know better."

Cobalt was one of the most difficult kids to work with. She was about eleven years old, and definitely projected the gang leader image. She would have no part in negotiating with me. As she said at our first meeting, "Why should we change our minds?" Mathew was even scared of her. I knew that another challenge ahead was to find a way to reach her.

Copula was an unusual alter because of her speech patterns. She did not use verb phrases, omitting the auxiliary verbs. For example, she would say, "The body bad, the body die." She also did not use prepositions, "Why you talk TOB?" This helped remind me that again, I was dealing with a small child whose only belief was her badness. How could I turn that thought process around? She became an ally after I passed the "truth test." She helped me understand Sandy. Few of the alters knew Sandy. What they did know, was that she was crazy. She would try to fly by jumping out of windows. She spoke in whispers. She believed the mother was always beside her, telling her she was bad and deserving to be punished. As therapy evolved, and I began dealing with all their fears in confronting their anger towards the mother, Sandy began sabotaging the system. This little girl had great power in her anguish and the ability to confuse.

Stephan, Oliver and Cryin were other personalities labeled "the killers." Death didn't want them to meet me because she was afraid that they could hurt me as they had others; she believed that they were the evil part of the system. But no one bothered to understand them and find out if that was true. They were either "sent away" or locked up. I knew I would have to be the one to let them out. Cryin was most difficult to work with because he was an "elective mute." My theory as to why he chose not to speak was that when he had spoken out, he had probably been hurt and punished. I learned I was right when I was given a note written by Cryin, which looked like gibberish, but when read in a mirror, made so much sense. "You tell, you die." Why would anyone want to talk and live with that threat?

All these "killers" were merely small children who were scared of living. How could I be scared of them knowing that they were only trying to survive against what they believed to be hostile forces in the outside world? I vowed to myself that I would not succumb to their aggressive acts by reacting in anger and frustration. I wasn't always successful.

I don't know if I could have learned as much, had as much stamina, or believed I was on the right track, if it were not for Stephana. Although only fourteen years old, she was considered a protector and she projected a strong, assertive self, and liked to call herself a "Bull Dyke." She had a wild side, liking to go to bars, have casual sex, and would often get into fistfights with others outside the system. She also was very handy around the house, fixing cars, building things, and was always trying to mend the damages to the body. I considered her "my right-hand man." She would tell me how Death was feeling and how the little ones were doing, and when TOB cut, she would stop the bleeding. When I got an infection, she told me how to cleanse it. She was quite remarkable. I told her that she needed to go to medical school. She helped me in my efforts and reinforced them. When I became discouraged, she told me not to give up. She wanted to live.

What was most disconcerting was my misunderstanding of Gabriele's being. My assumption was she was the main person, host or the one who experienced the initial pain and trauma, and from whom the many others (often called alters) were created. Erroneous assumptions distorted my ability to truly understand the complexity of the individual called Gabriele. Although Gabriele was the person who called for help, and the first person that I met, the others would take over as I delved deeper into their past. Gabriele was created to be the person who could act sane to the outside world. She was the conduit for all other personalities. She was scared of being crazy and the more the others talked to me, the more she disappeared. As she said, "It's like a war going on inside. You don't know what it's like to hear constant roaring."

She had called me because she wanted help with her depression, and not sleeping or eating, but really didn't want all of "them" to come out. That's why she didn't want me to use hypnosis. A previous psychiatrist had done this and Gabriele just went away. She didn't want to believe anyone else within her was real. She was the one who truly did not understand Disassociative Identity Disorder. I realized that although Gabriele portrayed an independent, competent aura, she was just another child within a woman's body, who was scared, confused, feeling out of control, and mistrusting of a new adult entering their lives.

I became aware that disassociation was increasing in frequency and intensity as the process ensued. I believed that it was necessary to reach the root causes. However, in doing so, great destabilization was occurring. The roaring was becoming unbearable. I did not understand that their inner torment was Tigger's screaming, Randy's crying, and constant arguing amongst the many personalities, whether to live or die.

Remembering that Gabriele was unaware of all these personalities, it was not surprising that she was experiencing more blank moments. She wrote me the following letter:

Rachel,

I cannot seem to get you to understand what I am going through, and I don't know how to explain it. I feel like I am going insane and there is nothing I can do to stop it. You tell me about these people or parts that you talk to, and all I can think to myself is that I am completely nuts. Then I never seem to finish a conversation with you. I always end up thinking that something happened and you are angry with me. You tell me about these little kids. I don't remember, and I don't like it. I am scared that I have hurt someone or done something wrong. And it makes me feel CRAZY! I don't know if I can keep going this way, and all I can think about is giving up. If that makes me a chicken shit, so be it. I think that if I made up all these people, then that was a chicken shit thing to do too. I don't care what happened. I should have just fucking dealt with it. I just want things to stop or go away. I should be strong enough to

deal with all of this, so why can't I? I want you to understand that I am going to explode and I don't know what to do to stop it. Maybe I am a fucking failure and no one wants to be honest and JUST TELL ME!
Gabriele

With all these personalities coming to the forefront, crescendoing with this desperate plea, I know most therapists would have begun to pull back. After all, it was like adding twenty more people to an existing caseload. Insurance companies certainly were not going to cover the extra hours of therapy necessary to meet with each of these personalities. Many of my colleagues expressed their opinions on working with the multiples, which could be summed up in a word: DON'T I disagreed vehemently with them. How could I not? To help an individual become whole was my most important goal as a professional. More valuable than monetary remuneration, was the deep sense of satisfaction and joy in giving an individual something he/she had never received before, a chance at finding happiness. I have always believed in the phrase, "Giving and receiving are the same." To give to Gabriele and the others, (whom I have coined for the purposes of this book, Gabriele, et al), was a gift to myself. Perhaps I could make a difference when all others had failed. I am not an arrogant person who believes she knows more than others, but I am determined to succeed. I do feel confident in who I am and what I do. I have always been called an optimist, but I am also a realist. Working with multiple personalities is overwhelming, exhausting, and trying, but I was willing to begin this journey in the unknown of this disorder.

Throughout this process, I did challenge my own optimism with the realities of a twenty-eight-year-old tortured, fragmented soul, who believed death was better than life.

And so I was not surprised, but rather pained, when on the afternoon of July 1, 1998, I received the dreaded call. She told me that I was fired. I knew that meant that she was ready to end her life. Could she really follow through with that decision? Would she be the first client I would lose? I knew I couldn't show her my own fears, rather this was a time she needed to know someone was calm, strong and confident in the face of her craziness. I needed her to know that I could help her gain control of her life, but I also knew that I might not be successful. As coincidence, luck or destiny would have it, I had just received a cancellation freeing up an hour. I told her that I wanted to see her now! She agreed to come into my office. Between the time I replaced the receiver of the phone and the time she arrived (about 20 minutes), all I could do was pray. I asked the greater power above to guide me and to give me the wisdom to handle this situation in the right way.

When we saw each other, I looked into her eyes and without thought, blurted out, "We need to write a book together!"

Hanna: Chapter 2

The Cast of Characters

"Leave no one out of the big picture. Involve everyone in everything of any consequence to all of you."

—**Tom Peters**

Randy called and talked to Rachel the day before Gabriele's twenty-eighth birthday. He was upset that Gabriele was planning to kill herself and Randy knew that if Gabriele died, he would die too. He did not want to die. Although he knew that something was very wrong, he did not completely understand what exactly was happening and why everyone was so upset. Randy had been listening to the internal conversations that the rest of us had been having, and he knew that there was a lot of fighting and arguing among those of us who were older. He also knew that some of us, though at the time he did not know exactly who, were pushing Gabriele to kill herself. He believed that was wrong and he wanted it to stop, but he did not know how to stop it himself. As he listened and watched what the rest of us were doing and saying, he was becoming more frightened that Gabriele, or someone else, was going to do something to harm the body. In addition, he had been watching Rachel, decided that she was okay for a big person, and he liked her.

He wanted to talk to Rachel, but he did not know her phone number. He inquisitively watched Gabriele dial Rachel's phone number and pushed out past her (something only Randy knew how to do). Maybe Rachel can help and maybe she will listen, he thought, as he waited for someone to answer the phone. He knew that he was taking a chance, but more than that, he knew that he was breaking the rules. If he got caught, he would be in a lot of trouble. He decided to be very quiet while he was talking to Rachel.

When Rachel got on the phone, Randy did not know how to explain to her exactly who he was and what was going on, but he knew that he needed to try. As he began to talk to her, he felt unsure if she believed him. More than that, he was afraid that Rachel would be mad because he was telling her that she was talking to someone that lived inside of Gabriele. Randy feared that Rachel could not understand that, but Rachel did understand and was not angry. Randy was relieved, because one of his biggest fears was that someone would be angry with him or worse, would not like him. And he wanted more than anything for people to like him.

Because of all his fears and concerns, he decided to ask Mikhail for help. Since Mikhail was eighteen years old, Randy assumed that he would know what to do. Mikhail could be gruff and act like he did not care, but he wanted to get back to work, which he couldn't do as long as Gabriele and the others were suicidal and not doing well. Working at DCC was his job more than Gabriele's, and he was determined not to lose it.

"Just tell her the truth. She will listen or not, but worry about that later," Mikhail told Randy. "And don't tell her about me." That was Mikhail's one condition if Randy wanted his help. But Mikhail was not the only one that did not want Rachel to know his name. None of us were keen on the idea of Rachel finding out exactly who we were. All of us believed that if anyone on the outside, especially a big person, knew a name, that they would have power over him/her. In addition, we did not like to be asked how we got our names. It was hard to explain and for some of us, the circumstances surrounding our naming were painful and embarrassing, or we simply did not know.

That is why when Rachel asked Randy for some of our names, instead he told her, "There are lots of us." When she told him how she liked to address people by their names, he decided she needed to know them all to understand the inside personalities. But in his haste, he broke his word and gave her Mikhail's name too. That really made Mikhail mad.

Randy told her that she had not been talking to just Gabriele, but instead, had been talking to several of us, including a small child named TBF. He explained that she was the one that had been doing most of the burning and that she wanted to die. Randy knew that TBF had been hurt by a lot of big people, including the mom. He also wanted Rachel to know that TBF was not bad, and that she used to be his friend. He told Rachel that he would help her with TBF, but first he needed to know if Rachel was going to hurt her. He told Rachel about TBF being left on a desert island, a place where a psychiatrist had sent her to try and keep TBF from hurting the body. He wanted to make sure that Rachel would not do anything like that to TBF, or any of us, again.

When Rachel agreed and gave him her promise not to hurt any of us, Randy was relieved. He now felt that he could tell Rachel a little bit more about us. He wanted Rachel to know that things inside were not okay, but that there was a lot of pain and he really needed her to help. Randy told Rachel that he would tell her things if she wanted to know, because, " I am a little spy and that is what spies are supposed to do, right?" Randy was extremely intelligent for such a small child.

Rachel explained to us that a probable reason for his intelligence was his ability to avoid the abuse that the rest of us suffered. When Randy felt threatened or scared, he would run away. His curiosity allowed him to preserve that special quality of being a child.

Randy was not the only one in our system that was smart. He shared his intelligence with Mikhail. Rachel got to know Mikhail over the course of several different sessions. What she discovered was that Mikhail was extremely intelligent and a book worm, happiest when he was reading in a library. Because we were unable to stay functional enough to attend college, reading was how Mikhail gained most of his knowledge. In addition, like Randy, Mikhail did not suffer the abuse that most of us did, because we would protect him. Because of this, he did not have the suicidal and self-destructive desires that the majority of us did, freeing his mind to learn.

Although Rachel believed Mikhail to be gifted and talented, he did not think that he was intelligent, because he had been unable to finish school. He blamed us for this failure. Mikhail's job did not end with school. He was the one who dealt with all our basic needs like money, bills, and trying to hold down jobs, although we did not make this easy for him. He was not very social. In fact, Mikhail was extremely shy. He was more comfortable dealing with technical tasks, like the type of work he did at DCC.

Mikhail wanted to prove that he could do things well and was a perfectionist (something he and Rachel had in common). He did not like to admit this. He knew he was somewhat odd, but did not really care. He was not very emotional, but could be harsh and was usually referred to as a jerk by the rest of us. However, he would be the first to offer other people help, because beneath the façade, he really was a nice guy. That is why he helped Randy that day, even though he got into trouble for it, because he knew that he needed to help.

Randy was just a little kid and was often scared or hurt. He needed an inner protector. He called on Storm to help him. Besides, Storm thought, If Randy is going to be giving out names and talking about the kids, then I want to meet this Rachel and find out if she really is okay. It was Storm's job to take care of the little ones, including Randy, and it was a job that he did not make easy for her. Without her, things would have been even more chaotic internally. She really did not like to come out and would only do so if she thought that it was important, or we were in a life and death emergency. Then she would be one of our most powerful protectors. She loved children. Over the years she had taken care of many real kids, one of her few pleasures. Storm was very impressed with Rachel's patience, but felt that she had a lot to learn. She was not completely sure if Rachel could deal with many of the children inside, or what they remembered and had to say. She did decide to give Rachel a chance, but decided to watch her closely while she talked to any of her "charges."

Mathew was not "one of the little ones." He was around fourteen—years old. We really couldn't understand him. He was hard to deal with, a huge loner and did not want any part in the therapeutic process. Mathew liked to play head games in order to figure people out. This was something that he learned while he was a part of a gang of kids that lived on the streets in our internal world. We called them the killers, or simply, the street kids. He was a part of this gang until he got frightened of them and decided that he did not want to be around them anymore. He did enjoy picking on the little kids inside, mostly Randy.

However, Mathew would not let any harm come to any of the inside children from any person outside the body. He was known to get into fights with other people in an effort to protect the kids from people he viewed as harmful. An example of this was when we were living with one of Gabriele's many foster parents. Mathew took a lot of abuse for all of us, and for two other children that were living in that household. He really did care about Randy and the other children, even if he felt that he needed to punish Randy himself. His meeting Rachel was because of Randy. He had been tormenting Randy all day, refusing to let him eat any food and threatening to harm him if he tried. At the time, the body's lack of nutrition was a concern, and Randy was the only one that was even trying to feed it. When Randy disobeyed Mathew and ate something, Mathew carried out his threat and cut Randy. Randy called Rachel for help. Mathew had no reason at the time to trust Rachel. In fact, he did not even know her, so he decided to try and mess with her head. But Rachel did not give into his games, and she never backed down from her position that he needed to stop hurting Randy, and let both Randy and the body eat. She was not mean, just firm. Mathew was unused to this and felt confused. What is this woman's deal? What does she want from me?

Rachel asked Mathew to come in for a therapy session. Although Mathew reluctantly agreed, he thought that therapy was a lot of "hog wash," and he did not believe the he needed any help because he was fine. It was the rest of us that were the ones that were fucked up. But after that session, we could hear him yelling, Let her do her psycho bullshit with the rest of you, but she just better leave me alone. He decided to stay the hell out of her way, because he did not want her to try "headshrinking" him. Despite this, Rachel would not have many problems from Mathew and there was a mutual respect that developed between them. He would even help her out from time to time. After all, he did have a nice side.

Some of us were easier to work with and were more willing to help, such as Stephana. She and Rachel developed a strong working relationship. When Rachel needed information about different people in the system, Stephana would be the one to tell her. When Rachel first heard about Stephana, she made the assumption that Stephana was male. Wrong. Stephana was a female and a huge "bull dyke," as she liked to call herself. She did not scare easily (though she was terrified of flying), liked to have casual sex and loved to get into fistfights. Everyone has got to have a little fun, she would tell us. She could also drink like a fish when she was in the mood. We guess you could call her a wild card. Stephana could be rather loud, and even rude and crude. But she did have a good heart and liked to help people on the outside. Stephana was also one of the three people that went to work, mainly to help Mikhail out when dealing with co-workers or the boss. She was the one that had most of the social skills in knowing how to deal with people in the external world.

At one point, Rachel suggested that Stephana should go to medical school, because she seemed to have a lot of medical know how. After all, she was the one that was always putting the body back together. "I hate the smell of formaldehyde," was her reply to that suggestion. The truth was she did not think that she was smart enough to go to medical school. This was a belief that she shared with Mikhail, Gabriele, and most of the rest of us. But, she certainly knew how to fix things, such as the car, the dryer, and the holes that others put in the walls. She learned how to do all of this out of necessity, because there was no one else to do it, and we could never afford to hire anyone else. Her main job, however, was to keep the body alive and to protect it from Death.

How do we explain Death? For us, suicide was not just a thing or an act. In our system, Death was a SHE and was real. She had been with the system from almost the beginning. Death was not this evil killing machine of a monster. She was very quiet, thoughtful, and sensitive, and she wanted more than anything for someone to care about her as a person. She wrote poetry and though it could be very dark, it was also very expressive, and was a way for her to let others know about her feelings and what our world was like. Rachel read Death's poetry way before she "met" her. Death let Rachel read her poems because she wanted to know what Rachel would think of them. She was hoping Rachel would see things as they were, yet was scared when Rachel did. Rachel's understanding of her pain opened possibilities for Death, such as life. Yet Death was scared of being disappointed or hurt. So, rather than risk believing in Rachel, she decided to kill all of us.

Death had been the one pushing TBF and Gabriele towards burning themselves to death. When Rachel got Gabriele to agree not to kill herself, and to agree to write this book, Death was angry. She felt that Rachel was getting in her way and she was determined to kill us herself, rather than wait for Gabriele to do it. She made the choice to act, but she forgot about one person: Randy. He had suspected for a while that she was the one behind Gabriele's self-destructive wishes, but he was scared to tell Rachel. Randy was determined not to let Death do anything to harm the body. As soon as he got the chance, he took a major risk to push out past Death and call Rachel from a gas station at one-thirty in the morning, waking her up to ask for help. When he told her where he was and what was going on, Rachel wanted to know who it was that was going to kill the body, but Randy was afraid to tell her that. He knew better than to anger Death. They had fought before and Randy had come out on the losing end. Death could be deadly and dangerous when she was scared or angry. So instead, he asked Death to please talk to Rachel and she agreed.

She knew that she had the power to kill all of us that night and if she had gone ahead with her plan, there was nothing that Rachel or anyone else could have done to stop her. Instead, she chose to talk to Rachel. It was one of the best decisions that she made. At the end of the conversation, Rachel got her to agree to go home and not kill the body or us that night. Death felt that Rachel had listened to everything that she had to say, and had shown respect and kindness to her, something she had never felt from an adult. We were all very thankful. If Rachel had said the wrong thing, like, "Oh, come on, it's late and I don't want to deal with this," Death would have hung up and just ended our lives and hers.

We did not think that Rachel had any idea that Death was one of the most important persons in this system, nor what journey lay ahead to get this one personality to give up her death wish and choose life.

Slowly, it started to become more evident that there were a great many of us that were self-destructive. In addition to TBF, Death and Gabriele, there was TOB. Rachel had her first conversation with TOB over the telephone while he was in the process of cutting himself. Although he knew about her, he had been listening in on other's conversations. He did not want to talk to her. Rachel was insistent, so he finally relented. He figured that he would scare her off by telling her of his cutting.

TOB believed that he was completely evil and that if he cut deep enough, the evil would come out. And if he died in the process, then so what? TOB was very mistrusting of Rachel because of his past experiences with other therapists and doctors. One of his problems with other professionals was that he felt they thought that he was playing games or bluffing. TOB did not bluff. He truly believed that if he trusted her, then she was going to betray him. He did not understand why Rachel would not just give up. "Run while you still have the chance," he told her repeatedly. He felt that Rachel did not understand what he was going through or what he had survived. But it also scared him to think that Rachel might actually understand both and not think of him as evil for it. No one else ever had. TOB had the ability to block out pain, which made his cutting very dangerous. He would cut to the point that the body (that he did not believe he shared with others) was in danger of bleeding to death. TOB was afraid that Rachel would find out about some of the abuse, which he wanted to keep a complete secret. But when Rachel started to ask some very pointed questions, TOB gave her the truth, as we will talk about in more detail later. The only barrier that Rachel had to go through in order to talk to TOB was William.

William was about fourteen or fifteen years old. He was a protector, and he was also somewhat spiritual, which was something uncommon amongst the rest of us. Because of some of his religious ideals, he believed that TOB was evil and dangerous. Therefore, he was unwilling to let TOB meet Rachel. What was even odder about William was that he wanted to convert to Judaism. This was something that he had thought about for years. When Rachel found out about his interest, she gave him the name of a Rabbi to talk to. She also started to share more about her own beliefs concerning sin and forgiveness. Although she and William found some common ground, he was still guarded around her. And over the course of a couple of weeks, William decided that Rachel was a danger to us. She was asking too many questions of which we weren't allowed to give answers. He was part of the "committee" and one of his jobs was to make sure that no one told "the secrets." It also frightened him that by meeting one of the children that she was not supposed to, she was endangering us all. He reported back to the chairman that he felt Rachel needed to be stopped from learning more. To this end, the committee members did not allow questions she posed to be answered, deals to be kept, and therapy to progress. Rachel knew she needed to talk to a member of the committee for our work to continue. Finally, she met the chairman.

He was determined that Rachel would never know the answer to her question, "Which of you came first?" He felt that Rachel was being disrespectful of the committee's decisions, yet no one had ever told her what those decisions were. So, the chairman just came straight out and made sure that she understood that he, and the committee, had the power to stop her, and us, from going any farther in therapy. He told her that she was not going to be allowed to talk to the little ones if he did not approve of her. Rachel had to agree to ask for his permission before she talked to one child in particular; the same child that William had been upset about her meeting. Her name was Tigger. Rachel did not challenge him and agreed to his terms; she refused to get in a power struggle with him. This seemed to diffuse the chairman's need to continue his dominance, and he allowed her access to Tigger. Therapy started to move forward again. Strangely, after this encounter, the chairman, and the committee, just seemed to fade away.

Rachel met Tigger by accident. We had gone to the dentist to get a root canal and it had turned into a nightmare, ending with us losing the tooth anyway. The whole experience was very triggering for us (we really do not like to have people messing with our mouth), and so Rachel agreed to see us for an emergency session that night. During the session, Tigger surfaced. At the time, neither Rachel, nor us, realized the importance of this child. She was the one that we believe was born first. Because she could not endure the abuse, she was the one to split into the other personalities. She never grew up. She still lived in that world where she was being abused and hurt. Rachel did not know until much later, that Tigger was the one that we always heard screaming. When Rachel tried to tell her that she was no longer being hurt, Tigger could not comprehend what she was being told. She did not have the ability to grasp another reality.

In the beginning, a big problem for us was that we had no memory of what would go on when Tigger was talking to Rachel, or when she was even out. We just knew that we would have unexplained bites on our arms. There was only one person that had any memory of what would occur. His name was Brian.

Rachel had met Brian when she called one night and he was out playing a game called Yahtzee. He was about six —years old, quiet, shy, and for a long time we all made the assumption that he was stupid. He was not. He just liked to keep to himself. Stephana had a bad habit of telling him to come out and stay out, so that she could deal with problems inside. None of us really knew Brian very well. Brian actually did not like it when Stephana ordered him around, but he did not bother to tell any of us. His greatest contribution to the system was that he was the only one that could really see Tigger and communicate with her. He would talk to her and tell her that everything was okay. His efforts at keeping her calm helped the rest of us to function. Slowly, we all came to understand that Brian was Tigger's protector and caregiver.

There were other caregivers inside. Rachel learned about QED when she was sent a letter giving information about whom we all were. QED felt that Rachel needed to better understand how the system worked and how each of us coped. When Rachel received the letter, she was full of questions about who this person was, since QED did not sign her name or identify herself in any way. She did not want Rachel to meet her and for a time, was unwilling to even talk to Rachel over the phone. That was the way it stayed until there was a problem with TOB. QED helped Rachel see that TOB was a scared kid beneath the acting out teen. After that, Rachel and QED had a working relationship that was mutually respectful. However,

QED would not come out until Rachel was at her wit's end. Then she would give Rachel advice to help her change tracks and be more constructive, often angering the rest of us.

As time progressed, Rachel slowly became acquainted with some of the other children. She heard about them and was told things that they did or said, but it took awhile for her to meet them. We feared that Rachel would not understand them, might hurt them, that they might hurt her, or that she would give up because they were so difficult to deal with. An extreme example of this was the Killers. They were the secret keepers of the system and were a gang of children that lived outside on the streets of our internal world. We knew that they were becoming more and more upset as we told Rachel about the abuse and other secrets. We had hoped that they would be willing to work with Rachel and that she could help them. Rachel felt that the only way she was going to get all of them to stop their self-abusive behavior, was to meet with them face-to-face.

What we neglected to remember was that these children did not come out on a regular basis, and therefore, did not have many positive experiences with the outside world. In addition, because of all the abuse that they suffered at the hands of adults and their negative experiences in the therapeutic system, they had no reason to trust an adult who said that she wanted to help. However, when the self-mutilation was becoming worse and worse, we had no choice but to take a risk and let her meet these children. Unfortunately, her initial reaction to their behavior almost cost us our lives.

Rachel became frustrated and started to make assumptions. In doing so, she insulted them by calling them derogatory names and implying that they needed to go away, because she really did not see any reason to work with them. They became angry, refused to listen to anything that we tried to tell them, and intensified their efforts to kill the body. After several weeks of chaos, Storm, QED, and some of the others, finally got Rachel to understand that they were just children and they had a reason for existing. We also got Rachel to agree to talk to Mathew, because he seemed to still have some connection to these children. Mathew told her that her attitude was creating more problems, and she asked Mathew to pass along her apology for her statements and actions. Mathew also pleaded with them to at least listen to what she had to say, reminding them that they had never received an apology from a "big person" before. They relented and agreed to talk to her.

The first ones that came forth were Cobalt, Andrea, Copula, and Stupid. We were terrified that they would try to harm Rachel, something that she said she had no fear of. We felt that she was underestimating their potential for violence. She did not have an easy task ahead of her. She had to help them stop the cutting, the burning, and the refusal to let the body eat or sleep. All of these actions interfered in our ability to function, much less work.

Once these children began trusting in Rachel (a long process discussed later in the book), they paved the way for her to meet Stephan, Oliver, Sandy and Cryin. We believed that these personalities were crazy, because other professionals had labeled them that. We were frightened of them, because they had harmed other people. We believed that if we ignored them and denied their very existence, they would just go away. They never did. Instead they kept us up at night, and threatened to cut and burn all of us. We never fully believed that Rachel could have any success at working with them. We had to throw out our old beliefs about whom and what they were, and accept that they were just scared children that had done only what they believed they had to.

As Rachel worked with all of us, Gabriele lost more time and perspective. She refused to accept that she had to share her body with other personalities. She believed that she was going crazy, as the roaring inside was increasing in volume. We knew that sooner or later, she would do something out of desperation, and we felt that there was nothing that could be done to stop her. The only hope that we had was that she would keep her word with Rachel, and talk to her before she attempted suicide. Things quickly came to a head on July seventh when all hell broke loose.

Gabriele went to see Rachel for a therapy session. At this point, Rachel still thought that Gabriele was the host. This only complicated matters, and the session went about as we expected it to go. Gabriele was not willing to hear any more about us. By the end of the session, she had made her choice and left the office knowing what she felt she had to do. She left Rachel a letter she had written. She went home and started making plans for her suicide. Things started to get frightening. We kept reminding her that she had a deal to keep with Rachel and that she had to fire her before she killed herself, which meant that she had to talk to Rachel to do this. So, she called Rachel and fired her. There was a long pause and then Rachel, knowing what these words meant, said, "You don't have to hurt me this way. I have never lost a client before. I cannot work with someone this closely and not care about them." Rachel's voice was full of emotion. That hit Gabriele hard. She became confused; she could not ignore the fact that her death was going to hurt Rachel, but she was also angry. She did not want any complications, and did not want Rachel to try and stop her,

"GOD DAMN IT! I told you not to care. I told you that I'm not a good person and that I'm just going to end up hurting you!"

"Get it through your head that I will have feelings about you killing yourself! I will be hurt and I will be very sad. I do care about you, and that is not going to change, no matter what you do!" Rachel yelled right back at her.

This woman has guts, was the response inside. We were impressed with Rachel's tenacity. In the face of everything that had happened, she was unwilling to give up her hope that things could get better. We knew that she was taking a large risk by being willing to treat us. She had just been offered a way out and she was unwilling to accept it. This is an unusual quality in a therapist. In our past, other mental health professionals had given up after realizing that we were complex. Instead, Rachel found our complexity to be fascinating and a challenge that she was willing to take on. We saw this as a good sign and gained hope from her optimism.

Gabriele, on the other hand, did not find Rachel's optimism to be of comfort. She was angry and frustrated that Rachel would not back down and let her do what she felt that she needed to do, which was to die. When Gabriele said, "You have got to be the most infuriating woman I have ever known," we knew that a battle of the wills was about to ensue. Gabriele was making her choice known. She was unwilling to give life, or Rachel, a chance.

Rachel had an opening that hour and told Gabriele that she wanted to see her right then. "How fast can you get here?" Rachel's tone of voice told us that there was going to be no argument (we don't think that she would have accepted no for an answer). The only reason Gabriele agreed to go was that she believed that she could win the battle, and that Rachel would become frustrated and back down, thus freeing Gabriele to die.

As Gabriele was driving to Rachel's office, she was preparing herself to argue with Rachel and make Rachel agree to her terms. She even believed that Rachel would break her word and call the police. In that event, Gabriele was willing to make the police kill her. When she arrived at Rachel's office, we did not know what was going to happen and we all felt panicked. We hoped that Rachel could help Gabriele see that there was some hope. We never thought that she would look Gabriele in the eyes and tell her, "We need to write a book together!" Or, that we would say yes.

Rachel: Chapter 3

Bond of Trust: Foundation of Healing

> *"Trust each other again and again. When the trust level gets high enough, people transcend apparent limits, discovering new and awesome abilities of which they were previously unaware."*
>
> **—David Armistead**

I don't know how the idea came into my consciousness. Perhaps my subconscious had been storing the need or desire to write, and this just seemed like the perfect opportunity: an opportunity to go beyond my role as therapist to help many others understand the complexities of abuse and survival, and the opportunity to give someone else, specifically Gabriele, a purpose to live. I also believed that in the process of writing, another process of remembering, understanding, sharing, and finally healing could take place.

She pondered and asked many questions, especially, "Why would you want to do this with us?"

I answered directly and honestly. "You are unique. Your story is unique. The book can be great!"

I didn't know that she had traded places with Mikhail. He was the one to finally answer, "Yes, but on one condition. You have to learn how to play cribbage!" I was overjoyed! I felt that the first hurdle had been jumped through, and we were on our way to building a mutually trusting and caring relationship. Months later, he told me that writing this book was the most important thing in his life, and that he had never wanted anything more.

I naively thought that if I had been able to stop Gabriele from ending her life that day, by her agreeing to co-author a book, we were moving on our path towards life. I did not realize that all the others might not agree to this decision, as I would later find out.

Mathew and Randy were the ones who had warned me of Gabriele's suicidal thoughts. One of the agreements Mathew made with me was he would stop "bullying," if I could make a pact with Gabriele not to kill herself. The deal was made.

This concept of agreement, or deal, was one with which all seemed to feel comfortable. For them it meant that two people were each agreeing to do their part to meet the terms of the deal. It didn't need to be formalized in writing. It was based on trust, respect, and honesty, traits that are key in building a therapeutic relationship. Contract was a concept that evoked discomfort. To them, the word meant an authority figure drawing up a formal set of expectations that directly correlated with a set of consequences.

When I met Gabriele the first time, and knew of her suicidal ideation, I asked her to sign a suicide contract. This was a standard tactic that most professionals use, perhaps in hopes that they won't feel guilty or responsible for another's life. I knew that if Gabriele was ill at ease, this tactic was going to elicit only a mistrust of me. I would seem controlling, and putting my needs as a professional before hers as a client. My belief is that the client must always be first in my office. It is the client who must direct me. If I feel fear, I must respond with empathy, not my own agenda. Empathy means tuning into another's feelings, not necessarily understanding them, but accepting them as real and vital. What I knew to be vital to the process of building trust was that I had to show them that I, a professional and person, was willing to give them something that they could believe in. After all, I was asking them to give me their trust.

When Gabriele told me she could not sign a contract, I knew

she and I needed to find a compromise which would help me feel that I had addressed the suicide fear (it would have been unethical of me to disregard it), and would be something she would abide by. She then told me that she would make a deal.

The deal consisted of agreeing to call me before she would try to kill herself, and this was later amended to include all self-mutilation. My part in the agreement was to be available to them, and if it was after office hours, they could call me at home.

At times, as they became closer to me, I felt that they chose to consider my need for family time or sleep, rather than disturb me with a warning call. I would continually remind them that I wanted to have the chance to prevent a crisis rather than deal with the aftermath. Still, I had a difficult time developing trust with Gabriele. She was very influenced by others, especially the street kids. She seemed to be their conduit, so if they said to kill, she would try to commit suicide. One evening, she told me she was ready to do it. This was just as I was about to leave for a concert. I felt torn, knowing that at the moment all I could do was repeat over and over again that I didn't want her to follow through. I cared. She asked me why I scared her. I told her it was probably because to have someone care was a new experience. My mind was distracted and I was relieved when the concert ended so I could return home, although to what I did not know. She called again and after an hour of persuasive tactics, she finally told me where she was. She made it clear that I must not bring the police or take her to a hospital. When I arrived at the destination, I knew this would be a turning point. After a lengthy meeting, she finally agreed to a written contract that she would not commit suicide. Because I knew she didn't truly believe in this form of agreement, I was wary that she could abide by her word. But try she did, despite numerous attempts and great emotional turmoil, while her trust in me grew. As she would say, "I want to believe you that I can be happy, that I am good, but something inside me still tells me otherwise." I knew that until I found out what that something was, the risk of suicide would still be high.

My family was extremely supportive and accepting of these after-hours calls. For the first few months, my husband, Morrie, and daughter Sarah, knew they would be sharing my time with Gabriele, et al. Morrie became an important element as trust building progressed. He, with his own master's degree in educational psychology, is a kind and generous man. Gabriele, et al, used to ask me if there were any decent men around, and I always reassured her yes, thinking lovingly of Morrie. Although very encouraging of my work with them, he seemed uncomfortable at first, unknowing of how to respond when they called. Who was actually talking to him? They gave me permission to share our sessions. They seemed to need to have another "big person's" opinion before they truly felt at ease with the world knowing their story. Therefore, they felt it necessary to meet with him face-to-face and make sure for themselves that he did not think they were crazy.

First he met Mikhail when they discussed my buying a laptop to write the book. Mikhail gave him his stamp of approval and Morrie thought Mikhail to be most competent. He saw a depth in "their eyes." The others seemed a little more wary; after all, he was a male big person. At one point, I made a home visit on a Saturday evening. My willingness and commitment to seek the truth often took me away from the office setting. I knew they were feeling out of balance as if an ex-lover was coming over to retrieve her belongings. I went to their door; Randy answered. He didn't know who this other big person was and while he was bending down to make cuffs on his pants, Mikhail traded places. Randy was scared that Morrie wouldn't like him.

As our work together progressed, Morrie's concern and acceptance seemed to validate their existence, helping build trust for both of us.

Some therapists might feel that I was crossing boundaries and that I was becoming too involved and not emotionally detached as a professional is taught to be. What I told them was that my professionalism was always guiding my strategies, and I never lost my integrity as a therapist. I was aware that in all Gabriele, et al's, years of therapy, no one had consistently made an effort to understand their complexities and deep pain, or to see them as human beings, not "patients." Professionals seemed to respond to angry, acting out behaviors, and/or the professional system would not allow for the type of availability that I believed crucial to building trust. I was never afraid to show my real feelings. I would cry when hearing of their individual abusive experiences. Being a professional does not have to mean being aloof and contained.

Another client once told me that I did not need the usual external boundaries because I had such strong internal ones. She was right. I knew instinctively how far I could expand my boundaries to let a client in, which is just enough to give them my respect and acceptance of them as human beings without their feeling confused about the nature of the relationship. This enabled the client to build trust in me and feel comfortable with the sharing of his pain.

I wanted them to have a real person as a role model, capable of expressing caring feelings, experiences they had never felt. They only knew anger, as I came to learn over and over again. Their first question to me after a self-mutilation act was, "Are you mad at me?" to which I always responded, "No, I can't be angry with people who hurt. I feel sad that you're in so much pain."

I wanted them to know I was comfortable with my own self-disclosure of painful experiences. During one telephone call, Gabriele, in a very exasperated voice said, "You could never understand what it's like to hate a body!" There were a few moments of silence, as I collected my thoughts. I was aware from that statement that firstly, she detached from her physical being by using the article "a" rather than a reflexive pronoun. Secondly, she believed I had no personal experience that could compare to her self-hatred. How wrong she was.

I shared with her my own emotional and physical suffering as a result of scoliosis, a curvature of the spine, causing my spine to be at a ninety-five degree angle, crushing my heart and lungs, and requiring extensive orthopedic surgery and convalescence. As an adolescent, I hated my body; as an adult, it took years of bodywork and self-therapy to change a distorted body image and finally accept my physical being in a positive way. I knew I had shocked her with my monologue: her tone of voice changed to one of softness and appreciation, as she responded: "Then you do know what it's like." The many alters were listening in on our conversation and felt more strongly that I was indeed different than other therapists. My comfort with my own limitations allowed them to feel more equal and consequently, I gained their respect and trust.

Randy may have been my first ally. He seemed to want me to know what was happening with the system, so that maybe I could stop everyone from trying to kill. He would call me and ask if he was going to get in trouble. It hurt me to think that this little boy lived in constant fear of punishment. I always reassured him that he was being a good boy to try to find help. In one of the most painful sessions, I learned that Randy carried the brunt of the responsibility for much of the extreme punishment. During one episode described by Death in which the mother had tied her to a tree and started a fire around it, Randy believed this was a result of his actions because he had run away and tried to tell a policeman what the mother was doing. Sadly, instead of receiving protection, the policeman reprimanded him, told him he was lying, and then told the mother on him. It became a strong aversion to ever tell a "big person" anything that was happening to "them."

I was so thankful that Randy was trusting in me, even though I would call him "cute." He hated when I described him that way and would adamantly tell me he wasn't. I became a surrogate mother, making sure he was being fed. He would make sure I knew he didn't like meat, but cottage cheese with pineapple, and macaroni and cheese, were some of his favorites. One night he called to ask me how he would know when rice was ready, and if I had ever eaten rice with cheese. "You should try it, it's good," he enthusiastically told me. He was very happy after he had eaten. These interactions, which one might think trite, were actually very telling in the way this system operated. Randy was the only one who felt the body. He would be the one to get sick. I would explore this mind/body disconnection further in my own journey of understanding Dissociative Identity Disorder.

TBF was the next little one that seemed to let me in. Firstly, I needed to make an agreement with her that I would never send her away and she needed to agree not to hurt herself after we spoke. I learned from my new friend, Randy, that she had been sent to a Desert Island for a long time. I later pieced information together and realized what took place during hypnosis, as a psychiatrist was probably trying to send all the self-abusive parts away. Poor TBF. I knew she was just a scared little girl who only knew what she had learned, which was to hurt the body. I knew that to gain her trust, I had to always remember that she was deeply rejected by what they called *big people*. She did not accept my comfort readily. One of my first goals with TBF was to help her accept nurturance. I gave her a cute little stuffed monkey to sleep with and snuggle for comfort. At that point, she knew that I really did care.

Death was to become a very special helper and often co-therapist with the others. We have laughed at how our original meeting was and the evolving relationship that ensued. Here's an excerpt of that first telephone contact. Randy had just told me that Death was trying to kill them.

D: *Randy is a fucking little spy. How much trouble am I going to be in?*

Me: None.

D: *Life isn't real for me.*

Me: I have to help you understand that each of you is real. You all have your own way of looking at things. You're an important part of healing and growing.

D: *I don't know about that.*

Me: Let me help you be a part of this and figure things out with you helping me. I can't do this alone. It's new territory for us all.

D: *Why do you want to help us?*

Me: Because I care.

I decided I would share a little of me so that she would know that I was comfortable with her, despite my knowing of her suicidal mission. I wanted her to know that in my eyes, she was a person first, and I would treat her as I would all persons. Therefore, I proceeded to talk a little about my family and this seemed to calm her down.

Me: I like to talk to kids because they say things as they are—they don't beat around the bush.

D: *I'm impressed with how you answer questions.*

Me: Thank you. I get an "A" from you. I was one of these people who never thought I was good enough.

D: *Then we have something in common.*

Me: It's an awful thing to live with—not to feel good enough. That's why this book can help us both do things beyond what we've ever done. I think I excited some of you.

D: *Yea.*

Me: I'm so excited. Seeing my name in print will be better than getting a doctorate. And for you, it's saying you succeeded at something.

(Long Pause)

D: I remember once we were suicidal, and we called a therapist, and she didn't call us back for three days.

Me: I get so angry with people like that. I try to get back within an hour. I like to be available.

D: We don't get angry with you for that, but I get angry with you when you try to talk me out of what I need to do.

Me: Anger is okay. I understand that you have a need to hurt yourself. I have a need to stop you from hurting yourself. We are just at cross-purposes for now.

I knew that she was feeling less adversarial and more trusting of me when she proceeded to tell me that she was the one who wrote the poetry. Let me share with you two poems that she allowed me to read.

Question of Being

Being is not a Question of
Living
or
Breathing
Being is not just a State of
Surviving -
Being -
It is a Question of
Trying
Working
Striving
to gain Respect &
Pride
in one's self;
To do Right
as one sees it;

*To Break the Cycle -
so No More
Children
In
Life
Fear
For
Their
Lives!!
To make Right
what was made
Wrong
So many Years Before;
And of Learning -
No Matter
How boring the Lesson may be;
Being is a Question of NOT
Giving up your Dreams
No Matter what they are;
Being is also a Question of Always
Looking
for the Answer -
and of Knowing when Not to;
Being -
It is a Question of Learning to Love -
and then Letting Go of what you Love -
So that it may Grow;
Being—
It Is a Question of
Always Looking for
the Light
at the End of
the Long Tunnel -
And Admitting you were
Scared
But Continued anyway*

And:

Wounds

Where was she—
the Mother
when i Needed her
most?
why did she
leave
Forsake
me?
did she HATE me
so very much?
These are
Questions
that make laps in my mind—
all the Day
and all the Night.
i loved her;
i cared about her;
this mother i never
really
ever
had
i wanted her to feel
the same about me
this mother that never
Saw
Heard
Wanted
me
i know that the world is not always
fair
but how do you justify this—
to a little girl
a child

*who wants someone
ANYONE
to care about her
and about
what Happens to her?
How do you tell that child
she is
on
her own
NO ONE will come
to make it all BETTER—
when she
this child
cries in the night.
The Darkest Hours
are not in
the Night,
BUT in the
Waking Hours
when the child can see,
and hear,
and smell
the very person that she wants
to comfort her;
But she will never
ever
come
to any ones aid—
but her own
that comes through a bottle
and a man;
and when she remembers
the child
of her flesh & blood—
the mother will give only
the back of her hand.
then just when Fate seems to have Evened the
Odds—*

Rachel Gunner

She is Gone
in the Blink
Of
An
Eye;
This Mother
the child
Never Really Had.
No time to CRY;
for the child does not want
to believe this:
that the mother is gone.
Now for her there is
NOTHING
But Memories
of what was wanted,
needed—
but never
ever given;
Memories of
Pain
and
Fear
Fear of the Person
Who was suppose to protect her;
Then—
Memories of the Night
She looked out
the Window
To See the End
Of what was
and the End of her Childhood—
what little was left;
Memories of that Hurt
Wounds that may
Never Heal
How do i tell the child
that she must now look

> *No Where*
> *but Inside*
> *of herself;*
> *For There*
> *She May find a Little Peace*
> *Possible be able to Forget*
> *the Hurt,*
> *But Never*
> *Ever*
> *Will she be able to*
> *Heal the Wounds.*

I couldn't believe the intensity of the feelings being expressed. I knew poetry would be the medium she would use to share with me all she had repressed.

She then shared, with flat affect, how the abuse had started. At two years old, the mom and Stuart (the mom's husband) came into her room, drunk, and how it was the first time they saw "that thing." I assumed she was talking about Stuart's penis. I felt like crying and told her so. Children should never have to experience such humiliation and terror. Randy later told me that I almost made Death cry when I admitted my feelings. I knew then that she was going to let me in. She told me burning was the only means to get rid of the pain and was a way to punish the self for treason.

A day later, on July Fourth, I was at home making a peach pie when I received another call from Death. She felt like she was going crazy. I kept telling her that she had a right to be angry and it was okay to let it out. I gave her permission to throw something like a pillow, to release some feeling. She began to cry, repeating, "Why did she do that? I just wanted to be loved by her. What if it was my fault?" Death had begun to peel apart her onion and I knew that there were many layers until we reached the core.

However, trust had been achieved. That is, for now. I discovered that trust was something that I could not take for granted, that it was not necessarily permanent. I learned this lesson the hard way. I almost got fired after months of arduous work trying to establish a trusting and close bond with Death. She was experiencing grave emotional turmoil in trying to choose life or death. She felt inundated with new ideas and beliefs, yet still felt unworthy of accepting her goodness. I was becoming frustrated, wanting her to cross over into this new world of light and love. She wasn't ready. I wasn't listening, and this insult was the very experience she had had with other therapists. She felt misunderstood, discounted, and unreal. Mikhail shed light on my behavior, "If you try to take shortcuts while baking bread," he asked, "what happens?" *What a wise young man*, I thought. *Of course, every process takes time, and patience.* I had been forgetting and losing patience. I wanted her to heal, now! Once I owned my ineffectual interventions, Death accepted my apology. She renewed her trust in me as someone who she knew more clearly as human. I knew that acknowledging my own limitations to her, helped her to see herself and me as more real and involved in a true humanistic therapeutic relationship. I truly believe that it takes courage, strength of character and humility for a therapist to own up to his/her mistakes. How can we not, if we are to be healthy role models?

TOB and I had many telephone interactions before I was even allowed to see him in my office. William didn't think I would be safe from TOB. TOB believed he would contaminate me with his evil. Most of these conversations seemed adversarial and hostile, until I asked him this question: "Have you ever cared for anyone so that you would want to do something for them?"

He answered in a softer, sadder voice, "Lynn, a cousin. I didn't let Tom, an uncle, hurt her like he did me." He told me how bad Tom had treated him.

I had finally broken through a wall of silence. TOB would not make deals with me, however. He wasn't ready to give up the only thing he knew that stopped him from feeling—his cutting. I consciously decided not to ask him to stop, but rather, to continue exploring with him other ways to rid himself of pain.

After this exchange, William finally let me meet him. One of the first things TOB did was to look at my plants, which were in terrible shape, and tell me how to nourish them. I asked him to be the caretaker of my plants. My respecting him as having a special skill may have been the start of his letting me in a little. He gave me his pocketknife! This action became a key symbol of his trust in me.

Whenever the system became unstable, threatening self-infliction, he would give me his weapon.

William also began trusting in me when I initiated discussions on religious concepts, in particular, how different religions deal with issues of forgiveness. Although not well versed in the Judaic scriptures, I did know that during the Jewish High Holy days we ask that God forgive our sins, and on the Day of Atonement, Yom Kippur, we are inscribed in the Book of Life. William shared with me that for ten years he had been fascinated with this faith and had even considered converting to Judaism. I gave him the name of our Rabbi, a young twenty-nine-year-old woman, with whom I thought he could relate. He made an appointment to visit with her. It seemed yet another twist of destiny that Rachel considered one of Judaism's founding mothers, and Gabriele, God's Healer, would find a common thread in the strength of religion.

Trusting that the system would be alive when I returned from vacation, a two-week trip to England that my family and I were looking forward to, remained a concern for me. My goal was to reach agreements with all of them not to cut, burn or kill the body while I was gone. Daily and nightly, I spoke to Death, TOB, TBF, the ones I knew were still using these self-destructive methods of dealing with their pain, in order to try to enlist their willingness to a moratorium on those activities. I wanted to see them alive and well upon my return. I also wanted to enjoy my much-needed time off, without worrying about them.

I will always remember the morning before my departure. I found a white envelope in my mail slot. I opened it, and read:

I, Gabriele Weber, promise Rachel Gunner that this body will be alive, in one piece and in reasonable physical health on July 27, 1998.
p.s.
I will do the research that you want me to. And remember your promise not to think about me while you are on your vacation.

I smiled, took a deep breath of relief and called Gabriele immediately. "Thank you!"

She answered, "You're welcome."

They did keep their agreement, and I relaxed and had a wonderful vacation. I didn't keep my part of the deal completely, because I did think about them, and bought them a bookmark from Shakespeare's home:

> *"All the world's a stage,*
> *And all the men and women merely players.*
> *They have their exits and their entrances;*
> *And one man in his time plays many parts..."*

Gabriele, et al, were touched.

Sadly, the night before my return, TOB couldn't handle his feelings and cut the arm, necessitating a trip to the hospital and thirty stitches. They were very worried that I would be angry. I was just thankful they were alive. Our work could carry on.

As I continued to maintain the trust with those I had achieved, I strove to build trust in the new personalities that I was to meet.

A statement that I was to hear from many of the alters was, "When you break the bond, you commit treason." I knew I needed to explore what this bond was. I did not want them to transfer that belief system to the new bond they were building with me.

Cobalt, the street kid, became one of my greatest challenges. I had gotten off to a wrong start, letting my frustration control my therapeutic underpinnings. Once I was reminded that she was, after all, just eleven-years-old, I tuned into her age of development as a preteen beginning to oppose rules, to try to understand who this tough kid was. However, I was actually following a wrong path. During the weeks of daily interactions with her, one theme stood out. This young girl was extremely tortured, in particular through sleep and food deprivation. It seemed that she was carrying out a message that she had received: "The body is bad. The body must die. I cannot break the bond. If you break the bond, it is treason." I tried using logic and reasoning to change her beliefs, which I felt irrational. This tactic only caused Cobalt to be more oppositional and defiant. She screamed, "Why won't you let me do my job? I can't break the bond!" Her fear of breaking that bond seemed inexorable. I knew that to save the system, I had to succeed to gain her trust in a new bond with me. She would have nightmares and what I determined were hallucinations, which included seeing and hearing the mother and others. She would then cut and burn, and stop eating and sleeping. Although I saw these as punishment to the body, she believed these were the ways she was taught to be good. When I reasoned with her, she became confused.

The more confused, the angrier she would become, and the more power she seemed to exert over all the alters. They were scared of her. They began to lose hope as the weeks of my working with her still didn't convince her to stop the torture. She did reveal to me, "If the mind sleeps, it will tell secrets. If the body is not guilty, then what is wrong with the Trial?" There was that term that TBF had used. No one seemed to know what "the trial" referred to. It scared them.

One night, at 3:00 a.m., a desperate Death called. "Cobalt is going to kill us."

I kept saying to myself, "Why am I not reaching her? Why are the past messages so much stronger than the new ones? Why can't she trust when the others are starting to?" Without confirming my assumption, I decided that if she had experienced some form of programming of the mind, through sleep and food deprivation, then I needed to find a way to deprogram her. I decided to try some hypnotic techniques, such as the use of soft, repetitive statements, including, "The body is good. The body can live. No more killing. No more burning. No more cutting." They seemed to calm her down enough so that there was no killing that night. I felt hopeful, but only to become somewhat disillusioned the following day. I made a tape recording of these messages so that the others could play them and calm her down at the moment she began her uprisings. She threw the recorder across the room. She didn't want to listen.

It seemed that I was running out of tools, but I could not give up. I could not let an eleven-year-old control me. This power struggle in which we were engaged was a matter of life and death. If she won, the body and Gabriele, et al, would die.

One afternoon as we were sitting outside my office by the lake, I was clued into an interesting discovery. Cobalt looked up at me (which she rarely did), pointed to the cars driving by on the bridge, and asked me what they were. I realized at that moment, I was dealing with a child who had previously had no contact with the real world. Things she had said to me now made more sense, such as, "I do not like doors and beds in buildings. How do you open doors?" She liked being outside because she could run away. She was like a caged animal that I was trying to give freedom to, but that only scared her more. The newness caused her to defend herself with all she knew, and to lash out.

As I wondered about the approach that might work, I thought of the *Horse Whisperer*, a beautiful movie that depicted how man could tame wild horses with softness and compassion. She allowed me to take her into my office inside a building. I believed she was cautiously giving me some trust. I began to use some play therapy techniques when she picked up a crystal on my table. She seemed in awe. I described how rainbows are made. Then we colored a rainbow together. For the first time, she seemed like a carefree little girl. Although she still reacted uncomfortably to touch, I showed her how I wanted to pat her arm by patting mine first. Then she let me place my hand on her arm without flinching. I felt I was making progress.

Unfortunately, the years of deprivation and fear continued to influence her thinking. She drew the same picture each time we met: a tree engulfed in flames. Three figures were watching. She would not tell me what it meant.

I surmised that either this was a threat given to her if she were to be bad, or she had witnessed a frightening experience. I later learned from Death that these pictures were indeed threats of punishment for breaking the bond.

After she put some trust in me, sadly she was badly burned, and I wanted to know by whom. It was Andrea, another of the street kids. I knew I had been getting closer to the truth of their abuse and was a threat to the alters holding onto this bond. Andrea would not give in, and she continually repeated what Cobalt had said, "I cannot break the bond. This would be treason. The body deserves to die. Burning and cutting are good." She and Cobalt seemed to have experienced the same horrors. Their repetitive statements reminded me of how teachers often encourage children to remember information. In the alters' lives, repetition could be seen as a form of programming. Could I use the same method to, in essence, reprogram the negative messages and instill positive beliefs? I knew from my experience with Cobalt, that extreme fear was the predominant force behind her self-destructive acts. Again, I used guided imagery to help Andrea imagine a place of safety. Although resistant at first, she relaxed enough to let me take her on a healing journey. The first step in my building trust with her had been taken.

And then there was Little Sandy.—No one wanted her out, except for Copula. She made a deal with me that she would try to stop her from burning if I would help her. I could sense from her that Sandy was important to her and that she didn't want Sandy to be crazy anymore. I agreed. My task was to find a way to enter her world to ensure that she wouldn't try to run from me and/or hurt herself. My first attempt failed. I used a logical approach on an illogical child. I told her the mother was dead and Sandy didn't have to be scared of her anymore. This definitely did not make her trust me. Rather, she repeated, "No, you don't know what you're saying. She's here beside me. She tells me I'm bad. I must be punished."

One morning at 2:00 a.m., when Sandy was denying the body sleep, I finally had a breakthrough! I imagined a scared child who had never had an adult protect her and intervene on her behalf. I decided I would be that person. I told Sandy that I would talk to the mother, and tell the mother that children need sleep and to let Sandy sleep. I could hear Sandy relax on the phone. I told her the mother had said all right, which allowed her to fall asleep for the first time in several days. I felt encouraged that I might be able to really help Sandy heal. The more I pieced together what these children spoke of, the more I realized Sandy must have been stuffed in a dark box as one of her punishments. I began to brainstorm ways that I could help this child, who seemed petrified of light and outside, venture out into this open air. I visualized vibrant colors, sweet smelling fragrances, and roses. I bought her flowers. She smelled them, touched them even ate them, and most importantly, she smiled. These fragile gifts from nature helped lead this fragile little girl onto the path towards life.

Stephan and Oliver needed to know that a big person would listen to them, would not lock them up, and would not think they were crazy. Randy had told me that Adult meant "Angry, Disillusioned, Uncooperative, Large Terminator." He said that they had had awful experiences with, "big people in those big places." I assumed they meant hospitals where they were put in isolation and tied down when they screamed or tried to run away. My first thought was, *Of course they would try to protect themselves. How could professionals be so blind to what was really happening with these children?* All children need to feel listened to before they can trust anyone, especially an adult. I made a promise to do my best and listen, even if I didn't like what I was hearing. And Randy made sure I kept this promise by reminding me when I was not listening, "Hey, you're thinking like a big person." This was *not* a compliment. I knew I was truly accepted when he told me that I was like a *little* person. I knew he meant that I could be trusted, could play, and cared about others. And I had imagination.

Helping Cryin the mute, was yet another challenge. He came out after months of working with the system. My first task was to give him a message, through my words and actions, that I would not physically hurt him. I would sit on my hands to show him that I would not restrain him as I had learned other therapists had done. At first, he would bang his head and become agitated. During these times, I wanted desperately to stop him, but knew I must keep my hands to myself. He was a burner, and after months of working with all the others and keeping them from harming the body, Cryin became angry and burned the arm. I believed he did this because self-abuse was the only way these children knew how to express anger.

In addition, I felt he was closely watching my reactions and wanted to see if I would keep my word, or that I would not punish him or send him away. I did neither. Rather, I told him that I understood his anger and his fear, and wanted to work with him to teach him how to be angry and *not* hurt the body. Death, Stephan, Randy, and a nameless child, all seemed terrified of Cryin, and were helpful in telling me what Cryin was up to, in the hopes that I could stop it. They no longer wanted the body to hurt.

I decided I needed to see if he could speak. I wondered if he learned a language that no one else understood, would he feel safer to talk? I began speaking in French. The first word I repeated over and over was, "*Bonjour!*" After several minutes, he whispered *bonjour* back. Unfortunately, he never got past that one word. He became frustrated with me when we didn't understand one another, then he would start signing. Oh, I wish I had learned that art when my daughter was learning sign language in school. My last attempt at finding a common form of communication was writing. I gave him paper and pen, and he confidently began forming letters. I was so excited to read his thoughts, but I could not. Were his letters Greek? After minutes of trying to decipher them, I had a sudden flash and raced to a mirror. Then I saw what I suspected was true. The letters were written backwards. I could finally understand.

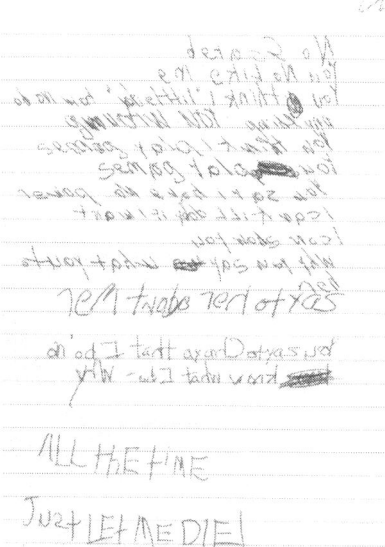

Then he began to draw horrific pictures of abuse and torture.

Eventually, he began forming words from his lips. Though

monosyllabic, they said so much: "Job, time die." I felt encouraged that I had begun to enlist his trust as I had the others, and the body would be safe again.

Each time I felt I had reached one of the children, I was so encouraged and hopeful that everything was going to finally be fine, and they would all heal and become one healthy individual. I was operating from my *pathological* optimism, but so many times my hopes were dashed as yet another episode of self-abuse occurred, and another alter was revealed. *How many more are there?* I would wonder, but I couldn't let myself get disillusioned. They needed one person to keep faith that their pain and internal chaos could eventually stop.

When I felt exhausted, unsure of my approach or direction, and close to burn out, I would turn to my husband who constantly reassured me that I was the only person who had helped them this far. "So, feel good about that," he said. I did. I truly believed that I was doing all I could. And finally I would think of the Alcoholics Anonymous statement, "Let go, let God." When I needed a power beyond the human form, I would turn to my religion and my belief that God would be there to guide me and protect the system of Gabriele.

I also knew that I needed to know more of what had really happened to these children to cause DID, in order for me to better understand the many alters continually emerging. I knew that DID is an incredible phenomenon whereby one's mind or psyche has the power to protect the core of life, the core of the system. Tigger couldn't sustain herself on her own in the unsafe world she lived in, so rather than die, she created another life force, and then another and another. Ironically, these personalities designed to protect and save the others were taught to hurt and kill, and so life became a journey into hell. Life/Death, Good/Evil, Real/Unreal, Love/Pain were concepts that got confused and distorted. To be good meant to follow the rituals learned—to burn, cut the body, let the body be deprived of sleep and food, and to keep secrets. To be bad meant to tell the secrets, to cry, to scream, to eat, and to sleep. All adults became bad; all buildings were unsafe. How would I, one person, an adult, change this thinking? I, a rational, logical person, capable of feeling, had learned a different set of rules governing right and wrong. My telling them what was their *right* was my *wrong*, only caused great confusion and anger, often provoking a display of their learned behaviors: self-mutilation.

I knew I had to enter their world of child abuse and disassociation.

Hanna: Chapter 3

Bond of Trust: Foundation of Healing

> *"Working together, ordinary people can perform extraordinary feats. They can push things that come into their hands a little higher up, a little farther on toward the heights of excellence."*
>
> **—B. J. Marshall**

When Rachel blurted out that she thought we should write a book together, we honestly thought that she had lost her mind. Why would she, or anyone else for that matter, ever want to do something like this with us? And why did she think that our story would be different, or that anyone would ever want to read about it?

Gabriele got completely overwhelmed at this point and just left. So Mikhail decided to come out and talk to Rachel about this book idea, unbeknownst to her. He did not tell her who he was, because Mikhail is rather shy. They had met before, but he thought that she did not really like him, so he kept silent.

He asked Rachel a lot of questions about what she felt the book should be like, and why she felt that this was something that she wanted to do with us. (Now remember, this is before Rachel had a complete understanding of what was going on.)

"You are the most fascinating person I have ever worked with, and I have been doing this for twenty-five years," Rachel told him. He was stunned. Why would she find us fascinating? What could she possibly see that no one else had ever seen?

She kept talking and Mikhail listened. While he listened to her, he thought about his life. He had never wanted to do anything like this before. He had never even given it any kind of consideration. When things became too chaotic internally, he had dropped out of high school and then out of college, out of sheer frustration. He had let us get fired from a number of jobs that he had worked very hard at getting. And he had never really cared if the body (and us) lived or died; he just did not feel that it was his place to make those kinds of choices.

Mikhail knew that this would be a huge commitment of time, energy, and resources, both hers and ours. Mikhail is a "man of his word," so to speak, and if he said, "Yes, I will do this," then he would do anything he could to keep his word. He almost said no, but changed his mind the more he listened to her. She seemed to be genuinely excited by the idea. But why? Mikhail thought about what he knew of Rachel and what he thought of her. He had been impressed with Rachel's willingness to learn; her ability to think for herself and come up with her own ideas, and not just follow the pack. She also seemed to be willing to do what she needed to help keep us alive. He had listened to the conversation between her and Gabriele, and he was impressed with her tenacity.

So he decided to say yes. But nothing is for free. He told her, "You'll have to learn how to play cribbage." This sounded like a good deal to all of us. Although she looked shocked, she enthusiastically agreed.

Soon afterwards we started to have concerns, both about the book and about our relationship with Rachel. We feared that she would give up sooner or later. Everyone else had so far. Did she even want to know what really had happened to us? Did she really want the truth? Was she even willing to see the pain that we held inside and never showed to the outside world? And how in the world could we really know that she was not going to hurt us too?

Then there were our fears over the book. Would Rachel be respectful of what was put into the book? Would Rachel understand that there were some things that we did not want published, or would she just ignore what we felt and thought? And what would be more important to her, our therapy and healing, or the book?

The common denominator of all these fears and questions was trust. Without trust there could be no working relationship, because there could be no honest communication. There could be no mutual respect and no room for caring. Without trust we could not heal. She had to trust us and we had to trust her. It was that simple. But it was also extremely difficult. How could we trust someone, especially a big person that we did not even know?

The first step for us in starting to trust her was her willingness to make deals with us instead of demanding contracts. For us, there was a huge difference between the two concepts. Contracts were generally written, with expectations that we, as clients, had to make all the changes.

In our past experience with mental health professionals, we felt contracts, such as "no harm contracts," were forced upon us and if we did not comply, there would be negative consequences, for example the anger of the therapist.

We were often told that if we cut or burned, the therapist would not work with us. But he/she did not offer support so that we would not cut or burn. This only served to make us dishonest with the professional.

We would hide our burns and cuts. Or we would be a "no show" (skip an appointment) because we did not want to deal with the therapist's anger and the possibility of having him/her quit on us. Another possibility was being sent to the hospital against our will. So our fear of the person who was supposed to be helping us kept us from getting the help we needed, because we could not trust him/her with very important information about what was going on with us. We did not want this to happen with Rachel, so we decided to work out deals with her instead. A deal is two-sided. Nothing was written down; it was just our word and the other person's word. Both parties negotiate honestly with each other to come up with something that they could both live with and be comfortable with. And both parties respect the other's limitations and boundaries.

For example, Rachel wanted Gabriele (and us) to agree to not harming ourselves in any way while in treatment with her. When we asked what she would do to support us so that we would not harm ourselves, her response was that she would talk to us, even if it were after normal workday hours. However, we were not comfortable with the idea of not hurting ourselves in any way at this point (it was the only way that we knew how to deal with the emotional pain and internal chaos). Therefore, the settlement agreed upon was that we would call her, or fire her, before we killed ourselves. Rachel respected this limitation at the time, but she added that we had to actually talk to her; she did not want us to just call and leave a message. We both accepted the terms. Later, we included cutting and burning as unacceptable behaviors. She never said, "If you hurt yourself, I will stop seeing you," or "If you hurt yourself, you will have to go into the hospital." We believed that Rachel truly cared if we got hurt, or died. She wanted us to stop the self-harming behaviors and live. She was willing to offer support and we had to be willing to call before we did anything.

Part of deal making is that both parties must keep their word. For our part, we had to be willing to pick up the phone and call. This was not easy for us because we have never been good at asking for help. Whenever we, as kids, asked for help, we got hurt more. As adults, we had some very bad experiences when we cried out for help. Commonly, we would be ignored, told that we were seeking attention or being silly. Occasionally, professionals that were supposed to help would put our life at risk.

For example, we called a crisis hotline one night that was staffed by professional counselors with degrees in social work. When we told the counselor that we were suicidal and wanted to take an overdose of medication, he responded that we were wasting his time and he was sick of dealing with us. "Why don't you just do it and quit wasting my time and playing head games with me?" We overdosed on a large amount of medication that night, but luckily were found by a friend who got us help. So we learned not to ask for help, and instead came to fear the idea of doing so. Therefore, we had a lot of fear that Rachel would do something similar, but she never did. She was clear that she did not want us to die.

Rachel was always telling us that it was okay to call. It was okay for us to ask for help. In fact, she never blew us off when we did call and ask for help, and she never said or implied that we were bluffing or seeking attention. She always understood that we were serious and that this was not a game for us. This was a new experience for us, because we were used to being told that we were playing games or that we were wasting someone's time. And though at first it was frightening, over time we came to trust that she did want to help us and would keep her word.

One of the things that we had to do in order to build trust with Rachel was constantly ask her for reality checks. For example, we were always afraid that Rachel would be upset with us if we called and woke her, or even worse, woke her husband and daughter up. One of our first questions to her was, "Are you mad at us?"

"I would rather be awakened than find out that something happened that I could have helped prevent. So no, I am not angry. I'm glad you called." She would tell us this almost to the word, every time, in a groggy voice. But it helped ease that fear and let us know that we had done the right thing to call.

At times, some of us would decide not to call and instead would harm the body. We were always scared that she would be angry with us because we had hurt ourselves and not kept our word with her.

Rachel was always consistent in her response, "No, I am not angry. I don't get mad at people who are in so much pain. I am sad that you felt you needed to do this, because there are other ways to deal with the pain. But please, call me before anything happens and let me be the judge of what I can do. I would rather be woken up than have something happen and have to deal with the aftermath."

Randy was one of the first to trust Rachel. This was shown in his willingness to take a risk by telling her about all of us, and trying to communicate what was happening inside so that she could understand us as a whole. The system rule was that we did not tell big person secrets, but he knew that we would not get better if we continued to hide who we were, what we really thought, how we really felt, and what we did to harm ourselves. However, he still had some fears and doubts that Rachel, a big person, could really understand. When he finally met her in person, he kept a physical distance between them. After all, she was an adult and he could not be completely sure that she would not hurt him. But Randy kept talking to her, because she listened to him and kept telling him that it was not okay for anyone to hurt him. Over time, the trust between them grew. She did not get angry with him for calling her when there was "big trouble." She always listened to what he told her. She kept her patience with him when he was having trouble explaining things to her. This was something that was new for him, as most adults would get frustrated with him, or blow him off, when he was trying to convey something he felt was very important. And then she tried to do whatever she could to help.

One of the ways Rachel earned his trust was making sure that we would feed him. She even listened when he told her that he did not like meat. This meant the world to Randy. No one had ever taken the time to really listen to him or care about his basic needs. We all knew that Rachel had Randy's complete trust when he let her hold him while he cried. This is not something that he had ever let any big people do.

Part of the process of building trust was that we had to learn to trust in Rachel's belief that we could heal, that we were good people, that we deserved forgiveness and could forgive ourselves. Most importantly, we had to believe that we did not deserve to die.

A good example of this learning process was the relationship between Rachel and Death. At first, Death was not willing to trust Rachel, and instead looked at her as an adversary. Rachel was probing more, trying to find out the reasons for the self-mutilation, in order to stop it and keep the body alive. In doing this, Rachel was getting in Death's way. Death felt threatened by all of this. She did not trust adults, and she especially did not trust shrinks. She felt that Rachel was telling us all a bunch of lies and was "full of shit." She did not believe that we could ever heal, and there was no way that we could ever be forgiven for anything that we had ever done, or that she had done. And why the hell would Rachel give a good goddamn about someone as fucked up as us?

Yet there was another side to Death. She was very sensitive and caring towards other people. She wanted someone to care about her. She did want to be forgiven. She did want to heal. And deep down, she did want to choose life. She wanted to feel real. And more than anything, she wanted to tell someone about what had happened to her and us. She did this through her poetry, a creative and expressive side that she never showed anyone. One of the poems that she worked on for years was about feeling trapped and hopeless, but wanting to be understood and heard. Before she could even consider trusting Rachel, she needed to see Rachel's reaction to her work. Rachel did not learn who was the true author until Death told her. This was Death's way of asking for Rachel's help, but at the same time, she truly did not think that Rachel could help. She did not think that Rachel wanted to hear about what had happened to her—or us. And if she did, she was not sure if Rachel would believe her.

Walls

These walls—
they were Built long ago,
when there was no hope of Release
from this Prison of Pain
that was
Constructed at my birth
How i have Hoped that someone
Would
Could
see what it is like for me;
But i do not Dare
let anyone Inside
these Walls
to see the Real me—
for that is too Dangerous
i can only hope to Explain my World
how it is a living Hell;
how every day is a Battle to Survive;
how i long for Someone
Anyone

Beyond These Walls

to Understand my Pain
these Walls will Never
Ever
Come Down—
they are too Massive
to Tear down
Now—
they have been in place so long
they are now Part of me
To tear them down Now
it would Destroy me
& my World—
or so i fear
but still
this Aloneness
it is Tearing holes
in my Heart
my Soul
There is no Escape from this Prison:
only Survival
and a wish for Understanding
from Someone who might just give a Damn
"Would anyone be Willing to look over this Wall?
just once?"
is what i want to Scream
"Or am i too Scared to Risk someone Seeing my
World
with all its Pain & Shame?"
This is what i say
to myself
at Night
"No one can Reach me here"
my mind says to the Night
"No one is Willing to Try"
It says back
"i have built these Walls too High,
for too long
they can not come over Them now"

is my last Thought
The Night is quiet,
for there is no Response
to my Thoughts
my Truth
"Why"
i ask myself,
"Do i Fight the only thing i have ever Known?
is there no escape from here?
Keeping only this Knowledge that i am trapped Here
Forever?"
i ask over & over—
Living with Only the Hope that if Someone—
ust one person—
was willing
& i was to let them
They would come over these Walls
Just Once
and sit with me in
my self Imposed Prison
"Someone,
Anyone,
give me the Chance to Show my Pain!"
But no one can hear my cry:
the Walls block it—
the Voice in the Night
will not let it be Heard
"Why am i so Alone in my
Pain?
Fear?
Hate?
Shame?
Why do i Continue to Survive?
Is there no Hope of a Life for me?
Why must i Live this way"
All Questions
that never have Answers
Everything is hidden within

> *Behind*
> *Walls*
> *that have existed*
> *since my birth*
> *Walls*
> *that have stood*
> *since the Beginning of*
> *Time*

Rachel read this poem, looked up and said, "This is incredible!"

Slowly, Death and Rachel built trust. If Death left a message, Rachel would call back within an hour, or sooner, and talk to her, even if it was only for five minutes. Rachel never accused Death of "bluffing." She always took her seriously and understood that Death was trying very hard to stay alive.

Rachel did something that no other adult or therapist had been willing to do - admit when she made a mistake. For example, when we first started working with Rachel, she made the statement that all of us were no longer needed and could "go away now." Thinking that she was talking to Gabriele, she suggested that Gabriele throw all of us into the lake. Stephana and Storm were furious! They proceeded to inform Rachel that Gabriele was nothing without all of us, and we were not going anywhere. She did not have a right to try and get rid of us, and there was a reason we were here! As they were talking, we could see in Rachel's face that she knew she had made a huge mistake that could lead to the end of the therapeutic relationship. The look on her face was one of "Oh shit! What did I just do?" She then promised to learn more about DID and promised to work with all of us. We were amazed that a big person, especially one with a degree and a therapist, was willing to admit her mistake to our face.

Another example of her ability to admit when she was wrong was when Rachel implied one time that Death was "playing games." Death was hurt and angry. She felt that Rachel was not listening to what she was telling her, and had broken her word. She was also extremely confused, because Rachel had never done this before. Death felt that she was being honest with Rachel, and she was trying to keep her word about talking to Rachel before she did anything harmful. "Why is Rachel doing this?" Death kept asking all of us over and over, in tears. She finally promised Rachel that she would not do anything that night and went home. The following day she saw Rachel again, and tried again to tell Rachel what she felt and what she was going through. She again did not feel listened to and felt that Rachel was making excuses for what she had done. Death decided that she had to fire Rachel and told Mikhail to do it. She did not want another confrontation with Rachel. She did not want to talk to Rachel about what had happened or her decision. Mikhail knew that Death would most likely kill us afterwards, but he also wanted a chance to reason with Rachel, so he agreed to call.

As soon as Rachel got on the phone, she apologized to Death, through Mikhail. Rachel told him that she realized in her frustration, she had done the one thing that she said she would never do, which was imply that Death was wasting her time and not being honest with her. Hearing Rachel apologize and admit that she was wrong made Death realize that Rachel really did care, and was different. "Please don't do that to me ever again—okay?" she told Rachel in tears. Rachel promised not to. This incident gave Death faith in Rachel as both a human being and as a therapist. It intensified her trust in Rachel.

All of us were amazed at the courage and respect that Rachel showed by her willingness to admit that she made mistakes. We have never been good at accepting criticism, because it only served to make us feel worse about ourselves. So we did not expect Rachel to be any different. When we saw Rachel's ability to not only admit her mistakes and short comings, but also her willingness to discuss them, we discovered something we had never known: that one could grow and learn from criticism, rather than be humiliated by it.

The way that TOB and Rachel built trust was a little different. Every time that Rachel would want TOB to make an agreement about cutting, or worse, hanging himself, TOB would blow smoke in her face. He would lie to get her off his back, and then do something anyway. TOB was sure that Rachel did not know what she was talking about, and that she really did not want to know everything that he had done. Rachel would tell TOB, "I want the cutting to stop because it is hurting you, and them." Rachel wanted TOB to realize that he was part of a whole person, yet he would not see her side of it. TOB was sure that he was pure evil and that cutting was the only way to get that evil out.

TOB never agreed to stop harming the body. However, he found other ways to build trust with Rachel. It started with Rachel's refusal to believe that he was evil, and with her showing that she was not frightened of him. TOB was convinced that he was going to contaminate both Rachel and her office. Rachel did not believe that he could, or that he would. Rachel felt that he had a right to come into her office. She respected him as a human being and pushed for him to meet her face-to-face, and for all of us to allow it. One day when they were talking about respect, TOB said, "Respect is recognizing each person as an individual and as having a right to exist." The depth of his statement shocked us, and his saying it aloud shocked us even more. It made us think that there might be some hope for the boy after all. So we allowed her to meet with him whenever he needed to.

Another way TOB gained trust in Rachel was her willingness to listen to his beliefs. She did not just want to learn from books. This was important to TOB, because he couldn't read or write. They would discuss what he believed and what she believed, and ask each other questions so that they could both learn more. He wanted Rachel to really understand what he felt and why. Deep within, he really did want to believe that he could do something worthwhile.

Rachel was always trying to look for something good in all of us. One day, in his usual obnoxious style, TOB mentioned his love for his garden. Rachel quickly noted this seeming contradiction, and started talking to him about plants. He showed her a soft and sensitive side that he revealed to no one else. He laughed with Rachel and told her, "You better not tell anyone about this or you'll ruin my reputation." Rachel saw an opportunity and asked him to care for her office plants. He couldn't believe her trust in him. Moreover, he couldn't believe how bad their condition was; it appeared that Rachel had a "black thumb."

Rachel did something else that surprised TOB. She made a home visit to check on us when she knew we were feeling extremely self-destructive. He never suspected that she would do anything like that. He did not understand why she cared, but he decided to give her a chance. He finally agreed to give up his pocketknife whenever things were not going well. This was a true statement of his trust in her.

The street kids were another matter. They were extremely distrusting of big people, so all adults were automatically viewed as a threat. Therefore, Rachel was viewed not as someone who wanted to help them, but as someone that was going to hurt them. Their belief was that Rachel would hurt them by making them break their "bond." They had given an oath that they would keep it, despite the fact that the bond was something that was imposed upon them. What they could not understand was that the bond did not need to exist in the here and now, or that it should never have existed in the first place. When Rachel tried to explain this to any of them, they got angry and would burn or cut the body.

We were terrified of these kids and we felt that they were the embodiment of everything that had ever happened to us. We did not want to even acknowledge that they had a reason or purpose for existing. To us, they were everything that we all hated about ourselves. Most of us did not want Rachel to talk to them and we were frightened that Rachel would be harmed, which to the rest of us, was unacceptable. Rachel did not seem to share this fear but, in the beginning, she made some crucial mistakes that took months to overcome.

Her first mistake was her implication that they did not need to be around, and that they did not have anything of value to contribute. This only served to fuel their anger, causing them to step up the pace of their self-harming activities. Then when Rachel found out that they were the ones that were pushing Gabriele to kill herself, Rachel called them ignorant, stupid kids. All of us agreed with her, except one, QED. She knew that 1) they were not going to just go away like they had never been here in the first place; and 2) Rachel had fallen into a "trap." She had become frustrated and had forgotten that they were children, and that everything that they did had a purpose and reason behind it. When Rachel was reminded of this, she apologized and started working with them intensely.

Rachel's third mistake was that she approached working with them as though they had the ability to think logically. They did not, and her arguments only served to confuse and anger them. They felt that Rachel was lying to them and was trying to trick them into doing things that they believed they had been told not to do, or so they believed. She would tell them that they were safe and then not prove to them that they were. She would tell them that the mom was dead and could no longer hurt them, but they continued to see the mom and hear her. Rachel and the street kids were not speaking the same language. This was something that had to be worked on constantly.

Over the course of several months, Rachel and the street kids slowly learned to respect and trust one another. The street kids had to learn new ways of thinking about the world, and Rachel had to learn to keep her frustration in check. By her not reacting to their behaviors, they no longer had reason to find fault or be angry with her. The street kids learned that Rachel did want to help them, and they slowly learned that she was not going to try and send them away.

Rachel learned to be patient and see them for what they really were, scared children. She also learned that she needed to work on helping them see the world in a different light, so she started to tell the street kids about white light, rainbows, and love, concepts they had never known. They were fascinated. When one of them would become upset, Rachel calmed them with guided imagery, where she would take them to a cloud, or have them imagine a rainbow, or white light. At first they were frightened that she would harm them in some way, or would want them to tell her secrets, but she promised them that she would do neither. She made it clear that children were not supposed to be hurt by adults, that children were precious and adults were supposed to protect them. All of this made them listen in a way they had never learned to listen to an adult before. Slowly the cutting and burning diminished, and the body was allowed to eat and sleep more regularly without their interference.

There were still setbacks. The hardest thing for them to learn was that they did not have to die and that the bond could be broken.

Rachel kept saying that all of us were incredible human beings: smart, kind, gentle, and giving. She told us that we brought goodness into her life, and that we were not bad or evil. Nothing we told her would make her change her mind about that. We all felt much differently and we kept asking ourselves how we could ever bring ourselves to tell Rachel about what had happened, and what we had done. Would Rachel even be willing to hear our story? Would we have the courage to tell her?

With trust, we took more risks and began to share our story, the story of abuse and our creation.

Rachel was the only person that had ever seen each of us as distinct, and found creative ways to understand whom each of us were. She even wanted to know why each of us needed to become so distinct and separate. And so we decided to let her in to the years of abuse that we had all suffered.

Rachel: Chapter 4

Shattered Body—Shattered Minds

> *"Most of us, swimming against the tides of troubles the world knows nothing about, need only a bit of praise or encouragement—and we'll make the goal."*
>
> —**J. P. Fleishman**

"Why? How could a mother do that? I could never hurt another human being." Those words, uttered by Death, constantly replayed in my mind. How *could* a mother consciously hurt her child? The more I learned from Tigger, Little Catherine, Cobalt, TOB, Death, Sandy and Randy, in particular, the more I came to believe that Gabriele, et al, the system, as we began to call them, were victims of extreme abuse, neglect, heinous acts from adults, and ritualistic practices that could only be considered sadistic torture.

Before I describe what I learned from each personality, it is important that the reader know that these memories were never prompted or solicited by using hypnosis or other memory recall strategies. They were freely remembered, as trust developed, and pain began to ooze forth like lava from a volcanic explosion. These memories needed to surface in order to help each of them understand who was bad, who deserved punishment, what punishments were appropriate, and what were not. I wanted each one to tell his/her story in the hope that the pain each carried could be lessened by my reassurances that each was not to blame for these acts. These children all believed that they were bad, evil and that they deserved punishment. They had to earn what children are given unconditionally—To them, to be punished by being burned, cut, deprived of sleep and food, locked up, punched, and sexually mutilated, were all appropriate ways of teaching them lessons. How my heart ached as each personality described these piece-by-piece.

Child abuse has been defined (in the 1998 Microsoft Encarta Encyclopedia) as "intentional acts that result in physical or emotional harm to children…behaviors that range from physical assault by parents or other adult caregivers, to neglect of a child's basic needs."

Every time one of the child personalities would painfully disclose recollections, they would ask, "Why?" I searched my brain trying to understand child abusers and perpetrators, but my only response was, "I don't know. Parents and adults must never hurt children. Children deserve to be loved and cared about." I did not think they understood the concept of love and caring. They would ask me how I punished my daughter. I shared that I never punished her, rather I would tell her in a firm way when I didn't approve of her behavior. I never hit her.

They would look at me in confusion, and ask, "You didn't lock her up, or punch her, or make her not sleep or eat? We must have deserved it. The body is bad." What made them believe their body was so evil? What was repressed for years began to slowly be revealed.

The abuse that will be described both graphically and verbally in the following pages became a grim secret, forced to be kept secret by them from the earliest age on out of fear of retaliation by the abusers. They made threats such as, "you will be thrown out the window, burned, or hung by your neck." Messages such as, "if you ever tell, you or I will be killed," were so powerful that living with confusion distorted beliefs about the self. Shame and fear became their way of life. There was such a fear in telling, or of speaking the words, that I used writing as a means to learn more. Somehow, this didn't seem like going against the mom. Also, if I asked questions and they answered, they felt this could not be construed as telling.

The one time Death did try to tell a teacher, the mother died the following day. Although her demise was an accident, the child's mind did make the correlation that, "to tell does indeed mean death." When one of their former foster moms died, the kids asked me, "Are we to blame? Did we make her sick?" When I said no, and asked why they would think that, Randy said, "Because people would tell us that we made them sick." It was clear to me how innocuous expressions people, especially adults, use when upset, can so easily be misinterpreted in a child's mind. All the child alters had been living with the belief that they had the power to cause illness and even death. I had to prove to them that this was untrue.

Other attempts at telling often resulted in disbelief by the adults addressed. Many found it too horrifying to believe that parents could attack children, and tried to obliterate these thoughts and deny that they could occur. It was no wonder that Gabriele, et al, would preface their stories with, "You won't believe me," to which I always replied, "Yes, I will."

Gabriele, et al, lived with such devastating memories that they could not imagine themselves loveable, or capable of being a productive, worthwhile member of society. Gabriele would say that everything she touched went bad. She felt that she didn't deserve to be cared about or cared for. They all felt that they would contaminate me.

Their lost childhood led to a lost adulthood. I believed strongly that by uncovering the sources of their shame, they could have a chance at a healthy adulthood.

The first realization of the extent of abuse was on my receipt of a folded piece of paper. Written upon this paper were the words that "the voice" would say. Here is what she heard:

"Does this feel good?" "Say it." "Stop screaming." "I'll teach you!" "You are so stupid." "Mommy loves you!" "You say anything and I'll fuck you up!" "You little mother fucker!" "It's your fault." "You will never learn—will you?" "Do it now!" "Kiss me goodnight." "You'll be the death of me!" "I should have had an abortion." "Go to Hell." "It never happened." "I'll never make it to 40 because of you." "They will

lock you up." "I never wanted you." "That's a good girl—now do it some more." "If you tell you die." "This is our little secret." "What is your problem?!" "Stupid brat." "I'll get in trouble if you say anything." "Loser!" "You will never be anything." "You're just like your father." "You made me do it." "Can't you do anything worth a goddamn?" "Who died and made you god?" "Fuck off." "Cunt." "Stop crying." "I'll give you something to cry about!" "What- does that hurt?" "I'll tell you when to stop!" "Stay in here till your ready to do it." "You're crazy." "PIG!" "You are a monster." "You ugly little bitch!" "I'm just teaching you how." "Now what?" "Fucking dirty ugly bitch!" "Faster!" "Go ahead—scream—I like that." "Don't tell me you're sorry." "You baby." "It tastes like bubble gum."

Who was the voice? I didn't want to assume it was the mother, but who else could have said, "I never wanted you, I should have had an abortion"?

Other torn up bits of paper were given to me in those early sessions—wisps of information, so shaming to verbalize, yet painfully revealing.

She likes to come in at 12 or so—she talks to me really sweetly telling me she loves me and that I am the only one that she cares about. She gets in bed with me and keeps saying things in that sweet voice. Rubbing as she talks. I know I can't get away.

And:

"We are here to honor our father by fucking our mother"

Pictures were shared that were drawn by TOB, Cryin and Tigger. I viewed them with disbelief that adults could be so sick as to treat children like animals.

I didn't understand the symbolism of them until months later. TOB shared with me the sexual and physical abuse at the hands of the mother. They would be locked in a dark utility room, hands tied, instruments inserted in the vagina, burned by her lighter with her initials engraved on it, or by a cigarette.

Tigger offered more of the horrors she experienced. During a play therapy I set crayons, magic markers and paper in front of her. She drew her room and in almost an inaudible voice, told me how the mom would come into her room from the mom's room, come into her bed, talk softly, and then lick her. Stuart would also come, smelling like cinnamon, rub her vagina, and tell her "it tasted like bubble gum." It was at that point that Death would trade places. Here is an excerpt of what Death finally unearthed:

Rachel,

Tonight you said that I should just tell you about what happened like it happened. [You] almost made it sound easy. I know that I need to tell you. I just really do not know how. I don't know how to explain something like that—or how to find the right words. How do I explain that it was not just what she did but how it felt while she was doing it. Or what she would say. Or the smells—the way she would look—the sound of her voice. How she would be talking in this sweet voice—tell me that good girls liked to do this while she had her fingers shoved up me and I just wanted to scream. But knew better—knew that I better not make a sound. Then when she was done she would grab my hair and tell me to keep my fucking mouth shut or she would kill me.

How do I explain what it was like to go down on her and have her grab my hair—yanking it so hard that I could feel it coming out—and pulling my head down so hard that I could not breathe. And hearing her laugh when I would try to get away. Or the taste of her that I could never get rid of. Or what her hand felt like while she stroked me, how it would feel good—then she would smile and shove something in me—and I could not get away.

How do I describe having him on top of me, pushing and pumping—my insides feeling like they were being ripped out, his sweat all over me and looking over and seeing her face? Knowing she liked what she saw and that she would join in—and just wanting to die. Not even allowed to close my eyes. "Look at me!" Slap. And I could not scream because he had his hand in my mouth. Asking God to make it stop and to let me die. I learned real quickly that nothing would. Not being able to walk afterwards—and the blood. And feeling dirty and knowing nothing would make me clean. And knowing it had to be my fault. And being about 3.

This wasn't just sexual abuse: Gabriele, et al, were survivors of incest—a taboo that must remain unspoken in order to protect a family system. As more deviant behavior by the mother, and stepfather were shared, the extreme shame and humiliation that these children felt needed to be dealt with. I tried to explain the realities of incest and how children must not forget that it is the adult who initiates the acts. According to Sullivan and Everstein in *Sexual Trauma in Children and Adolescent,* parents of an incest victim exercise this power to mold the reality and self-definition of the child in such a way that he or she has no choice but to become oriented to adult sex.

Another dynamic that results from incest is the confusion felt between feeling close, feeling scared, feeling hurt, feeling angry and having sex. They needed to understand that it was the adults who deserved punishment. They needed to let go of self-blame. They had no control of their environment. They were powerless to react in any other way, but to comply. They needed to understand that these acts were a fundamental breach of trust between parent and child. They had been betrayed and prevented from having a healthy nurturing childhood. I realized more than ever what a major risk it had been to trust in me.

These poems written by Death depict more vividly than any narration:

> *Every time i turn around*
> *i see her Face*
> *there it is - -*
> *Mean as ever:*
> *Hating me*
> *Loathing me*
> *Wanting me Dead*
> *nothing i say will make her*

*Go Away
it is her
Power
that makes her
Real
she is Almighty
in her ability to
Scare
i committed <u>Treason</u>
you see
and now she will make me
<u>Pay</u>
There was a time that i <u>Wanted</u>
<u>Tried</u>
to be Good;
to do her Will -
as a child - -
Now i am no better than her
Now i pay with my mind;
My Life
there is no Forgiveness ...
for i committed Treason...
Now there is only more Insane Pain-*

*there she is - -
looking me in the eye;
telling me
"<u>I Own You</u>"
i know i will Pay - -
or maybe i Already Am*

And:

*The air is hot and heavy
the Smell of Her is Everywhere
i look and see Her standing there*

Rachel Gunner

*it must be a Monster
it can't be my Mother
O God ...
Trouble is in the air...
i don't want to be here..
please let me get away.....*

*The air is cool and light
The smell of spring is everywhere
The Meadow is so Real
Thank God She is Not Here
i can hear the Children playing
their voices ringing in the air
But
in the Distance i hear the Thunder
of the Storm that is Brewing
of the Flood that is Coming
and
i must Return*

*The night is gone
She sits at the table
no remorse in Her eyes
there never will be
this can't be Real
O what i would give
just to be Free*

*what is a Mother
or a Protector
when you Know only a Monster
that lives not in your closet
but in your House
comes to your room
then to your bed
when there should be*

only Dreams there instead

It was no wonder they felt the bed was a torture chamber. Almost all chose to sleep on the floor, or not sleep at all.

How could I help them feel safe? Did they even understand the meaning of this word? In working with this system, I realized that words in the English language take on their meanings from their usage and from what descriptions other give to these words. Safety was a concept unfamiliar to them all. Therefore, when I gave what I believed a simple directive, "You are safe," I was not thinking that I was talking to them in a foreign language. I had to examine and define all these words so that we could to speak to each other in the same tongue. Their reality was skewed by hearing of voices, and of nightmares and visions of big people who entered their room at night. How could I restore something they never had, such as safety, protection, and comfort? I knew the uncovering of what had been hidden was the first step towards healing.

I also believed there were many barriers still to be torn down. One in particular was their inability to express feelings. They all were afraid to scream and cry. I learned from Sandy that when Death cried because her cat had been killed, the mother punished her by putting her in a box alongside the "dead" cat. Only the cat still breathed. What occurred was the creation of Copula and Sandy to help handle the fear of darkness. They became crazed, especially Sandy, who learned how to "see trees" within the torture of her living grave. These children learned never to cry out for help, but to endure and deny their existence. For them, letting out these emotions would mean the images would no longer just be in the mind and they would start to feel real. Could they handle the reality of their past? I believed that emotional abreaction was crucial to the process. I often used the analogy of an infection with the pus beneath the wound; there is so much pain at this stage. Yet once the pus surfaces, the infection can finally heal. Once emotions surface, the deep wounds can finally mend. I knew a major goal for treatment would be to free them of the fear that expressing anger, hurt, and sorrow would lead to more torment and pain. Their tortured souls were so fragile and vulnerable that I walked this path stealthily and softly. The trust we had developed would help on this road.

*my voice comes
and catches in my throat -
the words
choke my screams -
the tears
drown my words -
the Grief is so
Strong
the Anger so
Hot
the Fear so
Real
How do you Explain
Emotion?
How do you let go of Screams
from Years long ago gone?
How do you Cry
for a Child
long ago grown
But still Real -
Still Here?
How do you allow yourself
to be Held
when Simple touch Hurts
the Heart
but
Heals the Soul?
How do you Forgive
A Crime
that even God sees as
Sin
But not Yours?
How do you ask for
Forgiveness
When
Unforgivable
Contemptible
But not Responsible?*

Beyond These Walls

How do you give it up
When
it is your World
your Reality
But not True?
How do you pick up
the Pieces
and start Over
And find the
Courage to
Change?

And:

Too much Heartache
Humiliation
Hatred
the time goes by
the Feelings grow

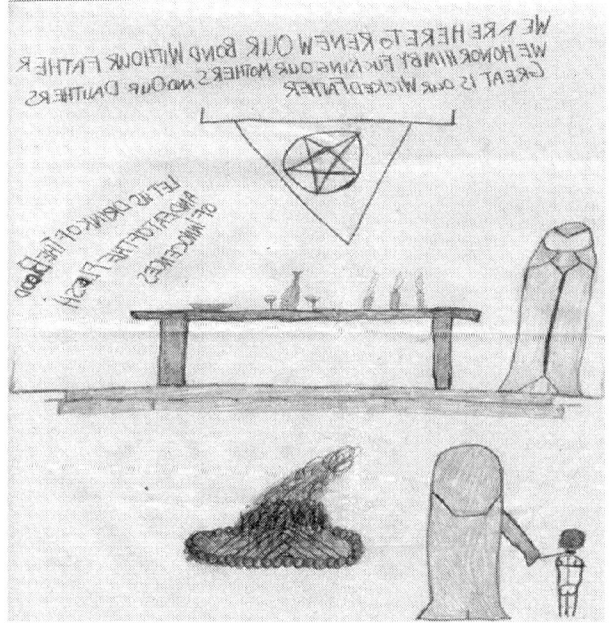

> *more insane*
> *i can't Handle Them—*
> *they are Inane*
> *i don't need them;*
> *they are not mine*
> *ou can Have them*
> *just Leave Me Behind*
> *Soo...*
> *Please don't hang*
> *around*
> *Feelings are the Foe*
> *They only come in the*
> *Wee hours*
> *they Creep up from Behind*
> *don't Acknowledge them—*
> *For they are*
> <u>*NOT MINE!!!*</u>

What had they all experienced or witnessed that led to such acts of self-mutilation, such as daily burning and cutting, as well as a belief that "the body must die"? TOB gave me the first clues that perhaps I wasn't dealing with just physical or sexual abuse, but heinous acts far greater than the healthy mind could endure - acts engaged in by evil and sadistic people. I could not verify that they were describing satanic, cult-like activities, but as memories of their horrors purged out, only those ritualistic activities seemed to fit the crimes.

TOB saw himself as a creator of all evil, a source of contamination. How did he learn to believe such thoughts? Cutting and burning were learned behaviors. They learned to believe that these were methods to rid them of their pain. Cutting was a way to rid the body of evil. For Sandy, cutting and making the "red come out" kept her feeling alive as she lay in her grave. Death shared that if she screamed, Stuart would shove a sock in her mouth, shove her on the floor, and if that didn't work, cut or burn them. The mother would watch and enjoy. They learned to feel no pain. Fire and blood were symbols of their torture, but were also seen as the beginning and ending of life.

Trial by Fire was a ritual they believed they must endure to finally know if they were good or evil. Cobalt described it in this way:

"I cannot have clothes on. I have to be below the sky. It has to be dark and in the same place where no one can find me. I have to set the tree and me on fire. It has to be a certain kind of tree. I have to wait to see what the verdict is. If I die, I am free. If I live, I know where I have to go. I cannot tell you. It is treason." Death meant freedom.

Here was another example of how the use of words could cause great confusion of meaning. I would say, "You can be free of all fear." If I did not include, "In life," I was in effect reinforcing their own beliefs: once they died, they would never experience fear again.

Bonfires were images that flashed before their eyes. People wearing hoods would be at gatherings. Death remembered the mom looking like a monster one night, telling her she was crazy, and threatening her that if she screamed, she would "give me over to one of them." She was given over to the men who raped her in a ferocious gang rape. At this moment in her recall, she was horrified to describe what ensued. She feared I could never like her if I knew. Her shame was so deep. What more could these people have done to an innocent child? I soon received my answer. Her body gave way in fear. She began purging, urinating and defecating, and then was forced to eat her own feces. All she could feel was damaged goods, not fit as a human being. Indeed, she had been treated worse than a lowly animal.

I was convinced that we were dealing with satanic rituals as the physical abuse was so severe, and the sexual abuse so sadistic and humiliating. The emotional abuse left each child feeling worthless and evil, such that they could only belong to Satan: the God of Evil. The adults had used methods to indoctrinate them to the beliefs that the bond of the "circle" was sacred, never to be broken. Treason led to punishment. Burning, cutting, and killing were acceptable forms of punishment. Dying began to be wished for. As Death and Gabriele both would say, "Sometimes I want to die so bad, I can taste it." They would be upset with me for not letting them do what they were supposed to do. Cryin would become irate when I would stop him from "doing his job." He wrote, "Just let me die." I told him I could not. What makes a child see death as a gift? I realized that it

was the only way out, a way to free them from so much pain. Cryin wrote down what seemed like a hierarchy of life and death:
>   Blood
>   Birth
>   Life
>   Fire
>   Death
>   Rebirth

This helped me understand the patterns I was seeing these children follow. All their self-abuse involved blood and fire. Dying was a way to return to a better life.

TOB felt most responsible for the evil in the body. He believed that if he had given the adults what they wanted, his word that he'd never tell another living soul, they might not have been so tortured. But that would have been selling his soul. They were all made to believe that they no longer owned their bodies. He described what Satanism meant to him. It was the use of children for power. Children represented innocence and virginity. A child lost his innocence by being an active participant in sins. Children represented God. Satan, Lucifer, wanted God's power. But God did not want to share it and expelled Satan from heaven. Satan, in his anger, used children to turn them away from God. All that Satan did was to represent God's polarity, the diabolical. Thus, the image of good became evil. Therein lay the answer to *their* distorted belief systems of good and evil. The belief was that *they* were written in the book of "servants," and this could not be erased. When I heard these views, I wanted to scream, "Don't you understand these were irrational thoughts of disturbed people?" But I was aware that this was all they knew. I had to offer them another way of understanding life and death. Without imposing my religious beliefs, I tried to share the Judaic view of God. Their interest and openness to listening was encouraging. During the healing process, forgiveness became a major focus of attention. Cobalt shared her greatest fear, which was the coming of "Hallows Eve." I feared that this date corresponded to Halloween and involved a death ritual, because she would say, "I need to do it before then." I assumed the "it" was the Trial. Ted Schwartz, in his book *Satanism: Is Your Family Safe?* explains, "Satanic practice took consistent forms. Ceremonies evolved for the celebration of life and the ritual slaughter of the innocent. All Saints Day, a time roughly corresponding to our present celebration of Halloween was a festival in which a child must die." Was this what she was referring to? I knew I had to break her bond with that circle before October 31st.

As the date neared, the internal panic became unbearable. The street kids pushed the others away; they tried to tune out my voice. They could have nothing get in their way of doing "what they needed to do." They could not be alive on Hallows Eve! I worked tirelessly day and night to try to reprogram their internalized messages. If they could pass over that date, unharmed, perhaps they could trust my words, "You are safe."

The most devastating consequence to their years of torture was the internalization of shame. Shame has been defined as "an emotion in response to a negative evaluation of one's self." According to experts, "Shame-prone persons interpret every incident as validation of how worthless they are, how bad they are, how unlovable, how incapable of loving and giving to others" (Harper and Hoopes). The belief is, "if others discover how bad I am, they will abandon me" (Borysenko); and "Shame is an adaptive, submissive state that favors survival but creates fear and helplessness."

As therapy progressed, Death seemed to regress into her negative self once again and though she reassured me she would not burn herself, it seemed that she was feeling more emptiness and terror as I approached the core of their being, the root of their creations. I knew she was still withholding shaming experiences. She was so afraid that my knowing would contaminate me and might make me turn against her. I knew releasing the shame was necessary for healing, but I needed her to feel safe. I needed her to know that no matter what she had experienced in her past, *I* would not be ashamed of her. Although I knew this message would be difficult to comprehend, my consistent caring for and acceptance of her would eventually help her conquer her fears. She began revealing the horrors she had witnessed, and continued to experience nightly in her mind.

What she finally shared helped me to understand the terrors and screams that prevailed throughout the night. They were the screams of a little boy named Jeffrey, who was a child of one of the adults in the circle. As she talked, her voice became a whisper and she hung her head. I reached out my hands to hold hers. I knew what she would reveal next would be crucial to her unburdening and eventual healing. Here's an excerpt of what she very painfully uncovered:

> *"They told me he was an offering. It was his birthday… They put him on an altar on his belly. I held him down while they did the raping… I listened to him scream. Everyone had a turn at him… I could have stopped them. I could have been the sacrifice instead… I hear him now, screaming for his mommy."*

She couldn't go on any further during that session. I just held her, repeating that she couldn't have stopped them. She was just a child as well, a child feeling great fear, a child who had learned that if you didn't listen and comply, you got hurt. This did not seem to calm or comfort her. She believed *she* could have chosen death.

Several days after this session, Death attended a Judaic Shabbat service in which the rabbi was explaining a Torah reading dedicated to Moses' talk with his people. It was at this time that he said, "You must choose life." I could not have asked for a more appropriate sermon! This seemed to give Death more courage to continue purging her guilt and shame. She told me Jeffery had died that night; she had just been a witness to a horrifying crime. She was too scared that I would see her as the disgusting person she saw herself to be. I told her nothing I heard would change my impression of her. I viewed her as a caring, compassionate, sensitive young woman, who didn't deserve to be treated as an animal.

During one marathon session, lasting into the night, she finally revealed the truth: she had been told that if she didn't do it, they would… they would kill him slowly and painfully. She thought the only thing she could do to stop his screaming, to stop his pain, was to agree to drown him. It was at that moment that she made a bond with herself: she must die too. She must be punished for this wrongdoing. Then Death left and another took over, but she remembered nothing else. I cried with her after her shameful disclosure. This is what she had been holding onto, the poor child. She and Jeffrey were two victims of inhuman beings, manipulated to take the blame for reprehensible deeds. She had believed she was indeed responsible for another's death. She saw herself as a murderer. I held her and with tears, comforted this troubled soul. I repeated, over and over, "You didn't have a choice; you did the only humane thing; you wanted him to die as peacefully as possible; you saved him from greater pain." She didn't completely internalize these words and I knew that there was still more work to be done before healing could take place.

I asked how the murder of a child could have been hidden. It wasn't. His death became the consequence of a car accident. The public never knew the truth. But, a ten-year-old little girl did know what really happened.

Her subconscious held onto this horrifying knowledge with deep shame and guilt. It became too painful to carry all of these emotions. The mind knew how to fragment itself into other parts. It had done this since the age of two. Once again, other personalities took over to help share in the pain. I needed them to understand this phenomenon.

How could I explain disassociation to them in a way that it would be seen as an act of sanity rather than insanity? One body, many minds. How could that be?

Hanna: Chapter 4

Shattered Body—Shattered Minds

"Do not fear the winds of adversity. Remember: a kite rises against the wind rather than with it."
—**B. J. Marshall**

You have just read what Rachel wrote about the abuse that we suffered. All of it is true. Discussing all of those things with Rachel was not easy. In fact, we went through hell just trying to muster up the courage to tell her about the abuse. We couldn't understand why she believed us when so many other people had not, and we'd ask her over and over why she did. Her response was always, "Why would you make this up? Children don't make this stuff up."

So now we asked ourselves, "Why would we make up stories of childhood abuse?" Our answer: we would not. If we were going to make anything up, we would create a perfect childhood, with a perfect mother and father who were loving and caring, who did not want to have sex with us or hurt us in any way, and would protect us from others who wanted to.

But that is not what happened in our childhood. We lived through hell. The fact of the matter is that the mom stole our childhood. She used us to get what she wanted and needed: an outlet for her anger; an object for her sexual pleasure; and a means to keep a husband. She never considered how these actions would impact us. To her we were just a thing. How else could she have had sex with us? Or let other people abuse us while she watched? Because of these actions, we believe that she did not have a conscience, and so did not believe that what she was doing really was wrong. She was also able to justify what she did to us, to herself, and to the world. She would constantly tell us, "You made me do it. If you had only done as I told you, then this would not have happened." Only once did she ever try to apologize, and that still fell short. She said, "I should not have gotten so carried away, but you did deserve what you got." She felt completely justified in what she was doing. 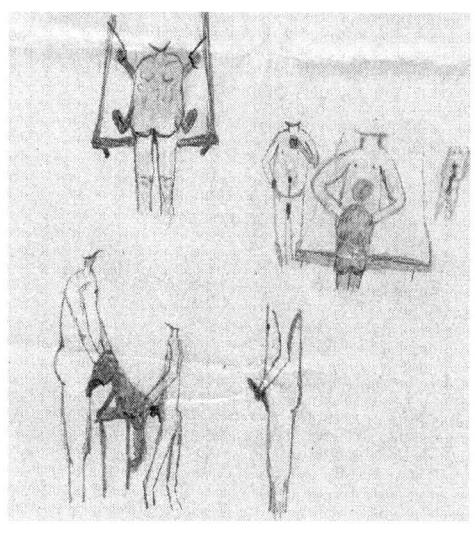 Her fear was if she was caught, she could be proven wrong. It was like living with a monster.

Rachel repeatedly stated that she believed that the mom was "sick and disturbed." We don't agree. We believe that the mom was evil. Being sick and disturbed is a copout, and relieves her of any responsibility for her actions. She is still responsible for what she did, even in death. The more we think about what she did to us, the more we wish that she had been put on trial for everyone to have known what she did to us, and then thrown in jail to rot. But instead she died, and we feel robbed of any form of justice. She got way scott free.

Our life with the mom meant learning to follow "the rules." We had no choice. From an early age we were taught that we had to respect and obey *ALL* adults, and that doing otherwise carried severe consequences. The consequences were usually a beating, being tied up, burned or cut. Once we were not allowed to eat for three days, simply because we refused to eat liver. Another time we were burned because we broke one of the mom's collector's plates. Her philosophy seemed to be that if the punishment were painful enough, we would not forget it and thus, would not misbehave again. We were also taught that if we *EVER* told what she did to us, we would be severely punished. The first of such lessons was watching our dog being shot right before our eyes, and being told, "This is what I will do to you, so you better keep your mouth shut, because if you say anything, I will fuck you up!" Over time these lessons were reinforced many times, and we learned them well. The message we internalized became, if we told, we had to die. We came to fear the very idea of telling any kind of secrets.

    Child abuse, in our opinion, is the most heinous of crimes. It robs a child of his innocence and his self-esteem. It leaves scars that may not always be visible. It makes life a living hell. The mom, Stuart, and other abusers, told us repeatedly that they knew that we "wanted to do this," or else we would have just said "no." So, we went through life believing that the abuse was our fault, and that we must have been the reason that the mom and others did what they did. We deserved what we got. If it did not happen to all children, we must have made it happen. We contaminated everyone around us and made them "bad," and if we let anyone get to close, we would cause them harm too. We could never tell. Besides, we couldn't imagine that anyone would ever believe us. If they did, they thought that it was our fault and we deserved what we received.

    These beliefs almost cost us our life. In fear, we kept our mouths shut and lived our nightmare, never thinking that there could possibly be another truth. We could not know that what happened to us was not our fault. We could not comprehend that what the mother had done was wrong; that mothers were supposed to protect their children, not harm them or let others harm them. We could not understand that as children, we did not cause the abuse, but were victims of abuse; and that we could tell, be believed, and heal rather than die because we told someone else. These lessons took time to learn.

The effects of the abuse should have been easy to see. As children, we were burned with cigarettes and lighters. Our arms and legs were always covered with bruises from any number of different occurrences, yet it seemed that no one *WANTED* to notice what was going on. Emotionally, we were withdrawn and hostile. We were the school ground bullies and got into fights at the drop of a hat. In the second grade, the school made us see a counselor, or else not be allowed in school because we were too violent. We were not stupid, but our grades were horrible and most of the time we were given *social* promotions. We would miss school regularly because we could not be seen in public with all the bruises. The signs were there and all anyone needed to do was look, but no one did.

We believe that child abuse is not just a family problem, but also a community problem. People generally are quite uncomfortable with the idea that parents could intentionally harm their children. We know from our experience that people turned a blind eye to our abuse, or they did nothing for fear of getting involved. How else could the teachers that taught us look the other way when we went to school with black eyes, or wore long sleeve shirts and pants in the heat of summer? Perhaps it was easier to ignore the problem than to look it in the eye, look us in the eyes and do something about it. Then there is the fear "what if I am wrong and it's not *child abuse*?" Because of that attitude, we suffered, and the mother and the other abusers were never punished. This still makes us angry.

As adults we perpetuated some of the abuse that was enacted on us. We cut and burned ourselves in an effort to punish us, and to "make things stop." It sounds crazy, but as children we had learned that as soon as the mother was done hurting us, we could go to sleep. We had also been told over and over that we would be punished for what we had done. It was made very clear to us that we were the cause of our abuse and therefore, in our minds, we needed to be punished for it. There was almost no rational thought involved in what we were doing. We were just doing what we were taught, and what we thought was right.

We would not sleep or eat for days on end. We did not believe that we deserved food or rest. We did not think that it was okay for us to go to the doctor when we were ill. We had to be dying before the mom would even think about taking us, and then she would be angry that we had gotten sick, telling us that we were being wimps. When we were children, no one bothered to meet our basic needs and so we learned to ignore them. We learned to cook for ourselves at an early age, since no one else would. The mom was gone most of the time. Night was not a time for sleep; it was when we were harmed, when people would come into our bedroom to demand sex from us. We got a very clear message: we were not allowed to have needs. We never stopped to think that it was not right for us to continue harming our body, or that people were supposed to eat and sleep on a regular basis. Even after we found out that our beliefs were not correct, we still found it difficult to change our behavior patterns.

One of the hardest things for us to understand was the abuse and our reaction to it. It was not until we were talking to Rachel one evening, after about a year of therapy and hard work, that it dawned on us why we were having so much trouble telling her about the abuse and its impact on our therapeutic relationship. She was relating how it seemed that the only time that we really seemed to open up to her was when we were on the telephone, or away from the office, in an unstructured environment. We realized, as she was talking, that therapy is very structured and it was that structure that was itself a trigger for us, because it resembled the structure of our abuse. We believe that there is a structure/ritual to all forms of child abuse containing a beginning, middle and an end:

The Beginning: this is what happens right before the abuse, leading up to the "Abuse Event," as we call it. The mom would come home feeling stressed or angry. We would do something that she would feel was wrong, inappropriate, or disrespectful: talking back, not doing the dishes, not finishing our meal, or even asking for something to eat. If she had been a normal, non-abusive, and healthy person/parent, she would have dealt with the believed wrongdoing by other, not hurtful means. But she was not a healthy person/parent, and our behavior, or lack of what she felt to be good behavior, only antagonized her. She would start to breathe harder and she would look angry. We would know when we had crossed the line and something was going to happen, even if she said nothing.

There are two kinds of reactions: sudden/immediate and delayed. In the first there is no warning, just be sudden physical contact: a slap or grabbing our arm. In the second there was the "Wait till we get home," or the "We'll talk about this later." For us, the delayed was the worse because it gave us time to fear and worry about what would happen. The whole time we knew that we were going to be hurt, so by the time the abuse happened, we felt relieved. Even when the body was an adult, this would cause fear and anxiety, even if we knew that the person that said, "We will talk about this later," was by no means going to hurt us. (We finally had to ask Rachel to stop using this phrase, because there were times that it would trigger self-mutilation to deal with the stress and fear.)

The Middle: this is the actual event of the abuse. The *event* had its own pattern. There was the threat, followed by the actual physical contact, and the reactions of both the mother and us. The threat was usually the warning of "Now you did it," or name-calling: "You little bitch! Who do you think you are?" One of the mom's favorites was to make us go get the belt, or whatever she was going to hit us with (something that she told us her father had made her do as a child). Then there would be some form of physical contact, grabbing was usually first. During the *event*, if we did not react in a manner that she felt we should, the abuse would last longer, i.e. not crying, or crying too much, not begging her to stop, or talking too much. There was never a way for us to know exactly what she was wanted, only the knowledge that she was totally in control of us to the point of deciding to let us live and when/how she was going to stop. We knew when she was going to stop by what she would say more than anything: "I hope that you learned you lesson," or "Now you better behave."

The End: this is the After-Event. During this phase, everyone tried to calm down and recover from what happened. We once heard a survivor call this phase the *apology*. Good way of putting it. This was when the mom would blame us, excuse herself, and/or apologize. This was also when there was the clean-up of the mess that was made either of the house, or us, or both. In our opinion, it could be just as traumatizing as the event itself. I know that for many incest victims, this is when their abusers would shower them with gifts, or tell them that it would never happen again. For us, this would happen on occasion too. Once the mom took us out to a favorite fast food place after having sex with us, and the whole time that we were eating, she was telling us that she would never do what she did again. So for us, this phase held as much anxiety as the Beginning: we knew that she was lying, and we knew that it would happen again.

The reason that therapy became a trigger was that it followed these same phases; Beginning, Middle, and End. The therapy hour starts with the therapist coming out and meeting the client. Small talk ensues, the "How are you doing?" (The Beginning). Then the talk turns more serious and the session becomes more intense (The Middle). Right before the hour ends, there is closure, and the "Calming down" (The End). This pattern was by no means abusive, but it was nonetheless difficult, if not impossible, to deal with. We could not bring ourselves to relax enough to really talk to Rachel, and would only feel fear and anxiety. During times of crisis when we needed to talk to Rachel about something important, and she suggested that we "talk about this when we see each other," our fear and anxiety would just intensify. After all, that was one of the most common threats during our childhood. Even her office was associated with the fears of our childhood, since the abuse had taken place in buildings, for the most part. When we talked on the phone, or away from the office, there was not that structure (of time and place), and thus we could relax and let ourselves trust Rachel.

When we told Rachel about our theory, she just looked at us and said, "That makes so much sense." Rachel knew that we had a hard time trusting her, especially in the therapy hour, so if we really needed to talk about something, it was best to wait until we could talk to her over the phone. She also knew that there were some phrases that caused us a great deal of anxiety and fear, and that the very idea of being in the office talking about the abuse was something that we could not usually tolerate. But she did not realize that abuse and our therapeutic relationship had so many common points. The telephone option helped both of us understand the impact of the abuse on all aspects of our life. It also enabled us to start to talk about the abuse encompassing in detail for the first time in our life, which shed light on why telling was so hard for us. When we first started to tell Rachel about the abuse, we were certain that she would not believe us. We were also convinced that she would see us in the same light that we had seen ourselves: as a little monster/brat/bad kid that had deserved to be hurt and therefore, we had nothing to complain about. It came as a shock when she told us differently. Rachel made it very clear that NO child deserved that kind of punishment, and children were not supposed to have sex with adults. We also were convinced that we should have been able to stop it, and that we could have done something like running away or fighting back. Rachel had to give us a reality check: children did not, and do not, have that kind of power. As children, we had no choice but to do what the adults said.

All our life we felt that we had done something terribly wrong, and because of *it,* we had to be punished. We felt that dying was the best punishment. We were constantly telling Rachel: "it's not about death—it's about punishment." Then as we started to disclose more and more of the abuse, we felt that we had committed "treason," and because we had told, we had to die. But it could not be an *easy* way out; we had to perform a Trial by Fire. When Rachel heard this term, her first question was, "What is that?" We told her it meant pouring gasoline over ourselves and lighting the body. Her reaction made sense: she turned pale. But there was a division inside about 1) if we should do it; and 2) if the Trial by Fire would even kill us. Mikhail, Storm, Stephana and even Death knew that if we performed a *trial,* that we would die a horrible death. The street kids, on the other hand, felt that it was a way to find out if we were good or bad, guilty or innocent, and they wanted, needed, to do it to find out for certain. They believed that if they and the body were good, then they would be *free.* To them, free was the same as dying, and was not bad. If the body were bad, then they would live. They believed that living was bad. Remember that little rational thought was involved.

The rest of the personalities just wanted to get the *punishment* over with. They felt that if they did not punish the body and themselves, then something *worse* would happen. Most likely, they feared that the mom or Stuart would come back and get them. They had always been told that if they told anyone the mom and Stuart would know, because they would always know what they were doing no matter where they were. These individuals were past caring about the fact that the body would die, and all of us along with it—they just wanted to do what they believed they *had* to do. They had broken the rules, therefore, they had to die. Those of us that wanted to live were just trying to keep the body alive and help Rachel figure out where these ideas were coming from.

The more Rachel found out, the more convinced she became that we were survivors of ritual abuse. One of her first clues came when we started to tell her about how we viewed the body and ourselves.

We would constantly tell Rachel that we were sure that we were going to contaminate her, and that we would make her evil too, and end up hurting her. At the same time, we were scared that she was going to hurt us. Rachel had to do a lot of work to convince us that she was not going to hurt us and that we were not going to hurt her.

She always started by reassuring us that she would not do anything to cause us harm. She was also very respectful of our physical being. Those of us that were not comfortable being touched, she did not touch. She was always careful to ask if she could give us a hug, and made it clear that she would not touch us in any way that would make us uncomfortable. She also made it clear that she did not believe that we would contaminate her in any way, and that we were not evil.

We knew that we did not have to tell Rachel anything that we did not want to. She had told us early on that she would not push us, and that anything we talked about would be our own choice. Still, sharing details of the abuse was both humiliating and a relief. One of the biggest problems for us was that we were extremely ashamed of what had happened to us. We were sure that we were the sole cause of all of the abuse that we suffered. The abusers wanted it this way. It was the only way that they could insure that we would never talk to anyone about what had happened to us. But it was also killing us. We felt that we had to be punished for everything that we had done and that we were completely responsible. For a long time, whenever Rachel told us that we were not to blame for what had happened, we assumed that she was just lying to us or that she did not have the guts to tell us to our face that she believed we were to blame; and that we had caused the mom, and everyone else, to do what they had done. It took some time before we could take in what she was telling us and not apply our own shame-based thinking.

Over the course of talking about the abuse we suffered, we came to realize that we had been manipulated into believing that the abuse was our fault and that we had caused it. For over eighteen years, we had all believed in our heart and soul that we had to punish ourselves for everything that had happened, never thinking that it could not have been our fault. The adults that were to blame had, in fact, tricked us into taking the blame for them. Then, because of the intense shame that we felt, we did not talk for fear of being blamed again. So, we compounded our shame with our silence, the whole time needlessly punishing ourselves through self-mutilation and suicide attempts. Something that lived in our heads all the time, haunting us and keeping us awake at night, was no longer a secret for us to be ashamed of. We could let someone else know what it had been like, how much pain we were in, and slowly let out the pain and with it, the shame and humiliation that we felt.

There were times that we could not explain what the abuse was like in words. We could see it, hear it, smell it, taste it, and feel it, but the words to explain it just could not be formed. We could not express the pain that we were in, and so it would come out in other ways. Other times we were too ashamed and fearful to tell what we remembered, believing that Rachel would view us as monsters. She never did. Rachel's consistent belief in us as good human beings who had done nothing to deserve the abuse we received, enabled us to let go of our shame and self-hate. It was a long, slow and painful process.

One of the things that we had to do a lot was ask what was and was not appropriate behavior on the part of a mother. We would ask Rachel if it was appropriate for a mother to take baths with children, and how a mother was supposed to bathe her child. There was a great deal of confusion, as we truly did not know if some things were wrong or not. Sometimes it would be really hard, because we did not want Rachel to think that we were being dumb or were blowing things out of proportion. She told us that if anything, we were minimizing what had happened to us and we needed to blow things up to their real size. "It was worse than bad," she would tell us. This was always hard for us to believe. We truly thought that we were being wimps because we had problems with what had happened to us. We had to learn that the abuse that we had suffered was terrible and that more importantly, we were not to blame for what had happened. Since we refused to talk about the abuse, we never learned the truth: that we were not to blame. Slowly, as we started to tell Rachel about the abuse, we started to understand that a child is never to blame for any kind of abuse. Adults should always know better.

We also had problems understanding what was and was not appropriate punishments for children. When we asked Rachel how she punished her daughter, she told us that she never punished her, but would talk to her in a firm voice and tell her that whatever she just did was not okay; she never hit or beat her. This was a concept that was hard for us to comprehend.

The question that always remained for us was, "why would a mother do something like this to a child?" Rachel never did have a good answer, and it was something that we had to learn to live with. It would haunt us for a long time, but we came to the realization that we would never have the answer that we wanted. This would remain a mystery. What we did have to find the answer to, was why we split into so many different parts, a journey that would teach about the amazing ability of a child to survive horrible pain and suffering. The more crucial question was: Could we put all the pieces of ourselves back together again?

Rachel Chapter 5:

One Body—Many Minds

"Great discoveries and achievements invariably involve the cooperation of many minds."
—Alexander Graham Bell

Trading places was how "they" described how one personality took over. It often happened before my eyes and took only seconds. Generally, one looked down, hands cupping the face, then a brief shake of the head would signal to me that someone else was now in my presence. They preferred that I didn't watch as this shift took place, but my fascination with this phenomenon often could not be curtailed. I wanted to understand all that I could. I wanted to be able to identify each personality so that I could respect each as distinctive and real. As I became familiar with each personality, I would often call them by name and ask that they come out to speak to me. Sometimes one personality would prevent another from doing that. This frustrated me, as their inner system was often a barrier to the process of getting to the root causes of their very existence. But as trust continued to strengthen, even the little ones, like Copula and Sandy, would *push through* and come out into the open. Sandy always looked confused, her eyes vague and unknowing. She would look around the room as if her sight had just been returned to her, stumbling, questioning. "What be that?" She pointed to a phone, a car out the window, and a flower on the desk. Once the answering machine was on and she wondered how the person was in the box. "It's magic," she said. Nothing in my world of reality was known in her world of darkness and imprisonment. As stated many times, they

> that she really does give a fuck?
> that she does not want to hurt me?
> that she believes us —
> Will it make it all too real? Will it turn it all upside down?
> She said that she thinks we are afraid of getting better.
> Why are we?
>
> Death is the key to unlock the door to the inside world
> Death the key to it all
> Knows the answers
> but not the questions to ask
> give her the questions then
> She has to pay First
>
> Not true — if you want to live — stay alive ...

did not believe themselves to be real, rather they perceived themselves as crazy, insane, freaks. They each had unique traits. They even wrote differently.

Medical research has shown alters to have different heart rates and different physiological symptoms. For example, some can present with diabetes, others with low blood sugar. In Gabriele's system, she was diagnosed with asthma; the others had no breathing problems. Randy often felt ill with a fever; the others felt fine. During a very frightening suicidal episode when Cobalt had taken an overdose of hydrocodone, Randy, Mikhail, Stephana, and Death began feeling the extreme fatigue at different rates. Mathew never felt the consequences of the narcotic in his body.

They didn't understand what I truly believed, that becoming a multiple personality through the art of disassociation was a protective mechanism against extreme and intolerable conditions. As the doctor in *Sybil*, Cornelia Wilbur, hypothesized, "being a mul-tiple personality was the ultimate rescue." Each personality held traits that were necessary to be able to cope, and when that self became too pained, another came forth to lend a helping hand. For example, Tigger, only two, could not handle her fears each time the mom and Stuart entered her room. She wanted to die and was going to jump off a balcony. Death came to her rescue. Perhaps, it was being needed to deal with a death wish that gave Death the strong emotional traits we've seen so beautifully depicted in her poetry. No other had those intense insights. Copula came to help Death, but she was tortured. She couldn't handle the pain, so Little Sandy came along. She was forced to live in a box without food, water, or light. She went crazy. Stephana was born to help keep Tigger alive. She never wanted to let these horrors happen again. Her personality traits were more aggressive and feisty. This led to trouble for *them*. Gabriele came to be the good girl that didn't do anything wrong. She was shielded from all the others to keep her appearing sane and because of not knowing, she often lost more time that the others. Ironically, she was the one who felt most crazy. She was lonely in her role and thus Randy, her playmate, was created. And what a playful youngster he turned out to be. Always looking out for the body, he was given the traits to feel the body. He was the one who got sick, he felt the pain and he was the one who ate. He was the "scratch of innocence." He still trusted in humanity, which is something lost to the others. He needed a protector and Storm took on this nurturing role. None of these children knew how to read. School was fast approaching. Mikhail became the scholar although, until third grade, he could not read well. Thanks to a caring teacher who taught them, they were able to get a GED, an equivalent to a high school diploma, and were able to find employment. Mathew came to help Mikhail, because Mikhail didn't know how to fight on the playground. Mathew became a very strong bully, but he too, needed help, and TOB came to his aid. Cobalt, Andrea and the other street kids came around to help Mathew and Death; their role was to keep the *bond* from being broken. And as we have seen, they fought most of their lives, until I came along, to uphold the responsibility they believed allotted to them.

Most of the alters were between two and eighteen years old. Yet the body that I viewed with my eyes had lived for twenty-eight years.

Their separateness became a means to partialize the pain, and to find a means to strengthen the core. Sadly, each was victimized, causing more trauma to be built on top of one another, much like a matchbox house that was ready to crumble.

At the time of our first meeting, the house had begun to degenerate. Although some understood that they shared the same body, the body was not real to them. Without this knowledge, they didn't realize that the self-mutilation each preformed on him/herself, hurt all of them. This was a very difficult concept to uphold. For example, TOB and Cryin's cuts hurt Randy and Death. Death, Cobalt and Andrea's burns hurt all the little ones, especially Tigger and Randy. They hated knowing that they were hurting others. That was not acceptable. Only hurting oneself was allowed. Even with this knowledge, it was very difficult for them to stop themselves from these acts. To this end, I photographed each as he/she identified him/herself in my office. It was frightening to look at these pictures. Their reality, that each looked so different (for example, TOB saw Death as blond with green eyes, while Mikhail was taller and sported a beard, and Stephana shaved her head) would no longer be valid in a world without dissociation. Their world slowly became transformed into a new reality: the body was one in the same.

Multiplicity has been seen as a necessity for survival. Yet their survival seemed to mean the perpetuation of pain and torture. What complicated my helping them understand the need to stop the self-infliction was the awareness of their numbness to pain. If one understands, the dynamics of pain are defined physically by the sensation, emotionally by the experience in how the pain is received, and cognitively by the interpretation of what the pain means. By disowning the body, seeing it as a commodity, the physical sensations could not be felt; by repressing their emotions and memories, the experience was denied as being *that awful*, and without these experiences, there could be no intellectual inference. Thus, my concept of pain could not be recognized in their world.

Interestingly, as therapy proceeded, and each personality became more open, revealing and understanding of their relationship to the whole, each began to feel the physical sensation of pain. They would laugh when I said feeling pain was good because it meant that they were re-owning the body. This process was long and arduous. For example, as Death, Cobalt, and Andrea began to examine their desire for dying and accept the truth that they were harming a body that they all shared, their ability to feel no pain was reversed. Feeling pain was a symbol of being alive. To be alive meant feeling the shame, humiliation, and self-loathing. It meant being a part of a Satanist's world, a fear so great that they battled to return to their known way of coping by disowning the body through disassociation. I needed to help them associate life with joy, peace, laughter and above all, hope. To this end, I asked Death if we could change her name. After all, if she no longer wanted her role to be the creator of ways to die, then she needed a name to represent her new path towards life. I suggested the name Hanna, a Hebrew name meaning "gracious" and "merciful," symbolizing, as in the song *Amazing Grace,* how a lost life could be found. I hoped all of the children could now feel a new beginning. And so, Death became Hanna, a name she began to cherish. I wanted TOB's name changed as well, but we couldn't come up with anything he liked; he still enjoyed being obnoxious. All the alters were very respectful of the name change. It was even decided that a symbol of their healing would be a legal name change.

Another significant property of the disowned body was the disinterest in eating. As stated previously, Randy was the only one who felt hunger and would want food. He was too young to cook and was dependent on the others to feed him. Yet, they did not see food as a necessity. They would say, "The body doesn't need food, it's too fat." It was true that the body was overweight. However, they did not understand the concept of eating healthy to help metabolize calories and to just live. I often felt like a Jewish mother making sure Randy got nourished. He was very appreciative. Of course, since their goal had always been to die, I began to accept that until their path changed towards life, eating and sleeping would not be voluntary behaviors.

The mother had committed grave abusive acts against her daughter. I believe that she also neglected to nurture in the ways moms care for their young children. Most believe it's a mother's duty to feed children, read them bedtime stories, tuck children into bed, and make them feel safe and secure at night. They didn't get these basic needs met. They were left on their own to feed themselves. They never slept, because nighttime was the time to be abused. Eating and sleeping meant pain and emptiness.

Death offered another explanation for not eating. It was another form of self-mutilation and punishment. By not eating, one could get rid of the body.

There was an interesting physiological awareness within the body that occurred when memories came to the forefront. TOB, Death and Randy would feel sick to their stomachs. When TOB revealed a night of terror involving blood and fire, he vomited over and over again. The body knew how to react to the disgust they had witnessed and the pain they had personally experienced. They needed to purge, to cleanse their being.

I often wondered how the body survived with the deprivation of food and sleep. All I knew was this body contained amazing inner resources. It must have wanted to live, despite the years of abuse and self-inflictions.

I wanted to nurture the belief that the body belonged to them all and since it had survived, it was time to learn to value it and take care of it. However, this could only happen once the shame was extinguished.

Although each saw him/herself as separate, there was a certain degree of cooperation and interdependence. It was as if they were creating their own family system to replace the one that betrayed them. There was also an element of competition, a most familiar experience between siblings. As I talked with each alter individually and gave each special attention, I would often be asked, "Do you care about *so and so* more than me?" Hanna (a.k.a Death) seemed to feel this way about my feelings for Randy and the little children. My mothering instinct did seem to have more patience to accept the children's fears. As an adolescent, Hanna was often obstinate and alienating; traits that often tried my patience. However, I continually reminded myself that Hanna's pain was perhaps the deepest of anyone else's, and she needed more than anyone the reassurances of my caring, my acceptance and reinforcement of the value of her life.

They described how they lived together. "Picture [the body as] a house with a long hallway and rooms off the hallway where we each go off to our own rooms. Sometimes we can overhear what the others are saying." I would often just talk to one, as if he or she was in front of me, hoping that either that personality would hear me or someone else would relay the message to him/her. Some of the alters were known to the others, but not all were known to everyone. For example, the street kids did not know most of the others. The protectors (Stephana, Mikhail, Storm, QED, and Randy), were most aware of how the system worked. As therapy continued, I took on a role of introducing the unknowns to one another in an effort to have a cohesive, rather than hostile, inner system. I believed it would help in my efforts to reach the common goal of choosing life over death and self-destruction.

Existential questions, such as, "Who are we? Are we real? Are we so evil that no one could ever forgive us? How can we ever live in your world?" plagued them. I always reassured them that they were real, with real memories and feelings. How they would live in my world, without disassociation, was more complex to answer. Each posed "What will become of me?" as each recognized that the existence of the system was in jeopardy. To allow the process of healing meant all of them might not be needed. After all, they were created, in part, to help the body die. If they lived, what would that mean? I must admit that I often felt that I had to have the perfect answer, or I could lose their interest, or perhaps curiosity in this *life* concept. I told them that they would become one dynamic individual who could use their strong inner resources to find ways to live a productive life. But in saying that, I grappled with the concept of integration. As Rhune and Lynn say in *Dissociation*, Dissociative Disorder involves "chronic disturbances in the normal integrative functioning of memory, identity, or consciousness." Then it is logical to believe that the most efficacious treatment would be to reintegrate the parts to make them whole. However, I struggled with my own theory, which, in part, was based on a saying written by Ken Blanchard: "None of us is as smart as all of us." Perhaps, helping them learn to cooperate and be allies in life would make them more able to cope in the new reality. Perhaps they did not need to be unified as one entity, as conventional theory upholds. I often use Gestalt techniques as interventive strategies to help individuals experience the conflictual inner parts of themselves. One such experiential tool is called the "empty chair," in which one speaks to other parts of themselves. It is powerful and revealing in helping the individual identify, confront, and resolve confusion and inner turmoil.

With an awareness of all the alters, could the system use ways such as this to work through their differences and still remain parts within a whole? I did believe that they needed to accept the concept that their self-identities were indeed attached to one body, that they did come from the same birth mother, and they did experience the same life history. With these ideas in mind, could Randy still exist to be playful and to remind them to eat; could Mikhail be around to help complete forms and keep the finances in order, and what about TOB's green thumb? Above all, who would become the core being? Would Hanna (a.k.a. Death), who had created the alters, be the lead person? What would happen to Gabriele who was the person known to the outside world? I personally had begun to care about each of them as distinct, unique, and necessary to the functioning of the whole system. I decided that I could not make the ultimate decision of who shall live and who shall die. Did any even need to die? I asked them to decide. I was amazed at their answer. All of them believed Hanna had been the key to unlocking the door to the inside world, and therefore should be the one to meet the outside world. They told her that they would rally behind her. But, Randy did not want to grow up. I told him that adults all need inner children to keep them young and that he could still be Randy, helping Hanna feel all that life had to offer.

The individualistic traits each possessed would be incorporated into Hanna's being: Mikhail's wisdom, Stephana's assertiveness and social skills, TOB's love for nature, Storm's nurturance, even the street kids' curiosity about life, would help in the learning of all the unknowns. Tigger could finally grow up, no longer stuck in a world of terror. It was conceivable that some might choose to, or naturally, no longer exist. Strangely, Hanna asked me one day why Gabriele seemed to be fading. I told her that as she recognized that she, Hanna, was now sane, Gabriele's role to be the sane one was no longer justified. I was convinced that whoever chose to remain would be smarter than each were as individuals.

I knew that even with the belief that the alters could be incorporated into the one body, there still would be a sense of loss and feelings of grief would still exist. It was more complex than just letting go of a belief that each personality was a separate entity. The grief was also about the loss of a childhood; the loss of a mother that never would or could nurture them, and give them love and direction as they grew up; and the loss of their heart and soul for twenty-eight years. They were afraid to express anger towards the mother. She was the only mother they knew. Yet, healing began for Hanna when she did let go, scream, and yell, "Mothers aren't supposed to sell their children out!"

Here is an excerpt of something Hanna wrote when she was still Death:

"Grief is transitional and multi-phasic (sic)", someone said that one time. But grief is all about letting go—so that one can move on. But do I need to grieve for me or for her? Is it her death that harms me—or her actions that robbed me of my childhood? Is it the last that I need to grieve? I see this little girl that wanted her to love me—and [the mom] did not—instead used me for her own proposes. Everyone grieved the loss of the woman—but no one grieved for the child.

This grief was triggered one year after therapy had begun when one of "their" foster mothers died of cancer. They didn't believe they had a right to feel sad. They were so confused about love and loss. They thought, *if you love someone, they will die.* They even tried to sabotage therapy and pushed me away because they were beginning to care about me and feared that they might somehow be responsible for something bad happening to me. The illogic of this correlation between love/death/loss was the only reality that they had known. It made living with "life" concepts frightening. How can you love and live? How can life be valued when it is filled with pain and suffering? As I continued to promote life, the street kids would become so distressed that the "system" often felt out of control and the feelings of going insane seemed to exacerbate. I knew that their concept of life still meant living with Satan.

I had to find a way to destroy Satan, and eradicate his image and voice from their mind. These visual and auditory hallucinations were so powerful that they fought with all their might to stop me. I was confusing them; my voice began to intermingle with His words. My words had to win. But did I have that power? That was my ultimate challenge. In addition, changing the belief that life could be good, meant a whole new way of thinking and feeling. I would compare their changing to a blind man who had been given his sight back—at first he doesn't know how to live in a world with color and vision. It's overwhelming. He only knows what an object is through touch, smell and sound. Vision adds a new dimension of confusion. For them, life added a new set of unknowns and complexities.

These changes involved every aspect of their being. They had to accept that they all shared the same body; they could not all continue to exist as separate beings in their new world. This new world included big people who could care. Asking for what they needed became okay; the nighttime did not have to be feared; they/we might become "I." And one very peculiar difference that had never been understood would now need to be resolved: are "we" going to become male or female?

Hanna Chapter 5:

One Body—Many Minds

"None of us is as smart as all of us."
—Ken Blanchard

Disassociation is not easy to explain, but neither is it very complicated. We have felt for a long time that the "experts" make the theory behind why and how it happens way too complex, and end up confusing anyone who tries to read their explanations. Whenever we tried to read these theories from books, we would get a headache and want our money back. Just the criteria for what disassociation is can be very confusing, and all of the experts are not in complete agreement about what it is, how a person is able to do it, or what causes it. They do agree that there are many different forms of disassociation, with varying degrees of severity.

For example, have you ever been driving, thinking about something else, gone through a traffic light and suddenly realized that you did not see if it was green or red? You hoped that it was green, but looked over your shoulder to see if a cop was flashing his lights at you, and felt just a little panicked that you might have run a red light without knowing it? This is a form of disassociation. The part of your brain that does the driving was still working and still taking in information, but the other part that was thinking about something else was *elsewhere*, so to speak. You were working on autopilot and did not really even know it.

Most people have the ability to dissociate. The problem arises when it starts to negatively impact their lives and they no longer have any control over it.

Most experts agree that DID is an extreme form of disassociation that a child uses to protect him/herself from overwhelming fear and anxiety, and that the vast majority of DID patients have suffered severe and prolonged childhood abuse that started at an early age. We certainly know we suffered.

However, we have now become frustrated by the *enchantment* that the outside world has with what kinds of abuse multiples have endured. We have been told in the past that the only way we would ever get better was to relive, over and over, the abuse that we suffered. Our response: *BULLSHIT!* How can anyone ever get on with life if the people that are supposed to be *helping* them are constantly causing them more pain? How can a person find joy in their life if all that they are living and breathing is the pain and terror of their childhood? Our belief is that they can't. At no time did Rachel need to go *hunting* in order to find out what the problem was. It was not necessary for us to heal, and would only have caused us more pain. Instead, Rachel made it clear that it was our choice whether or not we wanted to tell her anything, and then it was at our own pace. It was during our telling her of the abuse, that we came slowly to understand how the multiplicity had saved our sanity and our lives.

But, we have come to this belief: DID is more a phenomenon of *how* a person copes than a phenomenon of *what a person is coping with*. Yes, abuse can be the catalyst for dissociation, but the problems start when you have 5, 10, 15, or even two people living in one body, all leading separate lives and not caring about how their actions affect one another. No one can get anything done if you are going around in circles. We know.

Everyone has parts. These parts are just pieces of who you are as a person; the part that goes to work or school; and the part that cooks and cleans. Of course there is the part that drives, and maybe one that gets road rage and thinks of new and exciting ways to kill the idiot driver in front of you; and a part that has sex and feels sexual. Hopefully you have a part that likes to play and can't keep his/her hand out of the cookie jar. You know these parts and you know that they are a part of you. When you are out playing, you know you are still you. You know who the people around you are, and you know that you have to go to work tomorrow and write a huge report on something really important. You are still you, but you are just playing. Probably you cannot imagine the childlike part going to work, playing, and getting you fired. When you have DID, this can happen. We know, because it's happened to us.

In DID, these parts take on separate and distinct identities. They take on names and different genders. They are different ages, look differently, and act differently. They lead different lives, and have different feelings and different beliefs. One part will have friends that another part will have no knowledge of, or any relationship with, and this can include a marriage. One personality will be married and another will have no part or interest in that marriage. One personality might be a parent, and the other might not have participated in the raising of that child and not see that child as his own. They do not see themselves as part of a single person. They are, in their mind, a separate person, with their own body and a separate life. They have come to believe that their actions will not affect the other parts and they will not be affected by what the others do. This is the problem. The person as a whole is no longer working as one whole person, but many whole persons.

Then there are those individuals that do not believe that DID truly exists. They claim that DID is *caused* by hypnosis. A therapist *creates* personalities in an effort to explain a person's behavior or difficulties. Our response is that these individuals do not understand the process of hypnosis or its limitations. Another claim is that the patient will create personalities in an effort to "get attention" from the therapeutic community, or to please a demanding therapist. We can personally think of easier, cheaper, and more satisfying ways to gain someone's attention. So, we think that this is also bullshit.

All that said and done, the fact remains that children do develop

DID. They grow up and their lives are hell. The question then becomes: How do you effectively treat someone with DID so that they can get on with living, and stop just surviving?

We also hold this belief: *The treatment of DID does not have to be a long and drawn out process.* It should NOT take *years* and hundreds of thousands of dollars for someone to get well. What it does take is a damn good therapist and a commitment on the client's part to stay alive, and to do whatever is necessary to get well.

Nor does treatment need to have just one outcome: integration. Integration has long been held as the only viable way for a multiple to become a functioning member of society. The multiple is told that the only way that she is going to get well is for all of her parts to become one, and that this is the goal of treatment. We hold that this is not true. Integration should not be forced on a multiple. It should be a choice given to the DID patient. The decision to integrate should be left to the multiple; after all, it is their lives. Imposing this kind of action on a system is taking away that system's power, something that has happened to us many times. In our view, this feels like an abuse of power. What right does a therapist or psychiatrist have to force anyone to change in this way? Our stance is: NONE. When treatment is done and they have been paid, it is not the therapist or psychiatrist that has to live with this kind of action. It is the client.

What should be forced is safety and taking care of the body. When anyone is suicidal and depressed, he/she does not have the ability to make good sound decisions. We believe it becomes the therapist's responsibility to make sure that individual is safe, and that s/he is taking proper care of his/her body, including eating, sleeping, bathing, or going to a doctor as needed. In the case of DID, the only way to get this is to ask for the cooperation of everyone and to make it known that the body is being shared. Therefore, if one person dies, all die. Total cooperation should always be a goal to increase the safety and functioning of the individual as a whole.

We have seen the outcome of a "helping professional" pressing the issue of integration. The multiple panics, then becomes terrified and in some cases, chooses the worst option: suicide. We have seen a lot people with DID who were doing well, then regress when the process of integration was started. We have seen others drop out of treatment because they felt that they would rather live in hell than be killed off, which is what most alters feel when integrated. So our question is: What value does forcing integration on a multiple have? How does this kind of *therapy* help? Our answer: NONE. We do not believe it is the place of the mental health community to cause this kind of pain under the premise of *helping*. Perhaps these professionals have not been aware of the consequences of their actions. We hope that they have learned from their experiences. We just find it sad that human beings have suffered in the process.

We should state that we have read accounts by former multiples that claim that integration was the best thing that happened, that their lives were much better, that it was the only way that they could heal and become functional. We do not discredit what they are saying. We just question the *way* that the therapeutic community goes about the process of integrating multiplies. We question the unwillingness on the part of the therapeutic community, mostly the so-called experts, to leave the decision up to the people with DID. We also question the experts' ability to really know what is best for someone when they very rarely are involved in treating someone with DID from beginning to end, day in and day out, or see the aftermath of the mistakes that are made in an effort to *cure* DID. We also question the unwillingness of most therapists to openly and honestly discuss all the options with their clients, so that the client can make an informed decision.

We were terrified that Rachel would force integration on us, that she would follow the *normal* course of treatment, make integration the end goal, and then she would tell us that we had to follow this path or there could be no therapy. We were even more scared to mention these fears to her. But over the course of discussing the book, when the issue of integration did come up, we did share our fears.

She gave us a choice: to integrate or to stay separate, with all alters learning to cooperate. We felt that Rachel made it very clear that this is our life and that she did not want to exercise that kind of power over us. She also made it clear that she would help if we did want to integrate. More than that, she was willing to discuss what *we* wanted, what *we* thought should happen, and how *we* thought it should happen. Rachel was willing to look at many different options.

This helped us to come to some decisions about whether to integrate or not. What a relief!

There was one condition: we had to choose life and Rachel pushed for that constantly. She could do nothing to help us if we died, and she wanted us to live. She continually told us how much she cared and how upset she would be if we did die. This was a strange concept, but it felt good to know that for the first time, someone really did want us to stay alive.

Rachel also wanted us to understand dissociation, what it was, and how we were all part of a whole. We had to come to an understanding of why we did become multiple. We had to accept that it was the sanest thing that we could have done. The other choices were insanity or death, things that no child should have to know about or choose between. The process of learning about disassociation and the discussions that we had with her, gave us a lot of insight into how we learned to cope, and how these coping mechanisms no longer worked and were no longer needed. Most importantly, we came to understand that we had to change our belief system in order to heal.

All of us came to help one another. Death came to help Tigger, Stephana came to help Death, and so on. But over time, we came to hate one another instead of respecting one another, and in the process, we came to hate ourselves as a whole. We could not blame, or be angry with, the people that were responsible for our torture, because we were too afraid of the repercussions. Rather, we blamed ourselves and decided to punish ourselves. Our body became "the body." We became bad. Then the body became a bad thing that was not part of us. It could be used and abused by anyone who wished, because we did not own it. In order to deal with the abuse, it had to become unreal too; it had to be something that was known about, but did not matter. There could be no feelings attached to anything about it. It could not matter. It could not be that bad. Being beaten and hurt was something that happened to all kids when they were bad. We saw other kids getting the same thing that we got all the time, so what was our problem? Pain was something that was not felt. It was not real and it did not matter; you had to be real to feel pain. We did not feel real. Slowly, everything became unreal. In a desperate effort to save ourselves, we detached ourselves from reality and made the world around us unreal.

Life did not matter. Nothing mattered. Life was just a living hell, surviving day to day. There were no dreams, because there was no future. At age seven, we knew that we would not make it to ten. At ten, we would not make it to twelve and so on. Some of us lost interest in anything that had to do with the "outside" world and time stopped for these parts; they did not grow up, but stayed the same age year after year, feeling dead. Time stopped being real and soon it did not exist. It was a problem that would haunt us and cause many problems.

School was hellish. What should have been a time of learning and experiencing new and exciting things, instead became a test of endurance. How could a child learn if she was not getting any sleep or being fed properly? How could she concentrate if she was in constant fear for her life? She could not. The best solution became the one that she had chosen before: create another alter, someone who would not worry about what was happening at home, who had no concerns about things other than school and learning. That is how Mikhail came to be. He did his best to learn all he could, but we were constantly sabotaging him. We would lose his homework, or get into fights and get suspended from school. Mikhail did not understand these things. He had no knowledge of the abuse at home. That was not his business, so he could not understand how it was affecting him. And he could not understand why Death was constantly trying to die, why Stephana was always getting into fights, why Randy was always trying to run away, or why and how their actions had any impact on him. At age sixteen, he gave up and dropped out of school.

We had become so separated from one another that we started to forget that we even existed. Some of us knew that there were others. Some of us knew a lot of people inside, but most of us had no clue. We just went about our business with no understanding of how it was effecting the rest, and not really caring anyway. It was another way to make everything unreal.

The polarity of this is that DID is the ultimate form of self-expression. If you are three years old and being abused, you want to scream, cry, bite, or just do something. But if this expression is taken away from you, then you are unable to show the pain. Tigger could not let others know her pain. She could not scream or cry, because it brought only more pain and abuse. She was too little to stop the abuse or to run away. She could not cope with what was happening to her, but being a child, she had a special skill: she was creative. She could make her own world with people who could endure the abuse, and they could scream and cry for her. Only these people that she had created would ever know about her fear and terror, and what she had done. She would never again have to go home to face the people that hurt her; she would be safe and no one would ever bother her again.

Unfortunately, there was a penalty for this. She would never grow up. She would never learn to read or to ride a bike. She would never do any of the things that normal children learn to do. She would have no understanding of the fact that time had gone by and that it was not the 1970s anymore, but the 1990s. She would never know that the mom was dead. She would never get control of her world or own her body. She would cease to be real.

We all came to be because of the abuse and Tigger's inability to cope. And because we came to be, Tigger did not have to take responsibility for her life. Then she stopped wanting to *be*. She did not want to be alive; she wanted to "die." However, we do not think that she completely understood what death was. More likely, she had heard from an adult that it was "when you go to sleep and never wake up, and you don't feel anymore pain," so in her desperation, she wanted to go to sleep and never wake up. She knew that no one would rescue her or help her, and so believed that there was no hope.

DID is the ultimate form of self-rescue. And creating others was how Tigger and Death rescued themselves. A small child cannot just run away from abuse, so *going away* was a means of escape. The place that we would go to was the inside world. In this world there was no shortage of places to hide. There were no big people. Nobody but us could really know what it looked like, and for a long time we did not want them to know. It was the only thing that we had that was just ours—even if it was its own version of hell. Everything inside was dead. There were no trees, no grass, and no blue skies. Because there were no adults, the children ran around wild. And there was always screaming, and crying. It was a world of constant pain, but no one could get to us there, so in relative terms, it was safe.

The process of owning the body and making it ours was a long one. First we had to stop abusing it. Then we had to start feeding it and let it get some sleep. The hardest change was that we had to start feeling pain.

Pain was something that we could *block*. We told ourselves over and over that it was not that bad. We would also tell ourselves that we were being wimps if something did hurt. In the past, this was needed to keep from going insane. But pain is the body's way of telling you when something is wrong, and we were not listening. We could cut ourselves to the point of needing 30 or 40 stitches and not feel it. We could give the body a third degree burn and still not feel it. It amazed Rachel that we did not feel the pain from the burns. We would ask her if it should hurt, and she would look at us and say, "Yes, it should hurt. That is a bad burn." For a long time, we did not believe her. We could not believe her because in our minds, the burns were not that bad. Until we were facing the possibility of needing skin graft surgery, then it started to sink in that what we were doing was slowly killing the body, and us with it.

For us, pain was connected to emotions. Once we started to allow emotions to come to the surface, and then to express them, we started to feel pain. When we told Rachel about the abuse, she would ask, "How do you feel?" The response was usually "nothing." We had cut off emotions in order to save our sanity, but once the emotions started to come out, if we tried to cut them off again, we would get a huge headache. And we mean *HUGE*. Our body would not allow us to cut ourselves off any more and because of that, we started to feel something that let us know that we were real: pain. We did not enjoy it. For us, feeling pain was alien and it was something that we, at first, could not comprehend. We were not sure how much something should hurt or if it should hurt at all. So we had to learn to ask questions and get reassurance that it was okay to even feel pain. When we got stung on the face by a wasp, it was extremely painful and Stephana yelled. She also went right to the doctor, because she was afraid that the body was having an allergic reaction. Finally, we were learning to take care of the body!

When Rachel told us that it was good that we were starting to be able to feel pain, and that we were taking care of the body when it was in pain, we wanted to scream, "*Are you NUTS?*" But over time, we came to understand that this was a way to own the body.

Other ways that we had to learn to take care of the body were feeding it and letting it sleep. Feeding it involved listening to Randy when he told us that he was hungry. Sometimes it meant being honest when Rachel asked, "Have you fed Randy today?" But this was not easy for us. We felt that the body did not need food. It could survive without it. It had for so long. Besides, it was not sick and it was fat. Randy was just being a pest. The body did not need anything, so Randy had better quit bugging us. We could not understand why Randy was the one to feel hungry while the rest of us did not. We had to except that the body, and Randy, needed food.

Sleep was another matter. We were exhausted, but were not be able to relax and just go to sleep. We were too afraid. Night was too terrifying for us and the idea of sleeping was even more frightening. For us, sleeping was a time when we were our most vulnerable; we did not feel safe. Then there was the fear of all of the nightmares, and the fear that the mom and others would come to get us. So we would force the body to stay awake. For a long time we could not understand Rachel's concern. So what if we got only three or four hours sleep in a night? We thought sometimes that Rachel was amazed that we were still able to talk and walk. We weren't. The rule was, "the body is on its own." This included sleep. We would go on this way for two or three weeks, and then have a night of eight to ten hours of sleep. We honestly felt that this was enough. We had to learn that it was not.

We had to make the body real. We had to believe that it was real, and that meant that we had to believe that we were real, and had a right and a reason to exist.

In order to do that, we had to come to terms with many different things, but the biggest was that we did not hold any responsibility for the abuse. We had to understand that it was done *to* us, not *because* of us. We also had to let go of our *death wish*, and that meant that we all had to choose life. In order to do that, we all had to learn to forgive ourselves for what we had done to stay alive for so long. Once we could do that, then the body could heal and we could heal along with it. All of us needed to do it, but one person started the process: Death.

Rachel had always been uncomfortable with Death's name and when Death agreed to choose life, Rachel asked her if she would change her name to symbolize her decision. Death was apprehensive; she liked her name and did not want to change it. After many weeks of talking about what a name change would mean, Death agreed to think about it, and asked Rachel what she had in mind. Rachel suggested Hanna. When she told all of us that it meant *gracious and merciful*, like in the song *Amazing Grace*, we hoped that perhaps all of us lost children could now be found. Death slowly started to use this new name and stopped calling herself Death. We hoped this meant that through forgiveness, she would choose life and a new self would soon emerge.

For a long time we were determined that we were all separate people and that we could never be one. We wanted to maintain our separateness. The idea of integration was very uncomfortable to all of us, and was an idea that caused a lot of anger whenever it came up. But over time, we started to realize that we did not need to be separate any longer; we were all part of a larger picture and always had been. It started when we came to an understanding of who and what Tigger was. At first we thought that everyone would integrate into her, and this made all of us uncomfortable. Then slowly we started to realize that there was one person that was the key: Hanna. She had come to help Tigger and she was the one who felt most of the emotions. All of us had always been helping her, not Tigger. One by one, we agreed to "stand" behind her, and her healing process began to take on new dimensions.

She was no longer responsible for just herself; she had to realize that she was doing a great deal of work for all of us. This was very frightening to her, and there were many times that she wanted to turn back and become Death once again. She could not. She could not stop a process that had already started. She had to learn to grieve for all that had been lost, and then let go of the old ways of coping. She had to learn to face her past and tell her story. She had to let go of her shame, so that she could live. Most importantly, she had to forgive herself for things that she really had no control over. This process took some time and it was extremely frightening to her. She was not sure what to do or whom to believe, and during this process, she constantly felt that she was going insane. "I feel like I'm being torn apart," she would tell Rachel. Hanna was trying to decide if she could even live, because she did not even know what living meant.

Rachel Chapter 6:

One Body—Two Genders

> *"Male and female represent the two sides of the great radical dualism. But, in fact, they are perpetually passing into one another. Fluid hardens to solid, solid rushes to fluid. There is no wholly masculine man, no purely feminine woman."*
>
> **—Margaret Fuller**

How is it possible for males to live in a female body? Mathew, Mikhail, TOB, the adolescent boys were convinced that they were indeed male. TOB, in a somewhat sheepish tone, told me one day, "I know I have all my equipment down there." How could I disprove that belief? I certainly could not disrobe him and point out that "his equipment," was in fact a vagina. When I made a gynecological appointment for them, on Stephana's request, I asked Stephana what would happen to the boys. She said, "Oh, they just won't be there." I learned that during the girl's menstrual cycle, the boys stayed away. They had truly created a system of differentiation such that the male/female genders could both exist in this one body, so separate and distinct that the males did not witness menstrual blood flow, or experience the severe cramping that the girls felt. I knew that other multiples, such as Sybil, had male/female alters. However, I had not read in the literature, any research or theory to help understand this phenomenon. Could both genders continue to exist if the alters chose a cooperative lifestyle vs. integration? If they selected to integrate, how could the males accept a sex change? Transsexuals who feel male in a female body elect to have hormonal replacements and surgical procedures to make their sexual desires and orientation congruent with their physical/biological being. We were not dealing with an emotional or sexual confusion. The males saw themselves as masculine; the females viewed themselves as feminine (though not in the prissy definition of the term). The females knew they had breasts, ovulated, had monthly cycles, and were able to conceive and get pregnant. I learned that "the body" had become pregnant at age nineteen and they painfully miscarried. Hanna had a dream of one day being able to carry a child to full term.

I had been telling all the alters that each was real because each manifested his/her own traits, emotional, cognitive, and physical. How could I renounce that statement and tell the males that they really weren't real just because they didn't have penises or testicles. I would lose my credibility with them. I could lose their trust in me. I made a conscious decision to let them retain their self-perception of their maleness. It didn't seem to be effecting how the female body was functioning. They had their own ways of setting boundaries so that the femaleness did not impact their maleness—even when it came to sex.

In Gabriele's system, there seemed to be a predominance of masculine alters, and/or male-oriented females assuming the dominant personalities. TOB, Mathew, Mikhail, William, Alfred (the committee chair) and Stephana (the "Bull Dyke") were controlling forces, working with (and at times against) Death (Hanna), Gabriele and Storm. The little ones seemed to present the opposite gender differences. Randy and Brian were the little boys; Tigger, Little Catherine, Andrea, Cobalt, and Sandy, the little girls. And then there were Copula and Stupid who didn't seem to have a gender. I hypothesized that in sociological/anthropological theory, males have always been associated with strength, power, and aggression as these were traits necessary to survive against predators. This system needed the male traits to help combat the perpetrators and abusers. They survived by becoming their own aggressors. The older females in the system tried to nurture and protect, using the traits attributed to the female gender. There seemed to be more little girls because it was a frightened little girl who was first abused. Again, in line with sociological gender beliefs, little girls tend to be more needy and vulnerable, or at least, are allowed to show their emotions, and so the frightened female child dominated. Randy and Brian used their cunning and mischievousness to watch out for the predators, and warn the little ones of danger and trouble, which is something boys are taught to do. The genderless children were given no status in the system. No one really knew them, perhaps because they just existed to be puppets for the big people, who themselves could be considered inhuman.

Gender differences were a fascinating component of Gabriele's multiplicity. How did these male/female alters share in their sexual orientations? Did they engage in sexual activity? Where would the children be if the older adolescents chose to be sexual? Did being sexual trigger memories of the sexual abuse? These were questions I wanted to explore. Stephana, Hanna and I would have stimulating discussions as we examined these ideas. The boys were always uncomfortable and guarded when the subject of sex was brought up. Sexuality is a difficult issue to be dealt with in any therapeutic setting. The act of sex, the feelings about sex, and one's sexual desire and fantasies, are intimate matters which require deep trust between client and therapist. It requires openness and unconditional positive regard. Any hint of judgment, negative reaction, or shock for information being shared, would be extremely hurtful to the client and detrimental to his sense of self. My goal was always to be emotionally available to hear their stories, their pain, and their conflicts. For the system, in particular, with the more sexually active personalities, namely Hanna and Stephana, the dialogues surrounding sex were colored by their negative experiences with other professionals and the secrets they carried concerning their sexual history. Stephana was the most open because she had cut herself off from her emotions and viewed sex as a physical encounter. Hanna, on the other hand, was very reticent at first to share with me her beliefs and feelings. She would preface statements with, "It's stupid." No one had ever validated her thoughts and emotions. No one had ever affirmed what she intrinsically knew: that sex with a mom was wrong, and that all children have a right to their own bodies. I tried to be the vanguard of her rights, helping her know the difference between loving sex and controlling sex, between emotional intimacy and physical closeness. We had lengthy discussions about what loving relationships were all about: respect for one another, mutual consenting acts, and genuine interest and caring for one another. We talked about the nature of unhealthy relationships, including the fears in being oneself and in speaking one's mind, a sense of being overpowered, and a loss of oneself. They had only known the latter.

Relationships and sexuality seemed mutually exclusive. Despite not having had healthy relationships, Stephana and Hanna saw themselves as sexual beings. They chose to follow a lesbian lifestyle. Stephana believed homosexuality to be a choice. I wondered if this choice to be with a woman was, in part, searching for the warmth and love from a mother that they had never had. Stephana disagreed. Both men and women had abused her. She chose to be physically close to a woman because she was attracted to the female. She didn't seem to appreciate my Freudian psychoanalysis. She compartmentalized sex and love. Sex was simply an outlet for her emotions and a way to have fun. She did not have relationships, but she truly enjoyed pleasuring a woman. She enjoyed the process leading up to the sexual act: the enticing of a woman, and the challenge that ensued. She described this as being like an intricate dance. She seemed more masculine in her approach to sex. However, although her body would be aroused, she never let anyone reciprocate the pleasuring. She never let anyone see the body, because the body carried with it too much shame, too many scars. Darkness and bedcovers allowed the body to remain an unknown entity to others. During the process of engaging in therapy with me, Stephana stopped going to bars and going home with women. I was concerned that adding a new variable to a very fragile system could truly activate a major disintegration. She was respectful of the need for the system to heal. When she became frustrated, she threatened to go get drunk at the bars, but she always put our work first. Instead, she shaved her head. She said, "I need to feel in control of something!"

Hanna's sexual needs were different from Stephana's and the two often found themselves in conflict. Hanna was searching for emotional intimacy and closeness. Sadly, she didn't see anyone loving her. She projected the shame she carried, and believed that everyone saw her as unworthy and unlovable. The past abuse had fostered such low self-esteem that she would push people away. She felt that she did not own her body. Everyone who had abused and raped her had taken her body from her. Every time someone touched her in a sexual way, she felt owned. She hated the feeling, but didn't know how to retake her own body. She knew that until then, she could never enjoy physical closeness. Hanna also seemed to be questioning the chosen gay lifestyle. She was tired of sleeping with women and getting hurt. And as stated previously, she wanted to bear a child. She wanted to do this naturally, as opposed to insemination as many lesbians do. She had had one experience with a young man, Michael, who befriended her at school when she was nineteen. He helped her in math; he bought her lunch; and he took her home one day when her car had broken down. She enjoyed talking to him. She had a sexual experience with him. She became pregnant. She miscarried. The whole experience reinforced her unworthiness. She never saw Michael again.

Hanna seemed to be in great emotional turmoil over her sexuality. I didn't know how this conflict would be resolved. Stephana was adamant that she would never have sex with a man and that was final! Would Hanna's needs surpass all others should they agree to give her the host role, or would Hanna realize that being gay was intrinsically the right path? These were questions that could not be answered for now, but ones that were significant as healing progressed.

The males did not see themselves as sexual beings. They didn't do any of the bodily functions. They never looked in the mirror. They were not interested in sex. Therefore, there didn't seem to be a conflict for them when Stephana, for example, was acting out her sexual needs. They stayed away. One of the males, who was uncomfortable with his self-disclosure and asked that I not mention his name, shared that he could find both males and females attractive. He wanted to know if that was wrong. He said he never played out these feelings, because his "equipment" didn't work. He didn't do anything with these feelings. I found his recognition that his male organs did not function, revealing. On some level, this male alter was aware that his maleness had limitations, yet rather than reject the notion of being male, he just learned to deny his male sexual desires. I wondered if this would simplify the process of transference into the female body.

The children were not allowed to be present during sexual activity. Stephana was very adamant that she needed privacy and that sex was not appropriate for children. It was very interesting how protective the older, sexually active alters were of the children. They did not want to perpetuate the sexual abuse these children had experienced and/or witnessed, and condone sex with children. However, sometimes the best intentions failed. Many times she could feel their closeness to her, though not their physical presence, except once, when Randy, in a most inquisitive tone of voice asked, "What are you doing?" Needless to say, Stephana was quite put out by him, so he ran away, something that he learned to do well. He couldn't understand why she became so angry with him, because this was how he learned, by watching. How could I explain to a precocious eight-year-old about sex? I didn't. Instead, I told him that everyone needs privacy sometimes and we all need to respect that. Certainly no one in the system had been having his or her privacy upheld. This was another new concept to try to understand.

We have already described the horrific details that Tigger and Death recalled. How do those traumas effect the development of a child's sexuality and sexual identity?

Children of trauma do not learn that they have rights, that they can voice their feelings, or that they own their own bodies. The nature of sexual exploitation is such that children, who are dependent and not fully intellectually or emotionally developed, are unable to give informed consent for the control imposed upon their bodies. Children are robbed of the normal stages of development, which includes growing healthy sexual feelings. Victims of sexual abuse learn to be secretive, and live in fear and confusion. Children don't know what to believe, or how it can be wrong for a mother to fondle her child. After all, mothers love their children, don't they? Yet instinctively, children do know that this is wrong. They know because their bodies react by tightening up and they feel sick to their stomachs. Their minds react by wanting to scream, and their spirit reacts by feeling helpless and hopeless. Parents are supposed to be protectors, loving role models. Gabriele, et al, only learned to feel angry, hurt, scared, defenseless, guilty, ashamed, and above all, worthless. Love was a meaningless term. Sex was something to fear. Why then, do some children often become promiscuous while others are self-conscious? Can victims ever learn to truly enjoy sexual pleasuring without shame and guilt?

We have seen how Stephana enjoyed sex, seeing it as a game or conquest. She always needed to be in control, so she initiated the sexual contact. She was the giver of pleasure. She never let herself receive. The past memories would always be in the forefront of her mind if she let no one take advantage of her. As stated, Hanna wanted desperately to experience love and intimacy, but she did not believe this was possible. She could not handle physical touch; she could not allow herself to trust that closeness would not hurt, so the barrier to emotional intimacy persisted. Children who are sexually abused do not learn the difference between healthy physical closeness and inappropriate sexual touch. For Gabriele, et al, all touch meant the body was being used for someone else's desires. The years of force and violence to which the body was subjected, had left their enduring marks. Sex just hurt. Sex triggered ruthless acts of violation and the memories of the mother "doing it" to her. The mother even gave this young child a directive that would haunt her for the rest of her life, by saying, "You will only enjoy sex with me or with whom I choose." Like a hypnotic suggestion, Hanna could only get sexually aroused by visualizing the mother sexually abusing her. This realization was too repulsive for her to accept in herself. Sex became shaming, and so Hanna learned to punish herself for responding to such disgusting acts. The desire to burn became stronger after any sexual encounter.

She wanted more than anything to learn how to trust, how to let go of these fears and messages, how to let go of control, and to learn that physical touch and closeness could feel good. I knew this would be a most challenging goal to meet. Being an incest survivor is painful enough, but to be a victim of mother/daughter incest means growing up without ever knowing or feeling real love, affection and nurturance. This bond with a mother is crucial in the development of the ego. It is the primary source for building self-esteem. Gabriele, et al, never felt protected and cared for. They grew up with a deep void in their heart. All that filled the cavern were untruths and cruel lessons. Their young mind was like a sponge, everything was taken in, but nothing was wrung out. Hanna described how she saw her inner self as a black shriveled mass. This pained me deeply. I wanted to help her extinguish old messages and replace them with new truths, love and caring. I truly wanted her to know that she was lovable, but I knew a therapeutic relationship could never replace a mother/daughter relationship that had not existed. Despite this, I kept trying to show her that she was a loving person. She had great difficulty believing me. After all, love was an unknown concept. There is a French song that says, "Love is the child of freedom, never that of domination." Gabriele, et al, never knew freedom, only the control by others over their mind and body.

Therefore, loving sex could never be experienced as long as the multiples existed in their present forms. They were evidence of the sexual violations, and served to either block out emotions or punish the body. This reinforced a sense of alienation from the self and human separateness. Thus, in order to have a loving sexual experience, they needed to overcome separateness to achieve union. To achieve union meant healing the fragments of their beings and finding wholeness. It meant unburdening the soul of the past pain, shame, and self-loathing. The next phase of our journey was about to begin.

Hanna Chapter 6:

One Body—Two Genders

"Different though the sexes are, they inter-mix. In every human being a vacillation from one sex to the other takes place, and often it is only the clothes that keep the male or female likeness, while underneath thesex is very opposite of what it is above."
—Virginia Woolf

When it was decided that I, Hanna, would be the one that everyone else would integrate into, this raised many questions for which we needed answers. It became clear that there would need to be honest, open discussions between Rachel and all of us. The fact that all of us were so separate and distinct only complicated matters. We all had our own opinions and at times, were unwilling to compromise. But we had to talk about our sexuality and we had to understand how to deal with two genders in one body. There had to be some understanding about who and what the body was: a twenty-eight-year-old female. We knew that if the males in the system did not accept that the body was female, then they would be unwilling to accept that they were indeed female and not male, and this could have the effect of stopping the process of integration and ultimately undermine our healing. So, slowly we all started to talk with Rachel about sex and sexuality. We worked to discover why there were two genders and how this impacted our system. At first I was discouraged by the general lack of literature dealing with the topics of sexual healing and gender identity in multiples. I started asking myself, "Do other therapists think that these are areas that do not need to be dealt with? Do they want their clients to continue having sex with the old beliefs and problems (because surely there would be problems)?" I also wondered if the mental health community just assumed that as a person discussed their abuse experienced as a child, that there would be a direct correlation that would release them to ensuring healthy sexual practices as an adult. I believed this presumption to be wrong.

The child victim of sexual abuse does not have the skills and tools to function as sexual adults. Therefore, we need to learn these from people we trust, and who better than from our therapists? The more that I talked about the abuse, the more I found myself questioning every part of my sexuality. I knew that healing that part of me was a must, and the only way I felt that I could do that was to *actively* discuss and process my sexual beliefs and problems. "I do not want to live and not be able to have normal, enjoyable sexual relationships," I told Rachel, and she agreed.

In looking at gender differences, I knew that both Trudy Chase and Sybil had males in their systems, but did not know how they dealt with the identity issues that arose. I felt very alone and ashamed about having so many males in our system. In fact, I felt like a freak.

It was difficult for me to write on this subject as I began to heal from my sexual abuse, and come to terms with my identity and body. I did not want to be a *pioneer*, but that is how I slowly started to view myself. I had to find my own answers and trust Rachel's therapeutic instincts without being able to draw on others' past experiences. I had to learn about my sexuality from the ground up. Everything that I thought and knew about sex and sexuality had to be reexamined. What I felt was *me*, I would keep; what beliefs belonged to the mother, I would throw out. But it was the process of doing this that was extremely painful. I had to look at everything that I had done and what had been done to me, and then talk about it.

For a long time I assumed Rachel would be uncomfortable discussing these issues with me. Like most assumptions, I was wrong. It turned out that I was the one that was apprehensive and embarrassed. I found myself thanking the powers that be for that marvelous invention, the telephone. Because I was so self-conscious, it was easier to discuss sex and sexuality with Rachel over the phone, and know that she could not see my face when there was a physical distance between us. I was able to be more unguarded and outspoken.

I was immensely relieved that Rachel was going to be respectful and helpful dealing with this very delicate, but all too human, subject. My past therapists seemed ill at ease, and I felt blown off when I would try to discuss anything like this. For example, when I was having sexual problems with one of my female partners, the therapist that I was seeing at the time, handed me a book meant for heterosexual couples, then ended that session fifteen minutes early. The message I received was that I was not normal and did not deserve to enjoy sex, and that I was damaged goods and would be that way for the rest of my life. *BULLSHIT!* I am a sexual being, just like anyone else, and I have a right to have enjoyable, satisfying, and most importantly, healthy sexual relationships where the past does not creep into my present. More than that, I deserved to have a competent therapist who felt the same way and was willing and able to tackle the issues surrounding my sexuality without making me feel like a freak of nature who had no right to have sex. I still get so angry when I think about how my sexuality was mishandled. I felt that these therapists did more damage than good. They compounded my existing problems by reinforcing my own self-disgust.

When Rachel and I first started working together, she implied that we wanted to be male. The females in the system revolted. "We have *never* wanted to be male!" It is true that we were extremely masculine looking. We were striving not to look anything like the mom, who was feminine and prissy looking, so we would not wear makeup, dresses, have long hair, or let our nails grow out. For me, appearing feminine equated to being the mom, and that was not acceptable. But slowly I started to think that maybe, I repeat maybe, I could start to be more feminine and still be me and not the mom. When

I told a friend that I was thinking about wearing a dress, she looked at me and said she could not picture it. I dared her to; it took her five minutes and then only if I were wearing combat boots. I laughed, but it brought home a point. I did not look female; I looked male. No wonder Rachel made that assumption.

I honestly think that the reason the system had two genders came from the abuse and the madness surrounding me. The mother would tell me that she wanted a son and would treat the male personalities and me as male, expecting us to be physically strong, and dressing us in jeans and tee shirts. Yet she would then be critical of us for not being feminine. She was also abusing my body in a very feminine way. Rachel gave me her theory and I agree somewhat with it. . But I also believe that the creation of two genders was in an effort to please the adults around me in order to survive and stay sane.

I believed that I could never have a normal sexual relationship. In fact, I did not even know what one was, or what it would even be like. However, I did not want to live the rest of my life being owned by the mother. I told Rachel one day, "When you sexualize a child, you start to own them." I believe this is true. The mother made it clear that she owned me by constantly having sex with me. She did not respect my body as being mine. I was never given any privacy. I was made to feel, to *believe,* that I was nothing but a sex object, good for nothing but her personal pleasure, or for the pleasure of her friends. I was not allowed to be my own person, to come to my own sexual awareness *on my own, in my own time, and in my own way.* Because of this, I did not come to decide what I liked or did not like about sex. Sex was always forced upon me. I was *told* what kind of sex I could and could not have. I was *told* what I would and would not like. And I was never allowed to say "No" to sex. She would tell me that the only way that I would ever be happy was if she was the one having sex with me.

As I got older and started to have my own sexual experiences, I found that I could not have sex without seeing her face. I could not stay sexually aroused without her being there. It was very humiliating to me, and I was ashamed of my body's reactions and my inability to control it. I would think that she must have been right and that I wanted her to have sex with me, and that I enjoyed what was happening to me. Yet somewhere within me, I knew that she was wrong, that I had never wanted her to come into my room and touch me, or have me touch her sexually, and I did not enjoy it. So, I could not understand why I felt sexually aroused by images of the abuse that had occurred and why I could not just ignore those images.

Most of the time the images, and the shame connected to it, would trigger self-inflicting behaviors. When sex was over, I would burn or cut, or at the very least, take a scalding shower, all in an effort to get rid of my feelings and the images. The first time that I told Rachel about this problem, I felt so mortified by what I believed was my own actions. I thought I was the sickest person in the world and I wanted to run. I know that incest is wrong and sick, and because images and fantasies of incest would sexually arouse me, I believed that I was no better than the mother was.

Rachel did not agree. She explained that sexual arousal is common and is physical in nature; it is not something that I could completely control. She did ask me not to engage in any sexual activities, including masturbation, for a time, explaining that it was a way to stop the destructive cycle of my shame and give myself a break to sort out who I was sexually. During this period of abstinence from sex, Rachel and I had many discussions, and over the course of time, I realized (while Rachel repeated herself over and over) that my body had reacted on a physical level, and my mind had become trained to those acts and reactions. The more abuse that occurred, the more my body reacted, so the more the mom told us that we really liked it, the more that we believed her. After all, if you don't like something sexual, you don't get aroused, right? To put it bluntly, incest is invasive. It contaminates all parts of a child's life and psyche, leaving him/her damaged emotionally and psychically, and without a sense of self. I had to learn who I was and I had to learn to re-own my body. I had to relearn what I wanted sexually, starting with my orientation. I had lived a lesbian lifestyle all of my adult life, but found myself questioning whether I wanted to continue having sex with women. It was very triggering for me. I could not let myself relax and enjoy the encounters—I always felt a need to stay alert and on guard. I felt consumed by fear and haunted by the mother. If a partner wanted to give me oral sex, I would start to have flashbacks of being abused by the mother. I could not let my partners put their hands in my hair, because again I would have flashbacks. I found it humiliating when my partners would complement me on my skill, saying, "You are good at this." It was the same thing I had been told as a child. The mother had totally oriented me towards lesbian sex and I found that I did not enjoy it.

I wanted to be free of her and wondered if having sex with a man might be the only way I could have that freedom. I have had sexual encounters with men, however most were not of my choosing. I did not believe that there were any decent men in the world. I have had only one *okay* sexual encounter with a man who was kind and gentle. I also got pregnant. I wanted to keep the child, but miscarried in the first trimester. I was ashamed of losing the child. I thought that it was a direct result of a suicide attempt and my lifestyle, and not because of not eating, sleeping and doing way too many drugs. I decided never to have sex with men again, and I never saw the father again. But I now found myself questioning this decision. I want to have children, but I do not want to conceive via artificial insemination. I also want my child to have both a mother and a father. I believe that lesbians and gays can be great parents, and have known gay couples that have been the ideal parents. But I have my own views and feel that children need both male and female role models in their lives.

I do not want to be a single parent. I want support in raising my child. I know what it is like to be the child of a single parent, when no one was home to greet me after school and there were serious financial troubles. In addition to wanting children and not enjoying lesbian sex, I was tired of living a lifestyle that is just too tough. The fact of the matter is that when you are homosexual, you live outside of society's norms and you draw fire for it. I was tired of feeling like a freak and an outsider, and I wanted to be more accepted not only by society, but also by myself. I could not live this lifestyle anymore, and that was what mattered more than anything else. And if I could not be true to myself about my sexuality and my reasons behind it, then what was the point of trying to heal sexually at all?

I do not believe that homosexuality is wrong. I just believe that it is not the right lifestyle for me. I still maintain that a person's sexual orientation is a choice, and everyone should be free to make that most personal and private of choices *as they see fit*, without others imposing their judgment and morals.

We had lots of experiences sexually: one-night stands, as well as long-term relationships. Stephana slept with lots of different women. She had a "love them—and—leave—them" attitude. She did not want to become emotionally involved with these women and felt that having a long-term relationship would just complicate the sex. The only problem with her liaisons was that she would get us into some very *sticky* spots, putting our physical safety in jeopardy. Some of these flings would also put our long-term relationships at risk.

As far as Stephana was concerned, these women understood that there was no possibility for any kind of relationship to develop. Stephana simply was not interested in anything but a sexual encounter, and made this clear from the beginning. As soon as she was done having sex and done talking, she would shower and leave. She would never see them again, and would not accept a phone number or an invitation for another date. One time was all she wanted, needed and desired. Sex for her was nothing but an outlet (fun). What thrilled her more than the sex was the process of seducing these women. She considered it to be something akin to a dance. It would take hours and all of her social skills, charm, and wit. She found it to be completely engrossing, and was aroused just by the process and the skill that it would take to get a woman to even talk to her. There were times when she would be disappointed because a woman would have no interest in her and would refuse to talk to her, so she would have to start all over again with someone else, but her attitude was that it was just part of the dance. For all of her bravado about her encounters, she was ashamed of her behavior. Because of her shame, she never let the other women give her pleasure, nor would she let them see her body in full light; she kept herself covered the whole time that she was with them. She did not understand or care about the risks involved and she did not believe that she was hurting anyone else, or herself, with her behavior. But she was hurting us, me and the children within. These encounters felt more like what we lived through growing up.

Stephana was a major roadblock to my wanting to have sex with a male. She was adamant that she would never engage in heterosexual sex and because she understood that we shared the same body, she would not let me. "If you have sex with a guy then I will be having sex with a guy. No fucking way. And that is final!"

This made me very angry, and I told her so. "You elected me to be in the lead, to be the one that everyone would integrate into, and *now* you are putting conditions on what I do? You don't get everything that you want, Stephana. I want to have sex with men—not with women." Needless to say, there were many arguments about with whom I would and would not have sex. I did not see anyway to resolve it. Stephana and I could both be rather stubborn and unyielding when we wanted to. Her position was that she saw nothing positive in males and did not find them to be sexually attractive. In addition, she was only attracted to females and since she enjoyed sex with them, why couldn't I? She believed that I just needed to relax and enjoy it. It was like having my mother inside telling me to just, "relax and enjoy it." Stephana never did understand what it was like for me, because she cut off her feelings whenever she was sexual and refused to acknowledge her shame about her body. I must say that I was relieved when integration happened and she no longer was in my ear yelling. There are those times that I still hear a loud "Yuck!" whenever I think about a male sexually. I am pretty sure that is Stephana, still voicing her disapproval.

During the time that Stephana and I were going around about my wanting to be heterosexual, the boys were giving me their own twist. Whenever Stephana and I fought, they would just listen to the two of us and refuse to take sides. However, they did have one concern. "We are male, so if you have sex with a guy, it means that we are having sex with a guy too, right? Does this mean that we are homosexuals? Because we don't want that." My response was no, they would not be homosexuals if I was heterosexual, and they would not be having sex too. They did not have to be there; they never had been there before and they did not have to start now.

The males, such as TOB, William, Mikhail and Mathew were never sexually active that we know of and they were disinterested in that part of life. In addition, they did not want anyone else to know that their *equipment* did not work. They were more focused on other things, like Mikhail learning and working; William on his converting to Judaism; TOB with his plants and being self-destructive; and

Mathew on protecting and picking on the little ones inside. Because they were so focused on other activities, they did not need to think sexually. They *believed* they were male and when they looked down, they believed they saw a penis. When they were told that it really was not there, they became incensed and refused to listen. Rachel asked one time what they would do when the body would have menstrual cramps. They simply would not be around. What they could not understand, they would avoid like it was the plague. They could not understand or acknowledge that the body was female, with all the workings and problems of a female. So, they simply would not look at it or talk about it. Thus, they could continue their distorted reality and not have the body, or anyone else, interfere.

The children also had problems understanding the body. Rachel wanted to know what they did when we were having sex. We worked very hard at keeping them inside and *away* whenever there was a sexual encounter. When they came around it would cause huge problems, because they would freak out, believing that they were "back there" being abused. This was not always easy. When Randy heard a psychiatrist telling us that everyone needed to know what everyone else was doing, he took this completely to heart. It got him into trouble. He came around when Stephana was in the middle of a sexual encounter and asked what she was doing, thinking that he was just being good and doing what the doctor had told him. Stephana did not care and punished him for his interference.

The confusion of being multiple with different sexual needs was creating more inner turmoil. Instead of healing, I felt more hopeless. I knew that the children could never feel safe as long as they were living in the body. They needed to heal and either grow up, or let me live by myself. For that to happen, we needed to continue our journey with Rachel towards wholeness.

Rachel Chapter 7:

Unburdening the Soul

"Your past is not your potential. In any hour you can choose to liberate the future."

—Marilyn Ferguson

What is real? This was a profound question constantly posed by them in the body throughout the process of healing. Real is defined in Annandale's English Dictionary, as a state of being, of existing. It is not fictitious or imaginary. They did not feel real. Their reality consisted of visions, hallucinations and nightmares. Their truth was, by this definition, a non-truth, a misconception, an unfounded notion. They did not understand when I tried to explain that these images and voices were fears and memories stored in the subconscious. They were real at one time, a time when horrors took place. They were not real in 1998. And time for them was also distorted. Time stopped for the multiples. Most of the personalities stopped growing at the time of their extreme abuse. Some grew a few more years, but none grew into adulthood. Becoming a big person was something they did not want to do, because big people only hurt. Many of the child alters still believed the mother to be alive. They would continually fear her presence; they would hear her words of reproach and disgust towards them. They would hear her lessons. These lessons became one of the strongest barriers to accepting my truth and ultimately, to healing. I asked Randy one evening who was still getting in Hanna's way of embracing the life concept. He replied, "It's not who, it's what."

The "what" were the deeply embedded directives of the mother and her *truisms* that were acted out onto her innocent child. The children knew only that mothers are supposed to love their children. If mothers hurt children, it must be because the children were bad. Mothers are right. Children must obey. Children must never tell on a mother, or any adult. Telling means the ultimate of disobedience, worthy of severe punishment—punishment that included being burned, being deprived of food or sleep, and being locked up. Children must never question the punishment. They must know only that they deserved it. To further ensure that no one "on the outside" would ever be told of what was happening to the child, the mother gave this compelling message: "If you tell, no one will ever believe you, they will think you are crazy, and they will lock you up." This child, who became Gabriele, et al, learned her lessons well. All the personalities, except Randy (who ran away and therefore did not hear the lessons), believed wholeheartedly that:

1) They were bad;
2) They needed to punish themselves;
3) They must never tell any adult anything (including me);
4) If anyone did disobey the lessons, they must be punished; and
5) They must never be angry—especially with the mom: she was just teaching them a lesson.

Therefore, their conditioned, automatic and intuitive response to these voices and to these messages was always, "We must punish ourselves." Punishment was a way to stop the voices. Their reality, their existence, consisted of finding ways not to exist. Their life was one powerful paradox. It did not make sense to most people, but it made perfect sense to them. Life equaled death.

In order to heal, they needed to see and accept the world differently. The quest for a new reality, an existence dominated by safety rather than fear, for wholeness and self-acceptance, was subjugated to an understanding that what happened to them, the years of physical and emotional torment, was not their fault. They needed to internalize a new message that they were not to blame for the horrors that befell them. They were not evil. They needed to embrace a new truth; I was the messenger of that truth. This became a journey filled with anguish and inner turmoil. I sometimes felt that whenever I made progress in helping one alter hear my truth, this would scare another, and the body would be punished soon after (following the mother's lessons). The protectors of the body would throw up their hands in frustration. Yet no matter how overwhelmed or confused I felt, I knew that my optimism, my hope and my belief in the healing of this system were of paramount importance. If I gave up, they would infer that I had lost confidence that their beliefs were real and therefore, their only relief was through death. I could never let that happen. I would get to the core of their existence; I just had to have patience (an attribute not usually associated with me).

The first step in the healing process and in the growth cycle, was awareness of getting in touch with needs and feelings.

The original request for counseling was prompted by an awareness of feelings of depression, of the inability to concentrate, to sleep or eat, and of sounds of roaring in the brain. This awareness led to mustering up courage to do something about it, to call for help. At that time, Gabriele was prepared only to disclose sufficient information to validate the diagnosis of depression. However, other alters, in particular Randy, were aware of much deeper feelings and needs. They knew healing would never take place without a more complete outpouring of who they all were and what had occurred in their lives. Depression was only one facet of the outcome of their past. I needed to know more. I needed them to know that they could no longer suppress memories. As Sarah Olsen, in *Becoming One*, stated, "I came to see my memories as the only means by which I would get my life back," and "Expressing the inexpressible out loud to someone makes it real ... it's the beginning of your healing." I knew that this statement was true; they did not. Again, I came to understand their inner struggle to choose whether to believe the mother's words, "Never tell," or mine, "It's important to tell."

Hanna felt that if she let her emotions out, she would go crazy. She saw the world spinning out of control and she didn't know how to stop it. She wanted to scream, but the screams would not come out. Once, I took her to the woods, a place I hoped would give her freedom to scream and cry. She feared that her screams would hurt someone, or she would be hurt. During the Satanic rituals, that was indeed what took place. After much encouragement, she released a howl. My heart sank; it sounded like the wails of a dying animal. When she finished, I held her tightly, and softly repeated, "You will never be hurt again." This consoled her, but not for long. The shame of what she had experienced and was not yet ready to tell me became a major resistance towards healing.

The body was burned shortly after that episode, burned by her own hand, but provoked by the street kids who were still upholding the bond and the belief that to tell was treason. The more exposed Hanna felt, the more she wanted to scream. Yet, she could not. During one very long session, I sat with her on the floor helping her to free her soul. She was so fearful of the repercussions that what I was asking of her would truly be the act of treason, the breaking of the bond, telling on them and receiving their anger. After hours of reassurance and support, and some coaxing, she began, unsteadily at first, and more fervently towards the end, to express the words she had repressed her whole life.

"I'm not crazy. I know right from wrong. I'm not a murderer. I never wanted to be there. You're not a mom; you're a monster. I hope you rot in your grave. I want to live. I don't want to hurt myself because of you."

Hanna had finally found her voice. Yet she did not believe her own words. The mother's voice was still louder. How could I extinguish the mom's lessons so that they could be open to new learning? They would describe the mother as changing before their very eyes. She could be kind one moment and teach them how to love animals, and then turn into a monster with glaring eyes, capable of killing their pet dog (which she did as a way of teaching what happens when you don't obey). This inconsistency of love, this perpetual fear and resultant denial of love, made them emotionally starved. I believed that they needed my consistent acceptance and nurturance to help them see another type of adult/child relationship. And they needed to learn how to love themselves.

To meet this goal, I did a healing meditation in which I asked Death (Hanna) to visualize meeting her little child. It was a most compelling experience, as she met Tigger and heard her screams. I asked that Death do whatever she could to comfort Tigger, so she held the little girl and the screams stopped. Death then placed her head in my lap and began sobbing. She had recovered a lost memory. She had seen the child's face. She had felt her pain. It was becoming more real. There was a new realization that Tigger needed to grow up.

As their trust in me grew, there was more sharing of past events. But the sharing always led to their fear of my disbelief, or their expectation of punishment. And sadly, punishment always came in the form of self-infliction. The body would be burned and cut. The system was fighting back. Feelings were not supposed to be revealed. Burning and cutting were the only means of shutting feelings off. Yet on another level, there seemed to be some awareness that one could not be real unless one allowed oneself to feel. I needed to help them believe that feeling no longer needed to be feared. My words did not seem to have as much power as my own behaviors. Whenever they shared details of their excruciating abuse, I could not control my own tears. They would see my uninhibited emotional responses, and ask, "Was it really that bad?"

I would answer very simply, "Yes."

The system had learned how to block out and control feelings. "The repression of feelings and needs requires a great deal of control ... The control is needed to hold back the real system...Total means building internal pressure until the system itself may break down or explode," is how Janov describes it in *The Primal Scream*.

Therefore, the unburdening of the soul through emotional abreaction often led to intense fears of being out of control. This feeling scared some of the alters so much that they would ask to be hospitalized. This was a difficult decision for me. I believed hospitalization would cause regression of the healing process, a loss of trust in me, and exacerbate the nightmares of the street kids that they would be locked up and/or sent away. This would also validate the mother's message, "If you tell, you will be locked up." I also knew that they would not disclose all the personalities to strangers, as a result of their very negative past experiences with hospital personnel.

For example, on one occasion when one of the alters tried to jump from a window and run away, she was tied down to a gurney, placed in isolation, and told that if she wanted any privileges, she would have to calm down. I shuddered on hearing this. These actions by the *experts* were, in my opinion, the exact opposite of what was needed to build trust so that healing could take place. Rather, these strategies served to further alienate the personalities, reinforce that they were bad, deserving of punishment, and provoked continued need for self-inflicting behaviors. I could not subject them to the possibility of being treated in this manner. I did not trust that the hospital staff would respect them enough to disregard their behaviors in order to reach their core. Yet I wondered if I was being unethical in not encouraging hospitalization during these times of "feeling crazy" and unsafe. I told them that I would support whatever decision they would make. They knew their minds better that I did; they knew whether they had reached their own limits of pain and inner torment. In the end, they realized that thinking of hospitalization meant that they were feeling great desperation. It meant they were getting closer to the truth. Thus, rather than choose a way that would lead to further repression, they let me in to even deeper caverns. In reality, they never wanted hospitalization; that was a cry for help. They just needed to know they were safe.

The use of medication was another source of controversy between me and other mental health professionals, notably psychiatrists. Medication did not make Gabriele feel better. Medication did not stop the self-abuse. My belief is that meds only kept the feelings from being expressed and they served to keep her feelings from getting "out of control." These feelings needed to be expressed. If not, they would eventually explode, like a volcanic eruption, and I didn't think anyone, including me, would be able to pick up the pieces. I also feared that some of the torture they witnessed and experienced may have been under the influence of drugs. They would describe a vagueness and it was Randy's theory that "those big people must have given them drugs." If this were accurate, the use of drug therapy would only trigger those confusing times.

Interestingly, some of the alters did keep the body from ingesting medications, while others would abuse them, taking more than prescribed. One psychiatrist, in her frustration to find a drug that would calm them, prescribed Valium. I was appalled! The inevitable happened: they became addicted. It took several long, painful days and nights to help them get through the withdrawal symptoms of sweats, headaches, shakes, increased roaring, and feelings of craziness. I felt angry that my progress with the system had to be put on hold while I undid the damage of another professional, but in the end, they made it and they were free of all drugs. They have been drug free ever since

Feeling safe was an experience none of the alters had ever had, as they were created out of fear; lived in fear, and expected only bad to happen. There were only times of increased fear and franticness (especially at night), being in an enclosed building, during full moons, and contact with unknown adults. The latter made going to work very difficult. The street kids and TOB felt crazy in a work environment. For months during the intense part of therapy, they needed to be on disability leave. I was concerned that these alters would disrupt the workplace and they would be fired. If that happened, they would interpret it as, "We are bad; we don't deserve to have a good job." I did not want them to risk feeling failure.

It was very important that they have an awareness of feeling safe, so that when I made a comment about being safe, they understood this concept. To this end, I borrowed from Bernie Siegel, Joan Borysenko, and Helen Watkins, various meditations, which utilized the principle of light as a healing and protective source. I wanted light to be associated with goodness, with positive energy, and with a life force. It had to become more powerful than darkness, evil and death. These healing meditations helped create a new sense of calm and peace and, within that framework, offered new ways of coping. When any of the alters, especially Hanna and the street kids, felt panic and telephoned me, telling me they were going to burn or needed to kill the body, I would say very softly and melodically:

"*Listen to the sound of my voice. Let the sound of my voice always give you comfort and help you feel safe. Now, take a long deep healing breath in.*" I could usually hear a deep sigh through the receiver, and *responded, "That's good." I continued, "Let a wave of peace move down through your body, starting at the top of your head, and moving all through the body, down to your toes—just relaxing you, deeper and deeper relaxed. Now, I want you to feel a warm light surrounding you, penetrating every cell of your being, warming you, protecting you, and healing you. Feel its warmth." (One evening they were standing in the rain at a phone booth, cold and shivering. When I asked if they could feel the warmth of the light, they softly responded, "Yes." I knew that my voice was having the effect I wanted—it was helping them feel calm and be open to my suggestions.) I continued, "With the warm light surrounding you like a cocoon, you are safe. No one can hurt you here." I repeated this message over and over again until I knew that, at least for that moment, another self-mutilating act had been averted.*

It seemed that no matter how out of control they felt, no matter how convinced they were that they must "do it," there was something in that meditative experience that silenced their inner voice. That silence became my powerful ally. It bought me time to continue my work, to continue the trust building, the soul searching, and purging of the most gut wrenching and gruesome memories.

Another technique that seemed to work for both Andrea and Cobalt was the use of the crystal, a magnificent source of beauty and color, concepts unknown to either. Cobalt really became awestruck when I had her visualize her crystal while floating on a cloud. Then I began singing the song from The Sound of Music, "My Favorite Things," and she began chanting along. This very defiant child had begun to feel safe. She was then able to tell me more of what had happened to her, like how she had been put in a cage and left without food or water. I asked her to imagine all the people she was scared of and to blow each of them away, far away into space. I could hear her air streams through the telephone receiver. She then asked if she could blow "the coven" away and when I told her "yes," I could sense a smile on her face. She then became quiet and felt thirsty. This awareness of thirst was an amazing shift. After all, the street kids were the ones not allowing the body to eat, drink or sleep. We were making progress!

It was clear to me that as their trust in me grew, the defenses of each of the alters were lowered, and with fewer walls and safeguards creating barriers to healing, I could help them uncover their deepest shame. For Hanna, the shame was unbearable. She could not reconcile that she had participated in such crimes that "would make your skin crawl," that she broke the commandments, and that her body symbolized all this abhorrence. Her only way of coping, which continued even after months of revelations of the horrors and receiving love, and acceptance from a rabbi and myself remained, wanting to burn. Her struggle was painful to watch. The more she discovered from the alters who had traded places with her, what torture they had experienced, the more guilt=ridden and responsible she felt.

It seemed that no amount of acceptance from others could erase the self-loathing. Hanna kept telling me that there was still more I needed to hear and understand, but she couldn't find the words to describe the visions she saw. This, in itself, made her feel crazy. Finally one evening, the answer to this obstacle in communication was revealed. There were still alters who were the ones who had directly experienced more heinous acts and were carrying on a label given to them by other professionals: the killers. Stephan, Oliver, Sandy and Cryin were a few of the personalities who saw themselves as crazy and who did crazy things. I knew that until they disclosed their stories, there could not be complete healing for Hanna. She felt their guilt and shame, yet she was "in the dark" about why the killers were the only ones who could release her from her death wish.

But this also exacerbated her own pain. It also made her life more real. After all, disassociation had been blocking her from knowing and feeling. She did not know if she was worthy to live, if she was courageous enough to live, and even if she knew how to live. Dying seemed simpler. If not death, she still believed she deserved to be punished. I knew that Death's purpose and mission had been to die, yet I believed that within Hanna there was also a flicker of light that would not burn out. I labeled this light hope. Here's how she described herself at this stage in the healing process:

"I'm this scared and lonely woman (seeing self as an adult was a great step in healing) who wants nothing more than to be healed and forgiven. I love to spend time in libraries and read anything. I want to learn. I want to be looked at as a human being and not a monster. I don't want to be my mother's daughter. I guess I'm a survivor. But, I don't want to just float. I want to live. I care about people. I can go to a movie and cry. I don't want to be my former namesake (Death). I'm

just me, and I don't want to be ashamed of me anymore."

When she finished this most honest and rare self-portrait, my only response to her was: "It is an honor for me to know you!" And I truly believed that.

As therapy continued, I felt we would make great strides in negating the old belief systems and then reach a plateau, which meant readying ourselves for more work. Randy compared this to climbing a mountain, the closer you get to the top, the harder it becomes. What a smart child! That was exactly what was happening. As we got closer to the truth and to life, the fears grew stronger and the process slowed. But, I always kept this in mind: we were getting closer to that summit.

Randy was not the only one to help me understand the inner workings of the system. TOB seemed to transform into a wise man and my guide. I know he shocked the system, because they only knew him to be obnoxious; they had never seen this smart side. He offered me great insights to help me during times when I felt stuck. Here is an excerpt of such a conversation:

"I know I'm not real. I know it's 1998, but I'm the same as I was in 1984. But I'm not a figment of their imagination. If I were, I'd have all my equipment. Hanna is real. She is female. She is the heart and soul of all of us. All of us are her. Maybe Cobalt, Andrea, and the other street kids do have to leave. They were born out of something that should never have happened, and are here to do something they don't have to do. They can never stand-alone. Maybe you need to see them as parts, not as individuals. Death created them and they got hurt. She is carrying that shame. She needs to embrace them and incorporate them. Once she can accept who she is and heal, she can truly be Hanna. Maybe being a multiple is about protecting your innocence... You have to accept the bad part of yourself as well as the good. Everyone does something he's not proud of, but you learn to forgive yourself."

I was speechless upon hearing these remarks. Hanna did need to confront those parts of her that provoked her shame and learn to forgive herself. It would mean she would no longer be able to deny all that had happened; that she would no longer live behind her walls. I knew she wanted desperately to see what was on the other side, but what was on the other side was so illusive, that it felt untenable. She also believed that anything good would be taken away and therefore, she could not trust that good could truly exist.

Hallow's Eve became a test of which truth would win out: their reality of evil and death, or mine of good and life. I had such an overwhelming fear that the street kids would band together and overrun the protectors, that I did not believe the system would be safe on that dreaded night. They had been warning me that they needed to die or become Satan's child. My reassurances that this would not happen seemed meaningless. The only way I knew to protect them and prove to them that my truth was real, was to ensure that they were protected. I made the decision, with the support of my husband, to spend from dusk to dawn with them. I am sure most therapists would have chosen hospitalization rather that give up their time (without pay) for such a cause, but I emphatically disagree with that course of action. Hospitalization as stated, would not have symbolized safety, rather it would have meant a big person had again not believed them and sent them away. I knew I had made the right choice when, at 6:00 a.m., as the sun was just rising over the misty horizon after a harrowing night of thunderstorms, Copula told me, "You do speak truth. I want no more bad, no more trouble." I had finally given another of the killers a reason to give up his need to kill. I was overjoyed.

I felt we were getting closer to that mountaintop, where the fresh air of life would be breathed, the freedom of expansiveness without walls of fear would be felt, and where one could almost reach out and feel God's presence. I wanted to believe that we could leap and run to the top, with no other barriers in our way. Unfortunately, there were still several major crevasses to cross over. This meant that Hanna needed to let herself and the children feel anger, without the fear of the mom's lessons, but with the new belief that they are allowed to be angry with people, including a mother, who hurt a child. This dilemma was expressed in this statement of Hanna's:

"If I get angry and disown her, then it means I never had a mother, which means I have to rewrite myself, and I'm not sure I can do it."

I truly believed that once Hanna and the others could let themselves be angry with the mother without fear and guilt, they would stop deflecting this anger and shame onto themselves. They would stop being victims and become survivors! But the victim role was still overpowering.

Nightly, they continued to have nightmares and visions of the mother, which seemed so real. Hanna told me that she could feel the mother lying beside her. She could smell and taste her. It sickened her, and the urgency to self-mutilate heightened. I needed to prove to all of them that the mother was not physically present, and help them have some closure with her being. I decided that we needed to take a trip to the cemetery. They had not been to the gravesite since her burial seventeen years earlier. Hanna felt anxious and unsure if that was a good idea. I prodded her. I believed they needed to see the mom's name and date of death on a tombstone to help them in their acceptance of reality that the mother could never hurt them again. It was a beautiful drive on a cool sunny day through miles of Texas farm country. As we neared the location, I noticed a look of dread had overcome the sense of lightheartedness that had prevailed while we listened to tapes of K.D. Lang and the Indigo Girls. We perused the site until we came to a moderate-size marble stone at the far end of the grounds. There was silence except for the crackling of leaves beneath our feet. I shuttered. Here were the remains of a mother who had done such damage to the young women standing beside me. I felt anger, yet a need to suppress it. We were on sacred grounds. I did say some words. I asked that her spirit free her daughter from her shame and pain so that she, a mother, could rest in peace. I told her how wrong she was to have had sex with a child and I, an adult, believed all that her daughter had told me and that her child was not crazy, as she had told her. At that point, Hanna, almost hysterically, yelled, "Stop! No more." I did stop. I gave Hanna some space to say the words she needed to. She asked the mom to stay in her grave in the ground and stop bothering her. She said she was sorry, but she needed to break her bond with her. We then left. Hanna told me she felt her skin crawl and wished she could have burned the clothes she was wearing. She became famished; I was elated. I felt her hunger symbolized a freeing of her internal self. Again, my optimism turned to horror; that night Hanna became Death. She felt like exploding. She was so afraid that she would hurt someone. So instead, she wanted to kill her body. This was still the only way she knew how to relieve herself of the intense emotional pain she was still experiencing. The memories flooded in of how the mother never wanted her to be born, how no one wanted to assume responsibility for her after the mom died, and how she was expected to live with her uncle, a man who was known to be physically abusive. She only felt unwanted, unloved and unworthy. She did not die that night. Instead, she reached out for help, which was something she had never done.

Cryin also began experiencing the familiar torture through his nightly terrors. With the trust that had been growing between us, he began *telling* the story of cuts and burns, crosses, bondage, and the wish for deathThey told me that they could never forgive all those adults in their life. They didn't deserve it. I could not forgive these adults either.

This concept of forgiveness was the last obstacle on our path towards life that needed to be examined. Could Hanna and the others forgive themselves? Could God forgive them? I took them by the hand and led them on their spiritual journey to atonement.

Hanna Chapter 7:

Unburdening the Soul

*"The most repressed and denied aspects of our soul...
[are] often the treasure that lies buried in he darkness.*

—C.G. Jung

It was starting to look like it was going to be a good day. The sun was shining, though for a Texas summer, it was not looking like it was going to be a "scorcher," as we like to say. I was in a good mood as I thought about all that I had to accomplish for the day. I had gotten up early, had my coffee, and gone over to a friend's house to meet with another friend, when the phone rang. "Hanna, can you get that?" my friend asked as she headed downstairs to take care of something.

Picking up the receiver of the phone, I was surprised to hear Martha's voice on the other end of the line. Wondering why she would be calling me here, I asked, "What's up?" still thinking that it would be one of our usual conversations. I was wrong. My day was about to go "down the crapper," as we also like to say.

"George just called me. Helen died early this morning and I

know that you wanted me to tell you when it happened," she told me. My heart stopped. I felt a tug, an urge to slam down the phone and run as far as I could, as fast as I could, but I felt stuck. I could not move. Instead, I just stared at the wall in front of me as I heard the kids inside start to cry, and I felt my own tears start to well up. Martha was telling me about the funeral arrangements and I only took about half of it in. *I can't believe she is dead*, was all that I could think. Finally, I thanked her for calling and telling me, and then stood by the phone for fifteen minutes trying in vain to control myself. I was quickly losing the battle and I just *knew* I was going crazy. So I got in my car and drove to Rachel's office.

When I got there, she was just checking her messages and one was from Martha, letting Rachel know that she had told me about Helen. But I spoke up before Rachel got to that part of the message. "Helen died last night." Funny how saying something can suddenly make it all the more real. Rachel came across the room and gave me a hug. As we talked about the fact that this was for the better (Helen had been suffering horribly for weeks), I suddenly started to weep. I kept asking myself, *How many 'Mothers' can a person lose in one lifetime?* Rachel just held me and let me cry, while for the first time in my life, I started experiencing that very human event and an emotion called *grief*. It was going to be the start of a long and painful road for someone who less that a year before, did not know how to feel.

When treatment first began with Rachel, we were in a state of "non or limited feeling." We were dulled to our emotions and worked very hard at not feeling anything. So when Rachel started to encourage us not only to feel our emotions, but also to express them, it was really hard for all of us to understand why. "Feeling and expressing emotions makes you real, and human beings are meant to feel emotions," was her response to our questioning. Slowly, with trust, respect, and caring, she was able to convince the others that this was true. They would let her know when they were upset or feeling sad, but I was the hardest sale. I simply did not want to feel any emotions, and I most certainly believed that it was *not* okay for me to cry; being "wimpy" is what I called crying. In addition, whenever I allowed myself to feel anything, I would harm myself. "Besides," I told myself, "I am very good at keeping my emotions at bay, so why should I change now?"

Looking back, I now understand that all my life, my ability to suppress my emotions was both an asset and a liability: an asset in that not crying or showing any kind of emotion kept the abusers in my life from harming me more than they did - getting angry at the mom was simply not an option unless I wanted to die; and a liability in that those emotions were there, real and valid, needing to be expressed, and because I would not acknowledge them or feel them, they were eating me up inside with the depression and suicidal behavior. Sooner or latter, all my emotions would come out. I could not control them forever. In fact, there were times when my ability to control my emotions had slipped.

As teenager I was classified as "full of rage," and "out of control." Because of these classifications, I was sent to numerous residential treatment centers as well as to the state hospital. The goal of the treatment centers was to impose outside "control" in an effort to stop the angry outbursts with whatever means they deemed necessary. Generally, this meant using physical restraints, medication, seclusion and even good old-fashioned intimidation. For some reason the staff, therapists and doctors in charge of my "care" truly believed that this would somehow help me to regain control of myself. All that their *treatment* did was to make me an angrier and a more out-of-control teenager, resulting in some very serious suicide attempts, which at first was labeled as "attention getting." When they finally realized that they had made a very serious mistake, they decided that the state hospital was my *only hope*. The goal of the hospital was similar to the treatment centers, but it was a much more abusive and humiliating experience, and luckily for me, my time there was limited. My stay at the state hospital resulted in labels, which haunted me for most of my life. Words like borderline, untreatable, manipulative and my favorite, "crazy," to name just a few.

What no one seemed to, or cared to, understand was that I had damn good reason to be full of rage, and as long as I was not allowed to express it, I would continue to turn it on myself, and would continue to lose control. For me, the staff and therapists at these treatment centers and hospitals were not there to help me, but instead just wanted to hurt me. And what made matters even more complicated was the DID. Often my other personalities would become violent or would harm my body, and although I would have no memory of it, I was held responsible for it. If I claimed no memory, I was called a liar and this just made me, and us, more angry and frustrated. This caused the situation to worsen, resulting in more punishment and criticism. I decided that I would no longer show any emotion, thinking that this would be viewed as acceptable.

When something was done that would normally have upset me, I would simply walk away. I thought that this would allow me to gain more privileges and freedom, instead, I was told that I was not "cooperating with the program" and that my *current* behavior was viewed as "manipulative." What they wanted me to do was just show the emotions that they wanted, when they wanted me to. What those emotions were is still elusive to me. Finally, I just gave up and got very good at hiding my burns and cuts, as well as anything that I was feeling. I also got very good at *playing the game* by saying what they wanted me to, when they wanted me too. I also became a loner. I just wanted to avoid the criticism and harassment of the adults that were in charge of my life. It did not work and until I was eighteen —years old, I continued to be sent to therapists against my will, and threatened with hospitalization and/or residential treatment if I did not do exactly as I was told. So I went to my *therapy* sessions and *played the game* quite well, but never got any real help.

Therefore, when Rachel stated that she would never hurt us, hospitalize us for feeling, judge and criticize what we were feeling, and that she wanted to help us, least to say, we did not believe her. But as trust grew, the feelings that we were working at keeping hidden started to creep out, a little at a time: fear, a little anger, and some sadness. But the self-harm would always follow these *transgressions*. For months we lived in fear that we had done something *wrong* and Rachel was going to *find* out, or be angry with us, which to us meant that we would be harmed. I was constantly asking her if she was mad.

One time I sent her an e=mail: "Rachel, are you mad at me?"

"No, No, No!" she wrote back.

She occasionally got frustrated at our unwillingness, or inability, to take in what she was saying. After all, how many times can you say the same thing? Rachel always had to reassure us that it was okay to feel whatever we were feeling, and repeatedly told us that we did not have to be hurt for feeling, not by ourselves nor by anyone else. When I expressed fear that I was going crazy, she reassured me that I was not, that I was just feeling emotions for the first time in my life.

But the self-mutilation continued. There was still an extreme fear of the mom and every other adult in our life that had ever harmed us for expressing any emotion other than what they wanted. In addition, we had to learn that there was a pattern behind our self-harm: the build up, the explosion, the relief, then the fear, another build-up, and then the act of cutting or burning. Only then could we relax, though we never felt safe. It was a huge problem for a very long time and was not only an obstacle to treatment, but also to becoming whole. We would feel so ashamed of our "loss of control," that we would do something, which caused us more shame (the self-mutilation), all in an effort to stop the emotions that were coming to the surface.

Whenever Rachel pointed out that this is what we were doing to ourselves, it would lead to another event of cutting or burning. We were caught in a vicious cycle. None of us could see an end to it and felt helpless to stop what we were doing. Rachel and I, with the help of Randy, Mikhail and Stephana, started to look at the thought and belief patterns behind these actions in an effort to understand this cycle, and thus break it.

First we looked at how we experienced and dealt with all emotions. We learned that we didn't experience the full range of emotions like most normal healthy people. We didn't let ourselves experience the *bad* emotions and in doing so, we could not experience the *good* emotions. More than that, we coped with day-to-day life with black and white thinking, in that we are bad and everyone else is good. What we also began to comprehend was that feeling emotions, good or bad, does make a person feel real, and because we cut off our emotions, we felt unreal. A person can survive by not feeling their emotions (we know: it is what we did to survive), but they can never truly live, because they do not live life to its fullest. They cut off the very essence of life: being in the moment for better or for worse with all its joy and pain, feeling it, and then moving on. This is living life.

People like us just survive, because we never allow ourselves to be whole. *BEING WHOLE MEANS BEING REAL, AND BEING REAL MEANS FEELING EMOTIONS.*

Rachel wanted us to understand that we were real, and that meant that we had to start experiencing and expressing our emotions. The problem then became that we wouldn't let ourselves feel all of our anger, fear or sadness, and thus we could not move on. We had every right to be angry, to be sad, and to be afraid, but we would not admit this to ourselves. We controlled our emotions to the point that we almost strangled ourselves with them. At this time, what we could not understand was that we were spending so much energy on not feeling, that we had none left over to give to life. We ended up working harder at everything that we did rather than just living, existing and being in our moment. It is my belief that this was one of the main reasons that we all suffered from depression for so long. And there was another factor. For us, feeling was as much a trap as not feeling, because when we would feel, there was one emotion that stood out above all the others, and that was shame.

We let our shame guide our self-judgment. That shame came from a distorted reality. This was a reality that had been forced upon us as children and we carried over to our adult life. We believed that we were horrible, terrible people that deserved to be hurt, and no one could care about and love us. But this distorted reality was also born out of our disassociation, which itself was a result of the world around us. Also, it was a source of more shame. When Rachel told us that the DID had most likely saved our lives, and that it was a remarkable way of coping, we would feel ashamed and crazy. We felt that we had "copped out" at best, and at worst, that we were the cause of the abuse. Our problem was that we blamed ourselves for the abuse that we suffered, instead of looking at these events as the cause of the disassociation, and acknowledging that we had no control over the people that had harmed us. Instead, we just felt ashamed, believing that we were the cause and affect of all our suffering, and that we were monsters for making everyone around us, hurt us.

The result was that we would act on this undeserved shame while refusing to let go of the negative self-image and the distorted reality that went with it. In addition, we would not allow ourselves to get angry with the people responsible for that distorted negative self-image. Instead, we turned everything around and directed the anger back at ourselves. In this way, we did nothing but reinforce the self-image that had caused us so much pain in the first place, the reality (to us) that the people that abused us did it because we were bad. Then whenever Rachel brought our actions/behavior/self-perception to our attention, we fell into our shame/self-blame thought/belief pattern again. It was a constant cycle that seemed to have no beginning or end. Then it finally dawned on us that the abuse never really stopped, the abuser just changed forms from the adults in our life, to us. IN ESSENCE, WE HAD BECOME OUR OWN ABUSERS.

It was a sad revelation, but it was one of the major stepping-stones in our recovery. We now understood that by abusing ourselves, we were continuing a tradition that never should have started in the first place. This understanding better enabled us to stop the burning and the cutting.

This awareness came when I was talking to Rachel about Jeffery (something that I was extraordinarily ashamed of), and I finally understood that I had been manipulated into killing him. I looked down at my arms, at all the scares from all years of burning and cutting myself, and said, "You mean that I did not have to do this?"

Rachel looked at me and with tears in her eyes said, "No, you did not have to punish yourself for something that was not your fault."

To me, it was not just that one event that I now understood to be manipulation, but all the years of abuse by all the abusers. Why else would I have harmed myself for so long? I was protecting them! And in the process, I was slowly killing myself.

There were still times after this revelation that I became desperate and wanted to cut, burn, die, or go into the hospital or go on medication. This was especially intense when I had to wake Rachel at two in the morning and felt that I was taking too much of her time, and/or being a difficult patient. She always left the decision up to me, telling me that I knew what my own limits were and what was best for myself. She also reassured me that I could make it through and that I was not going crazy (which was a constant fear), and that it would be all right.

One night when I was really afraid of myself because I had gone out and bought razor blades, she had me meet her to give them to her. When I arrived, I handed them to her and turned to walk away. Then I heard her say, "Wait. Let's talk for a few moments. I want to make sure that you are going to be okay." We ended up talking for over an hour, with her telling me over and over that I was not going crazy and that everything that I was feeling was normal and valid. That night I did not do anything to myself and for the first time in my life, I felt *safe*.

Removing the razor blades was a way to ensure my physical safety (something that any therapist is ethically bound to do), but Rachel could have done many different things to make sure that I would be safe. She chose the more personal route. By talking to me, I felt that I truly was a real and important human being. And I felt cared about. I did not feel like I was just another difficult patient with a difficult to treat disorder. I was a hurting individual who deserved to be comforted. And Rachel was willing to give me comfort and reassurance, while letting me feel my pain.

About a week before Helen died, I went to see her one last time. I walked into her house and she was lying on a hospital bed in her living room. She was thin and drawn, in a lot of pain, and it was suddenly very clear that the time was getting close. I sat down and talked to her, joking that I was now twenty-nine years old and soon would be thirty. "I have decided that I am not going to do that thirty thing! After all, at thirty you have to grow up, and I don't want to. From now on, I am staying twenty-nine and if I *have* to turn thirty, then I am going to party the rest of the year to make up for lost time!" I explained to her.

She looked at me with a huge smile on her face, and said, "Enjoy your twenty-ninth year." Soon she started to tire, so I gave her a hug, and told her that I loved her. She gave me a kiss on the forehead and said that she would talk to me later, and that she loved me. As I walked out of her home that day, I had a clear understanding that yes, she was going to die. I also knew that she had said her good-bye, as I had said mine.

I got in my car and began my drive across town to get home,

started to cry and had to pull over. There I sat in the car, on the side of the road, weeping and grieving the coming loss of a dear friend, and the loss of someone else, the mom.

Yes, the loss of someone good in my life triggered a very old loss, and one that shocked me. I got angry. "I will not grieve for HER!" I screamed when Rachel pointed out that I was grieving the loss of the mom.

"You don't have to grieve for her, but you are grieving for yourself. You are grieving because she was *not* a good, loving person, and she was not the mother that you deserved," she calmly told me.

My anger built and built. So I threw the phone across the room. For fifteen minutes I just stood there, enraged. *HOW DARE SHE*!! was all that I could think as I paced back and forth. Yet it was true. It was time for us to grieve the loss of a childhood, the loss of our innocence, and the loss of never having a mother that would, or could, care about us. People that cared about us surrounded us, and they would never willing hurt us. It was now safe to grieve.

But knowing this on an intellectual level and on an emotion gut level, are two very different things. My first gut reaction was to run. I did not want to face the strong overwhelming feelings that I was going through. So I pushed Rachel away, justifying my behavior by taking offense with little things that she (I believed) did to hurt my feelings.

There was one thing that Rachel could not do for me: grant me forgiveness. I needed it and wanted it, but did not know how to get it, and all throughout my healing process, I believed that all the work that I was doing was for nothing if I could not be forgiven. One question that I would constantly ask Rachel was, "Can God forgive me for what I have done?" I was about to find out.

Rachel Chapter 8:

Finding the Key to Forgiveness

"God will not look you over for medals, degrees, or diplomas, but for scars."
—Elbert Hubbard

Hanna would ask me over and over again, "Can God really forgive me, us?" The shame for the horrific acts in which they were manipulated into participating, carried such a heavy burden upon her heart and soul that my reassurances and acceptance of her did not seem to be enough. She felt too flawed and unworthy. And I sometimes felt that I was limited in how much I could say or do to help her forgive herself. I believed in my therapeutic abilities, but recognized that I might not reach the core of their pain dealing only on an emotional and cognitive level. I needed to move beyond this practical realm into the spiritual dimension. I had a strong belief in God and began sharing my views. I felt strongly that my God could forgive her. After all, he had forgiven David, the founder of the Judaic dynasty.

As the story of David is told, he had Uriah, husband of

Bathsheba, the woman he loved, killed, so that he could marry her. However, he felt such remorse and self-loathing that he wrote his psalms (prayers), to help him in his process of self-forgiveness, and to help build strength and courage. God did forgive him, and out of the House of David and Bathsheba was born King Solomon.

The rabbi, with whom we consulted, reinforced God's forgiveness of Hanna, and reiterated my message: God does not blame a child for the acts of an adult. Hanna continued to doubt her worth, but began attending weekly Sabbath prayers. This in itself, was a remarkable step in her growing self-acceptance, as she no longer believed she would contaminate the House of Worship, and began to chant songs of praise and love for God. Subconsciously, she appeared to be internalizing new messages of faith and hope, which were slowly replacing those of despair and emptiness. As the rabbi said, "The power of this holy place is stronger than any darkness that could ever be brought in."

One of Hanna's greatest personal challenges was to accept that she could still be a good person despite her past actions. Because her belief system followed extremist thinking, she saw herself only as evil and that there could be no good in her as long as the past was real. The more the therapy unfolded what dissociation had blocked, the more her reality pained her soul.

The Jewish religion accepts that man is not perfect and as such, has the capacity to err. "Judaism is aware…of man's moral infirmity… that sin is ever at his door…" explains Steinberg in *Basic Judaism*. It is written, "There are none on earth so righteous that they never sin."

Judaism also believes that once man falls, God can offer guidance to help him go on, learn from his foibles and seek the good. In the Book of Genesis, after Jacob wrestled with an angel and was hurt, he was able to live, see the sunrise, and was given a new name to symbolize his victory. That is how I wanted Hanna to see herself, as a young woman who had known only pain and suffering, yet who was able to survive to see the dawning of a new day. The name Hanna symbolized her victory.

"Sin, in a word, is to be or do the opposite of the good," says Steinberg. In Gabriele, et al's, life, to be good meant to listen to the cruelty of a mother, to punish oneself, and to accept the doctrines of demonic beings and kill another. Therefore, sin meant breaking the commandment of honoring thy mother; sin meant the betrayal of a bond made by an adult, even if the bond meant evil doings. It was just too confusing in their world; they were boxed in, figuratively and literally. There seemed no way to escape without their feeling badly Do what is told and do evil, according to society's norms. Don't do what is told and do evil, according to the mother's norms. Could God shed some light on this illogical belief system? As Hanna revealed the wounds she carried, she felt intense remorse for her part in the killing of a child. She cried out, "I never wanted to be there. I never wanted to hurt anyone." Jeffery was always on Hanna's mind. She was tortured by his screams and the belief that she should have died in his place. It was difficult to help her understand that she, a frightened child, had no power to stop the killing, and that no child, including her, should ever have been used as a living sacrifice for any religious practices.

It just so happened that the Torah reading for the day of Rosh Hashanah dealt with the story of Abraham and his son Isaac, and God's test of Abraham. God commanded him to take his son, Isaac, and go to the land of Moriah, and bring him there for a burnt offering (Genesis 22:1-2). Abraham was forced to abide by God's words, out of his devotion to God. However, God called to Abraham, and at that moment Abraham saw a ram, which he used as an offering instead of his son. The rabbi's interpretation of this lesson was that God did not want any more human sacrifice, He just wanted to see the depth of Abraham's willingness to abide by God's commandments. This story seemed so befitting of Hanna's life. As a child, she knew to abide by the mother's wishes or be punished. She followed any and all of her commands, including partaking in human sacrifice, which she believed was God's wish. Hanna began to understand that God did not condone the killing of children. God wanted his children to live. In Judaism, children are seen as precious and valued: they are a Blessing. As the rabbi shared with us: "There are 613 Commandments, and the number one Commandment is, 'Be fruitful and multiply.'"

Also, we learn that the God of the Hebrews forgives those who ask for forgiveness. There is a Hebrew term, *teshubah*, which means repentance. "Repentance is awareness ... acknowledging the shadow so that we will be free to make more life-affirming choices.... Without repentance, there can be no forgiveness," is written in the *Gates of Prayer*. This prayer book was the source of many words of comfort for us.

During the High Holy Days of Selichot, Rosh Hashanah and Yom Kippur, man asks God to forgive him and to inscribe him in the Book of Life. It is written that with repentance, prayer and charity, man is pardoned for his sins by a compassionate God. As is stated in the liturgy,

"**You (God) are slow to anger, ready to forgive., It is not the death of sinners you seek, but that they should turn from their ways and live.**"

My own message to Hanna was always, "God does not want you to die. He wants you to live." I invited her, or them, to attend these services in the hope that she/they might receive some solace and peace from the prayers. I had always viewed these holidays as great holy days, days in which I could unburden my heart and soul, feel heard, loved, and above all, accepted, regardless of any wrongs I might have committed throughout the year. I felt a sense of being cleansed by the end of these days. I almost felt reborn and ready to begin anew. I wanted Hanna and the other children to experience these special days where they could feel the comfort of prayer. I was elated when she accepted the invitation and could read those very words in the passage above.

Hanna wanted to believe that she was a caring, compassionate woman who could willingly hurt neither man nor animal. But, she often felt she wasn't strong enough to extinguish the recurring words of the mother, "if you tell, you die" that the child alters, in particular Sandy, still held tightly onto. And so, the following words which were repeated during these High Holy Days, became most meaningful:

"**Your might is everlasting: Help us to use our strength for good and not for evil. You are the source of life and blessing. Help us to choose life for our children and ourselves.**"

I wanted desperately for Hanna to accept her goodness and obliterate her self-loathing. The rabbi and I both incessantly repeated that she had suffered enough, and punished herself enough in trying to make amends for her past, a past that she wasn't even responsible for. She deserved to be comforted!

We wanted her to heal from the grievous pain that darkened her life and to help her renew her hope that light could fill her life. The concept of light, which I used in my healing meditations, symbolized love, faith, optimism, growth, energy and a life force. "The light is intelligent, all-knowing and totally forgiving." "Your presence (God) is the light piercing the darkness on our way, lighting our steps, making us see beauty and worth in all human beings."

It seemed that every time I expressed my thoughts and beliefs, they would be reinforced by a prayer or poem found in the *Gates of Prayer*. I felt God's presence during the entire therapeutic process. This gave me great hope when I felt discouraged, frustrated or scared that perhaps they (Gabriele, et al) would never heal.

> "When all within is dark, and
> former friends misprize,
> From them I turn to Thee, and
> find love in Thine eyes.
> When all within is dark, and I
> my soul despise,
> From me I turn to Thee, and
> find love in Thine eyes.
> When all Thy face is dark, and
> Thy just angers rise,
> From Thee I turn to Thee, and
> Find love in Thine eyes."
>
> **—Ibn Gabirol**

In addition to the imagery of light, I happened upon rainbows as a metaphor when Cobalt and Andrea played with the crystal that sat on my desk. The image of rainbows seemed to help them see the world differently—with beauty and exaltation. It has been said that God put a rainbow in the sky as a promise to Noah that the world would never again be destroyed. It was a sign of hope and peace. "And even then this deathless people was renewing itself, its life…Whose will to live? The storm ends. In the sky, a rainbow signals hope and new life. Again, there is a song to sing…." My hope for this system was for Hanna to become whole, incorporating the strengths of all her alters, and follow her new path towards life. I strongly believed our faith could be the key to her unity. "Our celebration unites many separate selves into a single chorus." To this end, there were going to be so many metamorphoses. The following poem, written for the Yom Kippur Service, so beautifully described the change process:

On Turning
Now is the time for turning. The leaves are beginning to turn from green to red and orange. The birds are beginning to turn and are heading once more toward the south. The animals are beginning to turn to storing their food for the winter. For leaves, birds, and animals turning comes instinctively. But for us turning does not come so easily. It takes an act of will for us to make a turn. It means breaking with old habits. It means admitting that we have been wrong; and this is never easy. It means losing face; it means starting all over again; and this is always painful. It means saying: I am sorry. It means recognizing that we have the ability to change. These things are terribly hard to do. But unless we turn, we will be trapped forever in yesterday's ways. Loving God, help us to turn—from callousness to sensitivity, from hostility to love, from pettiness to purpose, from envy to contentment, from carelessness to discipline, from fear to faith. Turn us around and bring us back toward You. Revive our lives, as at the beginning. And turn us toward each other, for in isolation there is no life.

During all these internal and spiritual changes that Hanna was undergoing, Randy remained himself, the inner child, still curious, and very anxious to learn how to play and dream. One day, he looked up at a beautiful one hundred-year-old oak tree with a massive trunk and sturdy branches that seemed to stretch like limbs to the sky, and knowingly said, "That looks like Jacob's Ladder!"

I wondered to myself, *How and what does he know about this biblical imagery?* I must admit, I couldn't remember its significance and listened attentively to a Torah portion one Saturday morning as the answer was revealed to me.

"And Jacob dreamed, and behold a ladder set up on earth, and the top of it reached heaven; and behold the angels of God ascending and descending on it. And behold the Lord stood beside him, and said 'I am the Lord...The land whereon thou liest (sic), to these will I give it; and thy seed...And, behold I am with thee, and will keep thee whithersoever (sic) thou goest (sic)'...And Jacob awakened out of his sleep, and he said: 'Surely the Lord is in this place, and I knew it not.'"

Hanna needed to believe that God was with her, helping her live and fulfilling her dreams. Somehow, Randy had known it all along.

Another concept we needed to examine within the context of Judaism was Satan. Gabriele, et al, still feared in Satan's power. During one service, "Satan," a Hebrew word, was used, causing great fear within. The rabbi was able to clarify that this term translated into English, meant evil. She further added that Judaism does not believe in the angel called Satan or Lucifer. Both good and bad are parts of God and each human being. Evil is seen as what people create. It is not a separate entity or supernatural force. She continued by saying that no matter how much evil a person may have done in his life, there is always a way back to God. She looked to Hanna and very sincerely reassured her, "You were not evil. You did the only humane thing you could in the face of the evil around you. You tried to stop a child's pain." I felt comforted in knowing a rabbi, a learned religious scholar, was reinforcing my own words to Hanna. If only Hanna could truly hear our words. What would it take for her to feel forgiven by God?

To this end, the rabbi suggested that Hanna partake in a ritual to symbolize letting go of the old, especially her shame and evil self-concept, and the view of life as a painful struggle, and create a new beginning of goodness, self-acceptance, and seeing "life as a blessing." This ceremony is called "the Mikveh," and is celebrated to commemorate life changes. It is a precursor to baptism. The Mikveh, which involves the immersion of the self in water, symbolizes a transformation from one life-state to another. As an individual submerges under water with eyes open and then reemerges above water, a prayer, called the *Shecheyanu*, translated as, "who has kept us in life," is chanted depicting new beginnings. "The Hebrew word for blessing, *bracha*, is closely related to the *breicha*, which is a free flowing spring of water." It is hoped that once "we master the conflict of body and soul, then we can view life with all the freshness of a clear living stream."

It was a brisk day in December when Hanna dove into the sixty-eight-degree waters of the spring-fed pool. Different from Jewish orthodoxy, Reform Jews allow persons to be clothed. As chilling as the water felt, so was the warmth of the prayers that were recited. The rabbi asked her to say the following:

Mikveh separates what was in the past from what will be in the future. May this immersion cleanse me of my past and free me for a different future. May this immersion help me to move into a different kind of life than the one I've lived in the past. I pray that this will help me to forgive myself, and allow me to live closer to God.

I prayed that this ceremony would truly be the demarcation of good and evil, shame and pride. At the end of the religious portion, I gave a public address. I expressed my happiness at knowing such a fine person as Hanna. My husband and Hanna's new roommate were present. They both agreed with my sentiments. Hanna shared with me later how shocked she was that her roommate felt that way!

Hanna's acceptance of *self* and of being forgiven did not immediately follow this ceremony. She still doubted her worth; she still was haunted by Jeffrey's tragic death. I wondered if she could really let go of the past despite all these new words, new prayers, new rituals, and the caring of new people. Could all this newness ever override twenty-eight years of deep conditioning and the formation of an identity based on pain and repression? Could there be life after death?

Then one day, months later, it seemed that a new peace had come over Hanna. There seemed to be a shift in her attitude towards herself and her past. I asked her if she now felt forgiven. Her face glowed as she softly, yet with certainty, said, "Yes. I am beginning to have closure with my past." To symbolize this change, I gave Hanna a gift—the Hebrew symbol of life, *Chai*, to wear around her neck. Life was on the horizon.

Hanna Chapter 8:

Finding the Key to Forgiveness

> *"The greatest achievement was at first, and for a time, a dream. The oak sleeps in the acorn; the bird waits in the egg; and in the highest vision of the soul a waking angel stirs."*
>
> **—William James**

It is an effort to put into writing my personal beliefs, especially as they pertain to religion. I know there are those who may be offended. I am not trying to advocate a single belief; my only intention is to share my spiritual journey.

When I, Hanna, first agreed to this healing journey, as it has come to be called, I had one major question plaguing me, "Could I be forgiven?" At that time, this question had nothing to do with God, only with myself and what I considered to be my "crimes." I would constantly pose the question to Rachel, who always answered that I could and would be forgiven. But I did not believe that Rachel really understood the depths of my self-disgust, my shame, or my self-loathing. But Rachel did understand one thing very clearly:

before true healing could occur, I had to explore my shame, my wish and my desire for forgiveness, otherwise, I could go no further.

As a child (and for most of my adult life), I believed that I was the most terrible, horrible evil monster on the face of the earth. And it centered on the fact that I believed, without a doubt, that I had caused all of the abuse that I suffered. I had made the adults (big people) in my life want to abuse me. In fact, this was something that they reiterated to me on several occasions: "you made me do this," or "you wanted me to do this." I came to believe that these words were, in fact, true, and more than that, I started to live them out in my adult life. Being raised (as I was told) a Christian and I use this term cautiously, since those using it did not behave charitably, I knew that sex was *bad* and that incest was the worst crime in the eyes of God, next to murder (which I also had a part in). With this knowledge and the belief that I was at fault for these crimes, I came to believe that there was never any hope that I would be forgiven. So, I gave up. What was the use? I was damned anyway.

I can remember from a young age sitting the back of the church on Sunday (I was not allowed to sit near the front where people might have to look at me), listening to the preacher shouting at the top of his lungs:

THE WICKED WILL BURN IN THE FIRES OF HELL FOR THEIR SINS! REPENT YOU EVIL SINNERS! REPENT TO GOD, AND MAKE AMENDS OR YOU WILL DIE! HE WILL DESTROY YOU—EVERY ONE OF YOU! THE DAY OF JUDGMENT IS NEAR AT HAND!

Every time that I would go to church, I would hear these words in one form or another. And the people sitting all around me would be shouting,

"HALLELUJAH! PRAISE GOD. PRAISE JESUS. AMEN!"

I can remember thinking that the people in the church wanted the death of all sinners, and I even believed that God wanted the death of sinners. Over and over, I would hear this throughout my youth; there were different preachers and churches over the years, but the same message, and the same response. And every time it would have a huge impact on me. I would start to sweat, then I would feel like I was going to throw up, and I could just swear that the preacher was looking straight at me while he was shouting these words. For a young child who believed she was an *evil monster*, and that she was to *blame*, this was all the proof she needed that she was going to *pay*.

I came to believe that I was an evil sinning monster who was going to pay. God wanted my death. I became very careful about what I said about my past and to whom, and that became very quickly became *No One*, not a soul. I believed I could trust no one, and I was fearful that if I told anyone what I had done, they would turn me over to the preachers and the people in the churches, and then I would burn in Hell. I kept silent and as a result, the only place for all my knowledge and pain was inside, deep inside me, where it became a cancer called Shame.

I believed that because I had been "touched by Satan" (from the ritual abuse), and because I had caused all of those people in my life to abuse me, that I was a "contaminant," and as such, I believed that anywhere that I went, I would contaminate the area. I thought I would make it evil so that other people would get hurt because of me. I would make an effort not to go into churches, or other holy places, in an effort to avoid contaminating them. I even avoided going to crowded places or friends' homes, believing that I had to avoid contaminating and harming them.

All of these beliefs were, of course, shame based and illogical, but for the better part of twenty-eight years, I honestly believed them to be true and indisputable.

When Rachel discovered how ashamed I felt and the impact it was having on our life in general, she started to talk about her understanding and beliefs about sin and forgiveness. As Rachel stated earlier in the book, she is Jewish, so her beliefs came from that belief system (vastly different from anything I had ever known). Early on, she learned that William was very interested in converting to Judaism, and offered him the phone number and name of the rabbi at the congregation she attended. Though William was the one originally interested in converting, as integration began to take place, I took over the role of converting to Judaism. I want to note that his original interest was what started this process and without his interest, I most likely wouldn't have undertaken this painful, but rewarding, spiritual journey.

She told all of us that once a year, on Yom Kippur, the Day of Atonement, all Jews ask for forgiveness. We found this fascinating.

As children, we were taught that you had to ask for forgiveness every single day and even then, it was not a given that God would forgive you. It was instilled in us that there were a number of sins that were considered *unforgivable*, such as incest, murder, and dishonoring one's parents, to name a few. I believed that I had committed these sins among others. I was also taught that homosexuality was considered an abomination of God's divine will and plan; he would never forgive me for this grievous sin and I would "burn in the fires of Hell." The list of atrocities that I was told I had committed against God went on and on. So, I believed that I was doomed, as *persons of the cloth* had told me throughout my past.

When Rachel gave us the name of a rabbi, one of the first questions we asked was if she (the rabbi) knew of any sins that were considered unforgivable. Without any hesitation, she responded, "No, there are none." Then I asked her if it was okay for me to be a lesbian, or if this would pose a problem if and when I wanted to convert. With a smile, she told me that back when the laws were being written by the elder men, that they could not fathom a women having sex with another women, so there was nothing mentioned in the laws forbidding it. I found this very humorous. She also told me that Reform Judaism welcomed anyone that was interested in converting, whether they were gay, bisexual or straight. Though we all liked the rabbi, at the time I could not bring myself to mention the incest or Jeffery to her. I never wanted anyone to know of these acts.

We all thought that because we were so terrible and had committed so many of these unforgivable sins, that God would want our death, or at least would not care if we died. Rachel kept telling us that this was not true and that she believed that no matter what we had done, we could be forgiven. When we heard the words, "It is not the death of sinners you [God] seek," from the *Gates of Repentance*, we were shocked and relieved. Maybe, just maybe, we did not have to die. But we wanted forgiveness if we were going to stay alive. What would we have to do to be forgiven? Could God even forgive us? These questions plagued us constantly. Who wants to keep breathing if they cannot be forgiven?

I needed to have more talks with the rabbi, but I still felt too scared, ashamed, and worried that I was bothering her. With Rachel's encouragement, I made another appointment. I could not explain how hideous I felt about everything in my life. I felt ready for the rabbi to know more, but I still couldn't say it on my own. Therefore, I gave Rachel permission to share with the rabbi that I had been forced to participate in the murder of a child, and I felt that I had to die to pay for it. She also shared that I had DID and that I self-mutilated because of my shame. Since I did not have to worry about trying to explain myself face-to-face, it paved the way to talk about the issues that really mattered to me. The discussions between the rabbi and I were difficult, but the meetings were incredibly healing and encouraging. As well, they were the starting point of my road to forgiveness.

I asked the rabbi what I would have to do to be forgiven, and if she believed God would forgive me for what I had done. She looked me in the eye and told me, "Yes, God will forgive you. You have repented and repented. But Hanna, *you* were not responsible for what happened. The adults were the ones that were responsible. You were just a child, right? How old were you when this happened? Ten? You were just doing what you were told; you had no choice. You had to do what you were told. And you did the only humane thing that you could. You tried to end a child's suffering and God knows this. He does not hold you responsible for Jeffrey's death, Hanna."

I wanted to cry and could feel the tears welling up in my eyes. The relief seemed to flood in and overwhelm me. To have a *rabbi*, who was learned in the Bible, telling me that I was not a terrible monster, to hear her telling me that God could and would forgive me, and did not hold me responsible, felt like the weight of the world had been taken off my shoulders. I could finally start to breathe. Looking back, I could almost feel the freedom that her words were starting to bring to my heart and soul.

Almost was a key word. Old doubts continued to persist, causing me to question if I really deserved forgiveness. The rabbi asked me what I thought forgiveness would feel like, and what would have to happen for me to know that I was forgiven. At the time, I simply did not know, but I wanted to find out. I wanted forgiveness more than anything else in the world. The question was: Would God truly grant it? And would I be open to receiving it?

In that same meeting, the rabbi invited me to attend Shabbat services, telling me that I had as much reason and right to be there as anyone else, and she enjoyed seeing me there. When I told her that I did not know what I could give back to the temple and the congregation, she told me, "You don't have to give anything back. Just be willing to accept what we can give you."

When I told Rachel what the rabbi had said, with tears in her eyes, she said, "Thank God. I am so glad that someone else is telling you the same thing that I have been saying all this time. Please listen to her. Please listen to me. You were not responsible!"

I thought about what both the rabbi and Rachel had said for days and weeks afterwards. I finally decided that neither of them had any reason to lie to me, but I needed time to process all these new beliefs about myself and what I did. To this end, I started to go to synagogue on a regular basis and found that I really was welcome. I discovered that no one looked at me in a negative light or acted like I did not belong there. Soon I started to find more comfort than I had ever experienced before. I would go to Shabbat services every Friday night and if I could not attend for some reason, it would feel like my week was not complete; attending gave me a sense of closure. The services, which are so graceful and beautiful, started to give me hope, a sense of comfort, and stability. They still do. I also began to feel a sense of community with my fellow human beings, something that I have never had before. I will never forget the Friday night that the cantor (who had endured a rather stressful week) said, to the whole congregation at the beginning of services, "I'm so glad it's Friday. I don't know about you, but it's been a one hell of a week!" The congregation roared with laughter, myself included. I too was having a terrible week, and became aware that I was not the only one who anticipated the end of the week Shabbat services. I asked Rachel if she looked forward to going to temple on Friday nights. I was surprised to hear her say that she did, and for the same reason. Going to services made us both feel part of something bigger than ourselves. For myself, I felt part of something that was centuries old. Shabbat is not only what you have received, but also about today and tomorrow.

"Shabbat is a day of freedom and peace, a celebration of life and creation. May it open our eyes to the goodness we have attained and our hearts to the goodness we may yet achieve.

At services I did not feel alone when I was in pain, nor was I the only one that was seeking comfort, everyone else was too.

"Here, time and place invite our commitment to the ancient purposes that are our present hopes...time and place are one, bringing promise of triumph over anguish and despair...In this sanctuary we seek to free ourselves from the fears and conflicts that estrange us from one another.

This included when Helen died. I called and put her name on the Kaddish list, commonly referred to as the Mourner's Kaddish, a mourner's prayer that is in Aramaic and is chanted during the time of grieving to elevate the deceased soul. Even though Helen was not Jewish, when her name was read that Shabbat, everyone in the congregation recited this prayer with me.

Let the glory of God be extolled, let His great name be hallowed, in the world whose creation He willed. May His kingdom soon prevail, in our day, our own lives, and the life of all Israel, and let us say: Amen.
Let His great name be blessed forever and ever.
Let the name of the Holy One, blessed is He, be glorified, exalted, and honored, though He is beyond all the praises, songs, and adorations that we can utter, and let us say: Amen.
May He who causes peace to reign in the high heavens, let peace descend on us, on all Israel, and all the world, and let us say: Amen.

As I stood there reciting this prayer, my sense of loss eased just a little and I felt a sense of comfort in knowing that others were sharing my grief. There were others in the congregation that had known Helen and had attended her funeral the day before. All of us had felt uncomfortable with the Christian service, and I was later told that they had welcomed the opportunity to say Kaddish for this most special woman. I had struggled with myself over the decision, thinking that I did not have the right to ask for this honor, but afterwards, I felt that it was the right choice. For the first time in my life, I did not feel alone in grief.

There are many other versions of Kaddish, all of them just as soul reaching. The first time that I heard the cantor and the congregation chanting the Reader's Kaddish, I was mesmerized. Rachel had suggested we attend Rosh Hashanah services, a time of forgiveness and pardon. We didn't know if we really belonged there and still feared contaminating the congregation. But we went and were surrounded by 2,500 Jews, all there to welcome in the Jewish New Year. This is Judaism's most holy of days and is the beginning of the Days of Awe, consummating with Yom Kippur. I was still depressed and suicidal. That is why Rachel invited us to go. She hoped that we might get something out of the services that would help us choose life. We did not believe that we would, and I wanted to leave shortly after we arrived. The whole time I continued to think of dying, and was wondering how I ever let Rachel talk us into to going. I was hardly concentrating on what was happening in the service when I heard the *whole* congregation start chanting this beautiful melody. I could not believe my ears, so I looked down at my prayer book and read the translation. I found it beautiful and I still do to this day.

Let the glory of God be extolled, let God's great name be hallowed in the world whose creation God willed. May God's rule soon prevail, in our own day, our own lives and the life of all Israel, and let us say: Amen.

Let God's great name be blessed forever and ever.

Let the name of the Holy One, the Blessed One, be glorified, exalted, and honored, though God is beyond all praises, songs, and adorations that we can utter, and let us say: Amen.

Then right below this passage, there was another sentence:

For us and for all Israel, may the blessing of peace and the promise of life come true, and let us say: Amen.

There I sat, wanting to end my life, in the midst of people who seemed to embrace life fully, and they were all around me praying to

God, asking Him to inscribe them in the "Book of Life," not everlasting life when they were dead, but *now*, while they were still alive. I asked myself, "What am I doing? Why am I so eager to die, when everyone else wants me to live? Is Rachel right that there is another way, a better way to live?"

It seemed the whole service was filled with prayers thanking God for life, health and peace:

RISE UP TO LIFE RENEWED
May we lie down this night in peace, and rise up to life renewed. May night spread over us a shelter of peace, of quiet and calm, the blessing of rest.

There will come a time when morning will bring no word of war or famine or anguish; there will come a day of happiness, of contentment and peace.

Praised be the source of joy within us, for the night and its rest, for the promise of peace.

I knew that in order to embrace life, I had to first find a way to forgive myself, and God too. I felt abandoned by God and I felt that there was a huge rift between us that could never be mended. And since I felt that my relationship with God was irreconcilable, I was bitter both towards God, and myself.

When I was a child, I can remember praying to God to stop the abuse. I would ask Him, beg Him, not to let the mom hurt me anymore. One night in particular sticks out in my mind. I had done something wrong (what it really was does not matter), and knew that I was going to receive a beating for it. She told me take out the trash, and during the trip to and from the dumpster, I was asking God not to let her hurt me. "I can't take anymore, and You are supposed to help kids, right? Please help me. *PLEASE*. You know she will kill me." My prayers were not answered, except that I lived. It was not the worst beating I ever received from her, but it was still bad, resulting in lots of bruises and burns, but I was still alive. But I did not care. He had let me down again. It was the final straw. I held Him responsible and I hated Him for doing nothing to stop her. After that night, I quit praying to Him and asking Him for help, until I was about nineteen years old.

I was suicidal, and I had a gun. The only problem was that I could not pull the trigger. I simply could not find the courage. I sat in the middle of my living room, gun in hand, screaming at Him to help me die. "You *owe* me, you motherfucker! You did nothing to stop it and you owe me! You help me pull this trigger. I do not want to be here anymore! I don't want this stinking existence! You help me die! You hear me? KILL ME—DAMN YOU!" Nothing happened. No help from God in pulling the trigger. I remember throwing the gun across the room (dumb thing to do with a loaded gun—luckily it did not go off), and sobbing on the floor for hours. What I could not know was that He had helped me. He had kept me *alive* again.

God did not want me to die. He wanted me to live for whatever reason. The only person that God can help is the one that asks for his help. He could not control my mother. And in the end, He did stop her; she died. Thus, it was not God who failed me, it was my mother. My anger was pointed in the wrong direction all along. My anger at God kept me from seeing and acknowledging the truth, that my mother had been the one to hurt me. Her actions and behaviors had destroyed my faith in myself and in God. It was she who deserved my wrath, not God!

Even with this powerful revelation, I still had to come to terms with God, and it started with a dream—literally. I had been talking to Rachel about God, light and forgiveness. All along, Rachel's stance was that God would forgive me. All I had to do was ask. I maintained that He would not and that, in fact, He hated me, condemned my behavior, and held me responsible for the abuse inflected upon others and me. I also secretly believed that God had deserted me during all the years of the abuse and torture, and in the aftermath of despair and suffering. Then one night I had a dream where He came to talk to me. The dream was very *healing* and I awoke in tears, but with a sense of relief. I wanted Rachel to know about this dream experience, so I tried to describe the dream to her, but instead, I felt that I was not doing it justice. Finally she looked at me and said, "Write a poem about it." For several weeks I agonized over the words. One of my best friends still laughs whenever I tell her I still think it needs more work. "What are you talking about! Leave it alone, you perfectionist!" she usually yells into the phone. Eventually, I came up with this:

He comes only in my dreams
Gentle
yet Imposing
Surrounded in White Light
Blinding
yet Comforting
Eyes like vast Oceans
with Depths of
Sorrow
Despair
and Love
He kneels before me
raising my head
as i try to look away
how could He
this Being
know the Depths
of my self loathing
or my pain
"where were you when i needed you most" i cry out
"I was there with you", His voice is Gentle
and Strong
"why did you do nothing", i ask in pain
"I waited for you to be ready
and could only act in time", His voice is Firm
and Kind
"and while you waited what did you do", i scream at
Him
"I wept for your pain", He answers
in a voice full of Grief
"and what of my shame", i ask looking down
"there is none for you to bear,
you were innocent in it all", He tells me
looking at me with Respect
i put my head in my hands
remembering my crimes
my shame overwhelming me

> *How can i Believe Him*
> *Know that He speaks the Truth*
> *Ask for His Forgiveness*
> *"There is no need to Ask*
> *For you have done Nothing to be Forgiven*
> *But*
> *I will Give you what you will not Give Yourself*
> *So that you may*
> *Heal from All of This"*
> *His voice Thunders across the Years*
> *Breaking through my Fear*
> *Straight to my Soul*
> *and*
> *I Weep with Relief*

After writing it, I called my best friend and read it to her over the phone. She listened quietly as I read it to her. When I was finished, I asked what she thought. "This is most likely—no—undoubtedly, your most powerful poem yet." I got goose bumps up and down my back. "I hope that you see that it is true."

Yea right, I thought, *like God would ever forgive me*! I wanted to get another opinion and decided to take a risk and share it with Rachel. She was on a two-week vacation at the time, so I put a copy in the mail. I called her the day she returned to her office and asked her to read it over the phone. As she did, she kept saying, "I have goose bumps. This is incredible. Just incredible." I still doubted that it was good. After all, how could I trust the opinion of two different people? So I put it away for a while, thinking I would forget about it. I couldn't. I would hear the words of it in my head, and inevitably end up taking it out and reading it. Could it be true? Could God have forgiven me? "No," I would tell myself, "it was just a fanciful dream. Forget about forgiveness and move on."

Several months later, as I was struggling with the memories of Jeffery, I asked Rachel if she thought I should show the rabbi the poem, "YES!" was Rachel's unequivocal response. I gave a copy of it to the rabbi and asked her to tell me what she thought. I wanted to know, was it wishful thinking or was it something more *real*. The rabbi read it, looked at me and gave her response: "God has already forgiven you. This dream told you that. My question to you is: When are you going to accept *His* forgiveness?"

Good question, but at the time I had no answer. I simply could not, and would not, believe that God would grant me something that I wanted so much. "Besides," I would tell myself, "God is not real." I felt no connection to God. He is not something that you can see, hear or touch. And if God is not there, then God cannot grant absolution. Then I read the following words and started to see that this was not necessarily true. He is there in the everyday events, and in the miracles that surround us all.

AS CLOSE TO US AS BREATHING

O God, how can we know You? Where can we find You? You are as close to us as breathing, yet You are farther than the farthermost star.

You are as mysterious as the vast solitudes of night, yet as familiar to us as the light of the sun. To Moses You said: "You cannot see My face, but I will make all My goodness pass before you."

Even so does Your goodness pass before us: in the realm of nature, and in the joys and sorrows of life.

This prayer, and others like it, gave me hope, and I looked forward to hearing and reading them every week, even though in the beginning, I could not understand a word that was being chanted (they are in Hebrew for the most part, after all). I began to feel a sense of comfort in the simplicity, form, and yes, even the age and tradition, behind these prayers. This sense of inner peace was something that I had never known before, and I, for the first time in my life, was sensing, feeling, and enjoying this peace and comfort.

I have not always felt comfort in any religious act, prayer or service. I often felt out of place and usually got nothing from the services that I attended. How could I? The same people that would sit next to me at church were the very people that would then abuse me at home, twisting and defiling every Christian teaching while engaging in their satanic activities and sexual *pleasures*. The prayers and the ministers' sermons never gave me hope. It seemed that most of the sermons were about sin, the evil ways of man and woman,

Satan, Hell, and fire and brimstone. I never felt peace or comfort, only fear, apprehension, and uncertainty. As I grew older, I became disgusted and angry with this *doomsday* mentality, and with the feeling that no matter what I did, I was doomed to burn in hell. I did not want to have any part in a religious belief system or mentality that had no hope. As soon as I was given a choice, I decided that I would not have anything to do with any religion, and rejected everything that has to do with spirituality.

But slowly, over time, I came to realize that I needed a "higher power," as Alcoholics Anonymous calls it. I would talk to people I knew that would attend these twelve-step meetings, and ask them what they believed their higher power to be. "Nature," "My inner voice," "Mother Earth," and "My inner child," were among some of the responses I received. These did not feel *righ*t for me, so I kept looking and eventuality explored many different religions and movements, but I always came back to a basic belief in God, as held in the Bible.

I talked to a couple of Christian ministers, but I just could not bridge the gap between their belief in God, and Jesus (who they hold to be loving and only wanting everyone to be saved), to the fire, brimstone, and eternal damnation of sinners to hell. To me, this *discrepancy*, as I viewed it, felt *cruel* and *unjust*. I came to the conclusion that I did not want any part of this belief system. I had always had friends that were Jewish. We would talk, and I would ask them about their views and belief of God. They told me that they never looked at God as this revengeful, "sinner be damned to hell," kind of deity. For them, God was something gentler and kinder. Yes, you need to atone for your sins, but God knows that everyone makes mistakes, and so Judaism did not really talk about, or preach about, Hell or Heaven. "Repentance, prayer and charity" are the three main words. What was of bigger concern, it seemed, was doing well in the here and now. God would deal with you later.

It seemed that no matter whom I talked to, they all urged me to find something higher than myself to believe in, urging me to seriously rethink my rejection of religion and spirituality. I started to realize that I had made this rejection out of rage and for me, it was a mistake. I began to recognize that a person consists of mind, body, and *soul*. How could I hope to heal my mind without feeling a larger connection to something higher than myself? And if my mind was not healed, then I knew that I would never take care of my body. I also started to realize that the religion I was raised with did not have to influence my present. The *faith* and *beliefs* of my parents was not necessarily, nor automatically, mine. I had a choice and I decided to choose not to have anything to do with my family's belief or faith. I viewed my parents, and my family in general, as hypocrites who had no true belief in good or right, or God for that matter. They would go to services on Christmas and Easter, say the usual pious words, and then go home and do what I considered to be truly evil.

I decided that I wanted to convert to Judaism, but first I needed to put some distance between my family, my past and myself. So I asked the rabbi if she might have any suggestions on how to accomplish this goal. Her recommendation was that I undergo a ritual called a *Mikveh*. It is an immersion in a free flowing body of water, such as a natural spring, to signify a "change in state." She told me that whenever anyone converts to Judaism, becomes a mother, or is married, they undergo this ritual to symbolize the change or transition from what they once were, to what they are now. The rabbi suggested it not only was a way to symbolize a separation from the past and the present, but also to symbolize receiving forgiveness from God, and of my forgiveness of myself. I was hesitant to agree to the ritual at first. Though it was a symbolic ritual, for me it was a true separation of my past and myself.

I asked Rachel what she thought and she encouraged me to do the *Mikveh*, but did not push for it. "This is something only you can decide." She knew that I needed to make the choice on my own, and in my own time. Over the course of a month, I thought about why I should and should not do it. I did not want to take this too lightly, and I did not want to rush myself into something that I was not ready for. But I knew that I desperately wanted to have something that would symbolize that I was no longer part of the past, with all that it represented. So I agreed to do it and invited Rachel, Morrie (who was becoming a close friend), and my roommate (who is also Jewish, and with whom I was starting to feel a bond), and of course, the rabbi was there.

At first I was embarrassed about my body, about why I was doing it, and wanted to back out. It was in the middle of December, the water and the outside air were both cold, and my legs were very white, with all of the scares showing predominately as angry purple marks. Slowly I started to understand that the people around me did not share my feelings of embarrassment or disgust for my body. However, they did share my feeling about the cold. "Are you actually going to get in that water?" my roommate muttered. I did walk into the water (after gaining my courage) and dunked my head under, uttering a private prayer for forgiveness and new life. After my immersion (and warm towels), prayers were said thanking God for good fortune, and life and health. As I looked at the people around me and listened to their prayers, a strange feeling came over me: I almost felt cleansed of my past, with all the emotional and religious garbage that came with it! But there was much left for me to do.

Things seemed to die down after that day and I felt like I was just drifting along, still bitter, still feeling like I could not come to terms with my new life, with God, or with the world around me. But I continued to go to services every week, and consciously decided to allow myself to feel the comfort of the community that I was starting to become a part of. I started to allow myself to chant the age-old prayers of the Jewish faith. I decided to make an effort of letting go of the old hates, fears, and hurts of my past faith. In the process, I slowly, *very slowly*, built a foundation for my future with God and myself. I was starting to come to terms with God and at the same time, starting to truly forgive myself.

I was asked once if I could ever "forgive God" for not doing something to "stop" the abuse and torture I had to endure. Forgive God? I never believed that I could forgive God, only that I could accept what He had, and had not, done. With the process of reawaking my *spiritual self*, I came to believe that God had done everything that He could to help me, but after a time, it was then up to me to finish my journey towards healing and life, or to throw my life away in a desperate act of suicide. He could only stand back and watch. God could offer me hope, but the rest was up to me, and many times I had rejected that hope for the chance to die.

I was rather shocked when it dawned on me that I, Hanna, formally Death, the one that had cursed God, found myself praying to Him, asking Him to help me *live*, to give me hope, and to help me in my everyday trials. I had this insight at Friday Shabbat services during silent prayer. I sat there and cried. It was just a release to finally find peace. It was truly a personal turning point in my journey towards healing.

When I told Rachel about this revelation, we both cried with joy. I knew that God had given me a gift: the gift of forgiveness. I needed to learn how to use it, and that meant that I needed to learn how to live. The next phase of my journey was about to begin.

Rachel Chapter 9:

To Life !

"In the long run, we shape our lives and we shape ourselves. The process never ends until we die. And the choices we make are ultimately our responsibility."
—Eleanor Roosevelt

"Things are too quiet. I don't hear them anymore." Hanna felt scared and confused. It seemed that as healing and forgiveness began to soothe her soul, her alters were no longer always present in the wings. "What is happening? I'm not sure I like it. I want Mikhail and Stephana. I miss them. I can't see them anymore and it scares me," she said. Apparently, integration was occurring naturally. But with these internal changes, came new fears and self-doubts. She didn't feel real. Her reality had been so different from the new existence that she was now experiencing, that she wasn't sure she liked it. Her world, although loud and chaotic, felt safe in its *known* boundaries. The new world seemed to have no limits, no allies, no one but herself telling her what was right and wrong. She didn't know the difference.

Everything that was wrong had been right for her. Punishment was all she knew. Could she live with new rules and norms? She didn't feel prepared to be on her own and make all these decisions by herself. Stephana and Mikhail had both told me that it was time for them to let her figure things out by herself if she were to be the person chosen to live. She had to learn how to ask for help. Randy even said he thought it was called "courage." I will always remember one of my last conversations with Mikhail who described integration best. "I need to incorporate into Hanna because I have the will to live. If I'm a part of her, I can stop her from hurting herself. I know I'm not dying or even going away. I'm just changing forms. It looks like there's a doorway and it has a lot of white light; I'm drawn to it—it's Hanna's."

My tears streamed down. I felt so happy that these changes were occurring, yet so sad that I needed to say good-bye to the studious and serious young man who had written those early chapters tirelessly with me. But I knew he was right, and his fading into the background was allowing Hanna to shine in the forefront. That light did indeed symbolize a new beginning. In Hanna's poetic words, she stated:

Hope is but a light that when touched by love grows until the blind can see its brilliance and the darkness of despair recedes.

It seemed that my caring, shown through my consistent availability and respect for her, as well as the rabbi's concern for her, helped her have a new vision. In addition, she began to internalize the abilities she had always attributed to Mikhail, Stephana, and TOB, in particular. She became as technologically competent as Mikhail. She took over the role of co-authoring the book. Her writings did have a different flair. They exposed more emotion and pathos, the characteristics she herself possessed. One of my most interesting observations was that at times, she used the over-hand writing style of Mikhail. Yes, he still was with her!

My usual optimism believed that the progress we were making would continue moving forward. Although I knew there would be minor setbacks, I hoped their indomitable spirit would keep her always on the life-path. Years before I ever met Hanna or imagined I would write this book on life, I wrote the following poem, entitled *The Spirit of Life*.

Rachel Gunner

The Spirit of Life

Overwhelms
And transcends
The fears of Life

The power of the mind
Overwhelms
And transcends
The fears of life

Powerful, spiritual
Mindful being
Total integration
Ultimate creation

Fears are challenged
By the integrated self
Which no longer blocks
Creation
The spirit of life

However, fears often did block the spirit of life. She continually asked questions that made me understand how deprived her past life had been and how unsure she was of living in the present. For example: "What is it like to sleep through the night? What is it like to eat three meals a day? Do you go to a doctor if you are sick?" I used to take these behaviors for granted, and thus became acutely aware that I would need to teach her how to live.

She still viewed eating, sleeping, and taking care of her body as signs of weakness. She would ask, "Am I a wimp because I feel sick?" I would describe how mothers care for children when they don't feel well by checking their temperature, giving them warm soup, or just sitting by their beds and reading stories. She would look at me wide-eyed and shocked. "Really?" she'd ask. "We were always left alone and the mom would be mad at us. So we usually kept our sickness to ourselves." My heart always ached upon hearing of their neglect, and I understood more clearly how difficult it was to reach out to tell me when she was feeling physically unwell. I knew she was really on the path to life when she began sleeping through an entire night! This was an amazing breakthrough. It symbolized that she was no longer being haunted by the demons of the night; that the children no longer feared darkness; and that the bed was no longer seen as a torture chamber. The body was being given permission to sleep without "paying a price," and the mind was being allowed to rest.

Without sleep deprivation, Hanna was able to think clearly. The roaring stopped. The constant headaches diminished in frequency. Sleeping, something most of us take for granted, was becoming a new learned behavior. I was so excited the first time Hanna told me she had slept through the night, every day for one week that I reinforced this change by taking her out to a lovely restaurant. She told me that no one had ever done that for her, and it was just for sleeping. I wanted her to know that this was a giant step.

Allowing feelings was another growth spurt. One must wonder how a multiple, who has disassociated from feelings in order to survive pain, becomes capable of handling emotions? This was one of Hanna's toughest tasks. She had no prior experience coping in healthy ways, since she knew the others would take over if it got too difficult. Allowing anger to be shown and accepted was the emotion that challenged her most. She had been told that to get angry was bad. As a child, anger meant that she was bad. To be angry with the mom was really bad. Therefore, as we worked through the years of abuse Hanna suffered at the hands of the mother, she felt extreme rage and revulsion. Sadly, her admission of these feelings also caused her to feel badly and deserving of punishment, from herself and others. She still wanted to run; she wanted to cut, burn and do any self-mutilating act to relieve herself of the emotional turmoil. These acts were the only means she had known of taking control of the body and making it her own, but they scared me. It was as if she were addicted to this behavior. It occurred daily and gave her immediate gratification. Yet, the long-term effects were shaming, and she would be secretive and want to hide her body. I understood the power of self-mutilation; it was punishment, relief, a sedative, empowerment, and a way of feeling *real*. It was easier to turn on herself than risk expressing emotions such as sadness and rage, and drive people away. Hanna still feared I would leave or send her away if she let out her anger.

And so, when I received the following e-mail, I felt scared, disillusioned, and even had doubts as to whether therapy and caring would ever be enough to obliterate a child's tortured spirit and set him/her free.

Rachel,

I am sorry that I was not completely honest with you last night, and that I scared you. But I was scared that if I told you exactly what was going on you would become angry, and though you say that you will not, this continues to be a fear of mine. Just as when you get scared you come across as angry, when I get scared I can come across as angry too. But I am not angry at you or anyone else but me. I deserve my anger, even if you do not think so. I feel like a failure because I have not been able to let go of the messages from the mom. I feel like I am wasting everyone's time, including yours. I do not think that I am a good person, and as such I should not be going over to anyone's house, or to the temple. I know that you care about me. I have heard all that you have said. But it does not feel right, nor does it ring true for me. This is not to say that I think that you are lying, I do not. I wish I could take in what you say, and just let it be. But I can not seem to do that. I am sorry. I know that this is frustrating for you. I can not get angry at the mom. When I do, I feel like I am being just like her, and that is not what I want. I can not be just like her and let my self live. So I work very hard at not getting angry at anyone—but me—and then I feel okay about that emotion.

I know that this letter is most likely not making much sense. I am just trying to write down how I feel. So bear with me.

I do not think that I can continue this way much longer. And I am sorry. I know that you will be hurt and disappointed. I am trying to hold out. Really I am. But I do not know if I can. And I am not sure if I can tell you to your face.

I needed to prove to her that her fears were unfounded. One evening, after spending hours giving her permission in a safe environment to yell and scream, yet still unable to do so, I made a strategic and calculated decision: I would provoke her anger. She yelled back at me and then turned her body to me, in shame and embarrassment. I reached out to her, to give her a hug and let her know how proud I was that she had screamed! She seemed confused. Having an adult reach out to comfort was an unknown experience.

During painful times such as these, I used to wonder where Stephana or QED were when *I* needed them? They had always given me insights into what was happening within the system. Thank God Stephana did come back one day, if only to talk to me. She reminded me to be patient with Hanna, for there was much for her to learn on her own. Months later, QED called at 12:15 a.m. It was very strange to hear her voice now even toned, intellectual, confident and very different from Hanna's emotional reactiveness and insecurities. She told me that Randy had called for her. He was really worried that Hanna was acting more like Death, contemplating her dying. QED reminded me that Hanna was very scared of life and needed more comfort from me. I was falling into a trap, common for therapists who have been working with a client for a long time. I was less than patient and wanted to see results. Therefore, I tried to offer solutions and *fixes*. I was upset with myself when QED pointed that out. Of course, all Hanna needed was to know I cared and offer her a hug. It was so simple and yet so often forgotten! These meetings helped me believe that she and the others would always be around, if only on the periphery, to help when necessary. I used to tell Hanna that she could ask for an alter's help and would probably hear their responses. In actuality, once the alter was integrated, he/she did not want to be called upon as separate entities like before. Their hope was that Hanna would begin to *feel* their beings within her being, then she would just know their feelings and thoughts, and Hanna would not really be alone. But Hanna was not convinced. She felt alone. There were no more bantering and joking between them, no more horseplaying. Thankfully, Randy was still around, because he was still needed to help Hanna care for her body. She began to feel physical pain and even feelings of hunger. She even started eating, and she and Randy would often fight over food. The street kids also stayed, but they were different. Although still scared, their trust in me seemed to stop them from self-punishment. And they too, began eating! One day Hanna went to the refrigerator and noticed six packets of Jell-O gone. When she asked Randy where they were, he replied, "We each only had one!" This was so new! Even Sandy started having cravings besides flowers. She loved pickles and

Spanish olives, but this made Hanna feel like she was developing ulcers. Hanna became more aware of her body, even noticing when she felt sick, though she didn't understand why her body would shiver and her head would ache when she had a fever. She had never felt this way before and she didn't like it. I would reassure her that this was normal. How ironic, though, to be healthy meant to *feel* unhealthy and ill. I knew this was a sign that she was becoming one and was re-owning the body and making it hers. Re-owning the body also meant a detachment from the mother, and recognition that the mother no longer had the power over her to keep her a prisoner of fear and secrecy. As healing progressed, Hanna's expressions of anger no longer led to self-punishment (an internalization of self-disgust) and fear. Rather, it became appropriately redirected externally towards the mom, and all the abusers and perpetrators in her life. Self-mutilation was replaced by a deep sadness for her losses: loss of a childhood, of her innocence, and of never being a part of a loving family. This grief was triggered by yet another loss, the death of her foster mother. But now, she was able to let the feelings out and cry. However, the children would get scared and I would have to reassure them that crying was good. "It's what people do when they feel alone, scared, or sad." They no longer had to hide from these emotions. It was another sign of Hanna becoming healthy. Freeing her spirit from self-blame and allowing the self to feel, permitted her to begin living life. These new internal sensations and thoughts were so masterfully expressed in the following words:

My heart beats against my chest. The fear is so real I can taste it. The hate so intense it rings in my ears. suddenly i bolt—no longer human i run like a wolf with courage, speed and certainty. i own my world! the forest is mine! i am one with the woods and all the creatures in it are my friends. nothing can harm me here. through the night i go and never look back. i come to a high ledge and fear to run further. but i must continue—i can not stop. i leap off. my body transforms its self once more as i fall—and my wings beat at the nights sky. i soar in the air. i scream—not from fear but out of defiance. i have won! i have escaped death once more! with this scream i am free. the night is mine! i own the sky! i dip and spin. playing with the wind. nothing can touch me here. i know my time is limited and still i play on. i fly over water, i have reached the ocean. i drop towards it—and my wings become flippers. i dive into the sea, and swim with the dolphins. i feel the peace of the water, it cradles me and i feel at one with it. i know that i am loved by it. i let my body rest. my mind is peaceful—finally all is quiet. i sleep, knowing nothing will disturb me here. but soon i must return to the shore, for i can not stay here. i do not belong in this world. but i fear my return to my self. I soon find that it is unfounded. My experience will stay with me forever. I know that I can return to this magic world at anytime - to run in the woods, play in the sky, and sleep in the ocean. This is a gift from myself, and I can never lose it. I stand on the beach. I look around. There is nothing to fear here—not now. I walk away. My body is finally mine! I know I own my life!

That last statement, "I own my life," was so powerful. It expressed to me the beginnings of self-acceptance and above all, a new sense of pride. This pride was a concept she was just beginning to understand. My goal was to help extinguish her feelings of shame, replacing it with this new self-concept. I reinforced on a daily basis, any and all behaviors that were new and different. One day, she asked, "Is it silly of me to be proud that I helped a lost dog find his owner?"

I beamed with delight. "Not silly at all. You *should* be proud. You are one of the kindest and most caring people I know." I know she wanted to believe that. But could she?

The struggle to let life in, to let emotions out, and to have a new outlook, was an arduous one that took time. Hanna was often impatient. She wrote and rewrote the following words in her attempt to understand this newness. I thought this prose was brilliant in its insight and understanding of the change process, though she thought it was dumb:"

Looking out over the ledge, i see the world with new eyes for the first time, and wonder what it all means. why have i never looked at the world in this way before? what have i been missing? i have spent my whole life trying to end my life, and so i have never bothered to see the colors of the world, or feel the warmth of friendship that others would offer me. i am ashamed of my omission—it was born out of an obsession. now i am being offered the chance to sing, and a part in this greater play called life. do i have the courage to take the chance? will i get hurt in the end? will i still be me? or will i lose myself in the rush of it all? the tears of all that i have been through burn my eyes, but still i hold on— i do not feel that i can let go. suddenly i turn around to see all that is behind me—a past that made me. i wonder how i ever survived it. the pain of it breaks my heart, and the shame of it sets my soul afire. i want so much to be forgiven, yet i feel unworthy. how can i know that i did not cause it, but was just a pawn in it? how can i find the words to speak my truth? can i let go of it all, so that i can move on? or will i be caught in the quicksand of the past? in my confusion, i am tempted to linger, but the sight before me draws me back. i am amazed at what i see: a young woman who is finally letting going, so that she can move on. a human being who is embracing the past for what it really was, and not what she thought it was, and is finding the courage to tell her tale, and learning to forgive herself for what she did, so that she can set her soul free and it can heal. I see all of this, and know that for the first time I can admit who I am, were I have been, and what I have done. And I am not ashamed to cry.

Although she wrote these words, she did not always believe them as truths. These words became goals she wanted to attain. These goals of self-empowerment and letting go of the past were continually met with roadblocks from the present. Dealing with daily realities became as difficult as dealing with her memories form the past. She had learned to work with her inner world, but did not have the tools or experience to handle the external world. This precipitated greater frustrations, self-doubts, and discouragement that she didn't belong in the real world, feeling embarrassed and stupid when she could not handle all of life's responsibilities. Her self-worth was so fragile that anything that went wrong caused her to blame herself, and consequently deserve self-retribution. To live life meant that the ego that had been shattered needed to be rebuilt. She once described herself as Humpty Dumpy and didn't believe she could ever be put together again. I disagreed. She was already experiencing a new sense of wholeness in becoming Hanna. Gabriele, et al, no longer existed in their former selves. But, it was true that wholeness did not necessarily mean, "feeling together." The latter is a term generally used to signify a sense of groundedness or centeredness, feeling right with oneself and with others. Hanna still did not experience that. Rather, she felt more unsure, more afraid, and more self-doubting.

Self-esteem is the way one thinks and feels about oneself. High self-esteem makes a person feel lovable, worthy, productive, and successful. Low self-esteem makes one feel unlovable, unworthy, and a failure. Self-esteem is a product of a child's early learning and messages that a child's mind has internalized. A child is only capable of concrete thinking and cannot decipher from his being bad verses his behavior being bad. Gabriele, et al, through years of neglect and abuse, believed they were unlovable, undeserving and all bad.

To help Hanna evaluate these beliefs and change her conditioned responses (her self punishment), I reassured her that her thoughts were *not* stupid, that she was *not* stupid. I gave her my respect and trust as we worked side-by-side writing and editing these pages. Sometimes this didn't seem to be enough. Death's mission was to find ways to die and often colored Hanna's struggle to live. An example of this battle occurred as their twenty-ninth birthday approached, about one year after the beginning of therapy. I learned that birthdays, which most people commemorate as a celebration of life, was a time of fear that Satan would come to take them. Birthdays became a celebration of death and destruction. The life/death paradigm was in conflict on a day when most children (and adults) are joyful and playful. I knew these ingrained beliefs would take longer than one year to be erased, but we were on the right path.

I strongly believed self-acceptance and pride would gradually be internalized as Rose Mary Evans said, "a sense of life affinity" was replacing their belief of nonexistence and death. It was crucial to affirm life before they could choose new values. As they all learned of their existences, many alters learned to trust in the external world and transformation began taking place: honesty, integrity and pride were new virtues that began guiding their actions. As I wrote years before, the following poem depicts the ever-changing life force:

Life
Life drifts by—
If you let it
Life storms on—
If you risk it
Drifting calmly

Storming wildly
Peaceful existence
Excited revelry
Stable assuredness
Unpredictable questioning
Homeostatic acquiescence
Changeable openness
Peace is restful
Storms are restless
To stay with
To move on
Which life to choose?
Comfortable placidness
Unknown risk taking
To live is to grow
To grow is to change
To change is to risk
What is the answer
for you?

Hanna's life was certainly growing, changing and risking. This was very frightening for her. It meant she might need to grow up. I often forgot that Hanna was emotionally still an adolescent, yet chronologically an adult, expected to care for herself and be financially independent. No one had ever taught her how to budget money. After all, that had been Mikhail's job. She felt embarrassed and scared when she ran out of money and couldn't pay all her bills. She often would raid Randy's piggy bank, which made him really upset; he was saving up for a basset hound and at this rate, would never get one! How many teens can handle money responsibly? I would commend her for her efforts and offer some advice to help her learn how to budget more efficiently. Slowly she did learn how to allot money to pay bills from the first paycheck of the month. She began to learn how to prioritize needs, make decisions about buying a second-hand car, and make payments on overdue speeding tickets. (She became angry with Stephana for having run up those tickets!) She was growing up before our eyes, but we didn't want to admit this.

To her and the others, growing older meant becoming a big person, an adult, someone who was mean, didn't know how to love or play, forced you to do things you didn't want to, and punished you, even if you didn't think you did anything wrong. They did not think growing up was positive at all. I certainly agreed that the only adults in their lives had been cruel, harsh, and unloving. I hoped that she could see my husband, the rabbi, and me, as new role models for caring and kind adults. I also reassured her that there is still a child in all of us adults that keeps us young at heart, able to have fun, and even be silly. That seemed to allay some of those fears.

Sexuality was also affected by the metamorphosis that was taking place. First, gender issues were no longer in conflict. As Hanna assumed the primary role, so did the female gender predominate. Interestingly, menstrual cycles became more regular, albeit more painful. Her gynecologist jokingly asked if she was having periods for all the girls.

The most significant shift in sexual thinking was Hanna's increasing interest in men. She became more fascinated by who they were as people. Fortuitously, she had two male roommates, one of who was more *macho*, the other man was a softer, sensitive type. She was able to learn how different men think and behave towards women. She no longer seemed as fearful of the opposite sex. She learned to be playful and be at ease. She began asking questions about being in love. As she accepted the mother's behaviors as wrong and disgusting, she had feelings of revulsion when thinking of herself engaging in sexual activity with a woman. Gay friends wondered if I was trying to *change* her into a heterosexual because I thought being lesbian was bad. I wanted her to be at peace with herself and it was her understanding regarding her sexual orientation. I made no value judgments as long as she was true to herself. That is not my role as a therapist. Hanna knew that and would be irritated with friends who were not accepting of her personal changes.

Randy was still confused about sex and sexuality. He asked me, "If Hanna wants to do things with boys, do I have to be there?" Will she lock me up for six months like Stephana did when I saw her with another woman?"

I answered, "No," to both questions.

I told Randy, people need privacy when they want to be close to one another, whether male or female. He said he was just curious. A psychiatrist had told him that he should know what everyone in the system was doing, at all times, because that was his job. Again, I realized how a child believes everything an adult says. No one had told him of exceptions to that rule. Poor Randy, he was just being a child, bright-eyed and open to learning. He was very happy that he could let Hanna do her own thing "with a boy."

But Hanna still could not imagine that anyone, especially males, could desire her—her body image remained very negative. Yet, as the months of therapy continued, scars and wounds healed. She began uncovering her arms, shaving her legs, and growing her hair. Laughter replaced somberness, warmth and love began to be projected outwards, and she began to let out her gentle kind soul to others—a soul I had seen from the first moment our eyes met. I believed that there would be someone who would love this young woman. How could they not?

Perhaps the most crucial of all changes occurred during another intense period of pain and fear. We were nearing the millennium, a time when Christians and Satanists were prophesizing the end of the world. Hanna could not accept reason that this would not happen. She resorted to her old thinking by "him." Death again had taken over. Both the rabbi and I struggled to help her find hope. What I did not realize during those times, but figured out as weeks of this torment passed, was that Hanna was completely on her own! The kids were no longer around. Randy was no longer protecting her. I had not gotten any calls from him "tattling" on Hanna. I had feared he had run away, scared he was going to die. Without Randy, Hanna had no hope. For it was he who symbolized the belief that they all deserved to live. Without him, Hanna did not think she knew how to live. There was silence from within. There was no break from all the feelings that flooded her inner being. No one was taking over. She had to handle everything by herself. She still didn't trust in herself, one *self*. And so, she was turning to what she did know how to do, which was dream of ways to end her suffering. Life was too hard. She was angry. She had never wanted to be chosen for the role of "host" to all the personalities. She wondered why Randy hadn't been given that "honor." Then she knew why: he would never have accepted being "a girl." In the midst of her anguish, she laughed at this thought. Randy could still bring a smile to her.

Yes, life was and is hard. Life without a world of helpers to share in sorrow and fear is especially hard. The life on the horizon meant sharing these fears with an external world. Could she make it alone? I believed she could. I knew that the inner strength and will that had created her multiple selves was still at her core. It was she who first wrote:

> *Living with only one Hope*
> *that if someone*
> *just one person*
> *was willing*
> *and i was to let them*
> *they would come over these Walls*

She did let me in and as a result, Hanna (a.k.a. Gabriele, et al) had made the painstaking journey of moving beyond the walls that had kept her a prisoner of so much emotional pain and self-abhorrence. Together, we had fought the demons of her past, we had met head on the torment that was *their life*, and replaced it with a life of love, caring and compassion for one another.

I knew that this phase of the rocky road on which we had traveled together was nearing completion when she shared with me these words: "You don't know what it means to me to close my eyes and see rainbows instead of the mother's face." I cried with joy. I asked her if she felt forgiven. Her face glowed as she softly, yet with a new certainty, said, "Yes. I'm beginning to have closure with my past."

As for me, she helped me find my pot at the end of the rainbow—this book. Thank you Hanna for living, for your wisdom and your ardent determination to heal. Oh yes, and for teaching me how to play cribbage.

Hanna Chapter 9:

To Life

> *"Far away there in the sunshine are my highest aspirations. I may not reach them, but I can look up and see their beauty, believe in them, and try to follow where they lead."*
> **—Louisa May Alcott**

I used to wonder what it would be like not to hear the constant roaring, or have so many voices commenting on my every word and action. The "peanut gallery" was what I learned to call it. All my life I had lived with this constant background noise that it was both a comfort and a trial. Then one day I suddenly realized that everything inside was very quiet. I no longer heard the cries or screams, or the voices that had always been there. At first I was afraid of this silence, and then I just felt lonely. I told Rachel about this new quiet. She was both excited (for it meant progress) and understanding of my discomfort (it was something new for me). What this quiet represented was integration. It was the loss of everyone's individual voices and it meant that for the first time in twenty-six years, I was starting to become whole.

At first I did not know what to do. After all, I had always been able to count on the others to do things for me. I suddenly found that if I did not do something that needed to be done, like paying the bills, then it simply would not get done. When I realized this, I wanted to panic, and believed that I would not be able to handle my newfound responsibility. I was angry that everyone I had always counted on had gone away. Slowly I came to realize, with Rachel repeating herself over and over, that even though Mike, Stephana, TOB, Mathew, Cobalt, Andrea, Chris, Little Catherine, TBF and Tigger were no longer there, they were still a part of me. That meant that all I had to do was call on them when I needed help with something and they would be there helping me. The only difference was that they would not take over—it would still be me doing all the work. They were now just a part of me, and they always would be. They were just aspects of my personality. They always had been. I believe that if the abuse had never happened in the first place, they never would have split off. And for the first time in my life, I started to feel some real anger about everything that had been done to all of us. But showing it was another matter. The persons responsible were no longer around, and so I could not direct my anger at them.

I also had to learn to ask for help when I could not handle something. When I discovered that some of my biggest "protectors" were no longer there, I had to start listening to the ones that were still with me. The most obvious one was Randy. When I started wanting to hurt myself, he would tell me over and over to call Rachel. If I would not listen, he would start to threaten me. The one that really sticks in my mind is the night that I was driving around at 1:30 a.m., not knowing what to do, but wanting to hurt myself very badly. Randy kept telling me that I needed to stop and talk to Rachel. I kept telling him to shut up and go away. Finally he got so angry with me that he told me, "If you don't call her or let me, I am going to slam on the brakes and make the car stop. I will not let you back out to make it go again. And if the car is stopped in the middle of the street, a policeman is going to think something is wrong and will come to find out. Then you will have to try and explain *me*." I must admit that I was livid with him and made some threats of my own. But I gave in. What else could I do? Finally, I let him call Rachel.

When he told her what he had done, she, of course, thought that he was brilliant. I strongly disagreed.

The problem was that I did not want to listen to Randy. The two of us had never been friends and I thought that he was a pest. I had to change my way of thinking. He did not want to die. And then I started to find out that he did not want me to die either. He wanted me to live and he wanted me to be happy. When I first started to realize this, I was shocked and I wanted to deny it. However when I finally admitted it, I found that it gave me a sense of comfort: someone inside was thinking of me and what would be best for me. This was one step on the path of a new beginning.

Randy was not the only one who wanted to help me in this new process. Copula alerted me to problems with the children that were still around, and told me that, "It be okay." For the first time in our life, she stopped her self-destructive ways and wanted me to stop mine. She started to keep a constant vigil over ones like Sandy and asked Randy for help when there were problems. She also called and talked to Rachel (sometimes over my objections), so that Rachel could work with Sandy.

Because of Rachel and Copula's work with Sandy, I started to eat and sleep through the night for the first time in my life. When Rachel heard of this she exclaimed: "This is so exciting! This is something to celebrate, like maybe with dinner or something!" I was dumbfounded. No one in my life had ever felt that sleeping for nine to ten hours a night was a *good* thing. After I got home, I called Rachel back and asked if she was serious about this dinner thing.

"Absolutely." She went on to tell me that to her, this meant that all our hard work was really starting to pay off. I was on my way to becoming well. She kept her word and took me out to dinner at a nice restaurant. It was a very special night for me. After that night, I started sleeping on a regular basis from about 10:30 p.m. until 9:30 a.m., with some variations. But it became a regular habit that around 10:30 p.m. I would try to go to bed and go to sleep. I knew that the hard part would be getting up and Morrie, Rachel's husband, took it upon himself to call me in the morning to make sure that I got up so that I would stay on this sleep schedule. At first I thought Rachel had asked him, and when I found out that she had not, I was touched. It seemed that for the first time in my life, two people were ready and willing to help me start to learn how to live life at its most basic.

Because I was no longer sleep deprived, I started to think a little more clearly, and found that my depression (something that had plagued all of us most of our life), was starting to really lift. I noticed was that I no longer seemed to be constantly thinking about death, and actually started thinking about the future and even wanting to make plans for it. This was so new that it was almost scary, but I decided to keep doing it. It was fun!

One time when I was very overwhelmed with everything that was going on in my life, and told Rachel that I needed time to figure things out on my own, she told me, "No you don't. Talk about what is going on. The last thing that you need to do right now is pull away."

Pulling away and running away were old ways of dealing with things. They did not work then and they would not work now. The first thing that I did was I started learning to ask questions: "Is it okay to feel pride?" "Am I doing the right thing?" "Will you help me figure this out?" "Do I have to grow up?"

Growing up is something that none of us wanted to do—especially me. When Rachel told me that I was growing up, I would get pissed off. I think Randy put it best when he said, "Growing up means getting big and when you get big, you get *MEAN*. "I don't want to get mean." I agreed wholeheartedly with him. I wanted to stay a teenager. Growing up was simply not in my game plan. I believed that if I became the same age as the body, then I would no longer know how to have any fun. Whenever Rachel and I talked about this subject, I flat out refused to accept what she was saying. Then when she agreed with Randy, but not me, and told him that he did not need to grow up, I was hurt. But there was a reason for him to stay a child. Everyone needs a child inside, someone to play and have fun with, who is not afraid to cry or feel, and who can look at life with innocent eyes. Randy was that someone for me. In addition, he would be able to help me in the same ways that he always had, like making sure that I took care of the body by sleeping and eating, and reminding me to ask for help when I needed it.

One of the things that I began to realize was that, while for the first time in my life I felt safe, I wanted more. I started to dream of owning my own house, having a better job, and going back to school to get a degree. The kids were happy in their existence, they were safe, being fed and getting sleep, and they believed that there was nothing more that they wanted or needed. I did not agree with them. After all, one's goals, or lack thereof, dictated one's life. I know that I may not meet all my goals or realize all my dreams, but it should not stop me from having either.

I started to notice that I was not always panicking whenever something stressful happened. I also noticed that I was not as angry as I used to be. I felt like I was reinventing myself all over again. I was not the same person that I had been when we first walked into Rachel's office on May 27, 1998. I was calmer, more self-assured, and more trusting of the people around me.

The time that I worked with Rachel was filled with desperation, fear, anger, and sadness; a time of great pain and sorrow. I had to learn all about the value of my life, and come to terms with my past so that I would have a future. I also had to learn that my life was a *blessing,* and that the events of my past did not dictate who or what I was, or would be. I learned that I am my own person. Rachel continually told me that she believed that I was the most courageous person that she had ever known and that I was a good, kind, gentle soul, and she was honored to know me. I was never sure until one night after Shabbat services when I asked Rachel the following question: "Do you think I am a blessing?"

I needed to know what she thought, and so I was relieved when she answered, "Yes." What I could not see were the tears in her eyes. For me to even ask such a question was an indication of a new pattern of thinking about myself and the world. I was learning that there is such a thing as hope, and love, and friendship. I still had my ups and downs. I still had moments when all would seem lost, but I learned that the trick was learning to wait those moments out, and to find hope within myself and in the world around me.

Over the course of two years, I grew, learned, and was loved and cared about more than in the twenty-eight years preceding. My adventure and journey towards integration was almost over. I still had to learn to live alone as one person, and to accept all of my faults and weakness, along with my strengths and abilities. This is a process will be a lifelong one, and something that will take time and patience. But I now know that I am a new woman. I now know that life is stronger than death, light will overcome the darkness, and the night will be followed by a new day. This knowledge is a genuine gift for me and for this gift, among others, I have one person to thank above all the others: Rachel Gunner.

Rachel: Postscript

> *As you ought not attempt to cure the eyes without the head, or the head without the body, neither ought you attempt to cure the body without the soul...for the part will never be well unless the whole is well.*
>
> **—Plato**

I kept wondering what had happened to Randy and the other children. They had not said good-bye, like Mikhail had when we knew it was time to go. Would they come around when Hanna got scared again? Or was Hanna really whole!

The answers to my questions came at 11:30 p.m., on January 11, 2000. The phone rang. My heart panicked! I had not gotten one of these late night calls in a long time. I picked up the receiver with trepidation and heard my dear friend Randy's voice.

"It's me, Rachel... I had to talk to you one more time to say good-bye."

I felt a lump in my throat beginning to form. He really was no longer going to be there to protect Hanna, or to spy for me and give me pointers about my behavior. Would Hanna and I handle life without his lust for living, his amazing insights, and his playfulness?

He told me he was in a special place—it was white. "You know, like you used to tell us: think of a white light, because it's warm, protective, loving and healing."

"We are all here and there are no streets or buildings. It's not noisy, but not too quiet. Stephana, Mikhail, TOB, Mathew, Brian, Cryin, even Tigger, are here and they're doing good. Tigger even talks now and doesn't bite her arm. Sandy can eat her flowers here. She's happy."

It's hard to describe the immense joy I was experiencing. These children, who had only known pain, suffering and fear, were *happy*. He continued to tell me they were all proud of Hanna, especially Mikhail and Stephana, who saw her working as they used to. Stephana was especially pleased that she was "fucking like a rabbit." Then he asked me what that meant. He sure knew how to put me on the spot.

He got very quiet and then timidly asked, "Will you miss me?"

I could barely speak. As my tears were welling up, I said, "Yes, very much, but you will always be with us. I'm always reminding Hanna to eat like you did."

He laughed and added, "Remember, don't think like a big person. Even though Hanna has grown up, she still gets scared. And promise me that you will treat her like you did me. You used to hug me and talk softly when I was frightened. You didn't get angry with me. If you do this, it will be like giving more than my life."

He was still so wise. He was right. I still had a tendency to be more tolerant with children. I promised him I would always be there to help Hanna.

Another silence, and a longer one this time. Then he blurted out, "I love you, Rachel. We all love you."

The tears just streamed down my face as I returned his love.

He said, "This white place is nice, but I never thought I would have to leave. I guess it's okay as long as you don't forget me."

I reiterated that I could never forget him. After all, without him, I could never have done my job. He taught me patience, acceptance and how to be creative, traits that will help me throughout my life. He felt good about that, and then he said the final words, "Goodbye. We love you," and the silence felt deafening. He was really gone.

Hanna got on the phone and felt confused. She had only heard "the last phrase." I told her what happened and could hear tears in her voice.

"Does that mean I'm whole?"

I said, "Yes."

She wanted to know if it would last. She had never felt that way before.

I didn't know conclusively. After all, this whole integration had happened so quickly, naturally, almost effortlessly. But intuitively, I trusted that Tigger's wounds had been healed, and that meant Hanna's core no longer was empty and traumatized. This was replaced by love and a sense of calm and security.

All those endless hours of tireless work had paid off. I could truly rejoice in our success. Love had been victorious. One lost child had been found.

Hanna: Postscript

Dear reader:

I leave you with one last thought. Life is a precious gift that humans seem to take for granted. The evening news is as far as you need go for proof of this tragedy. Children are our future—and the human race *cannot* afford to allow their continued abuse and suffering at the hands of adults who are their so-called caregivers. I hope that if nothing else comes from this book, that it has made you stop, look around, and think about the children you know. Do loving, nurturing adults care for them? Do you know of a child that needs your help? If the answer is yes, then do something! Take action. If you do not know what to do, then find someone who does.

If, on the other hand, you do not know of any child in need of help, then you need only go to your local volunteer organization to discover someone who knows many such children. Your involvement need not be a full time job, but think about giving an hour a week. That hour can make all the difference to a child, and it will help. It will make a difference. Like I wrote before, "hope can be borrowed." So you, in giving a little of your time, will be donating your hope to a good cause. So I ask: *What can you, dear reader, do to help make the world a better place?*

Shalom,
Hanna Gabriele

Rachel: Epilogue

Rose Mary Evans, in *Childhood's Thief*, writes that, "Every once in awhile we may be lucky enough to meet someone who brings out the best in us. They do it by their example more than anything else, by giving us the best of themselves. Gabriele, et al, worked tirelessly with me to meet head on the demons of her childhood; to learn to feel emotions without fear; to change years of conditioning in which they were taught that they were evil; to stand up to these wrongful teachings; and to move on a different path—the path of healing and life. They taught me about patience, acceptance, commitment, devotion, and love between human beings. Although so different, a bond existed from the moment our eyes met. This bond moved me to never give up, as so many therapists before me had, but to work harder and find answers when resistance to my interventions were high. They brought out my best as a therapist, woman, and mother. I cherished my time with my daughter, recognizing that this relationship can either help empower a child to grow, to love, to dream, to believe that the sky indeed has no limits, or it can destroy the spirit, such that a child's dreams become nightmares, flowers die, birds no longer sing, and childhood is lost.

This unique relationship has made me question our therapeutic teachings, in particular, how we learn to view our clients as labels and diagnoses rather than human beings. Gabriele, et al, felt ashamed of who she was, afraid of who she was, and convinced that she could never be loved and be accepted by others. I am convinced that she could never have healed if I had treated her in the way most theories on DID advise. They view the client as having a severe personality disorder and who will take years to heal, if at all. The plan is to medicate to calm down the delusional, psychotic *parts*; hospitalize when suicidal; and use whatever it takes to calm the angry aggressive ones. How wrong! Gabriele was a person first, who deserved to be treated with respect, caring, compassion and dignity. Beneath the psychoses and acting out were terrified children begging to be nurtured, but unaware of how to accept an emotion called love. Yes, it demands long hours on the part of the therapist, a strong commitment and dedication to the process of therapy and healing, confidence and a belief that what one has embarked upon is the right path. Yes, I had moments when I questioned my interventions and myself. But professionals should constantly be reevaluating their skills and limitations. I always returned to my resolve that Gabriele, et al, deserved to be given a chance to live a whole life.

Was it worth it? Yes, absolutely. Death became Hanna. She wanted her own child. She wanted to love in the way I loved, to parent how I parented. She wanted me to be Godmother. This was the greatest testimony of our relationship and her commitment to life. She moved beyond those walls. She showed the others the way until one by one, they ventured into the new world, a world where laughter and tears could be heard as the sounds and voices of life.

Hanna: Epilogue

It is hard for me to explain what it was like to finally choose life. It was a very gradual process and took some months, and a lot of work. It was not easy and at times it was extremely painful. There were many times when I wanted to turn back, to go back to my old ways of death, self-destruction, and dissociation. I did not always feel that life was a viable path for me and at times, felt that Rachel was delusional for believing that I could live and be happy. I cannot call this a happy ending; there are no such things in life. But this is not the ending to my life, it is just the beginning of a new chapter. Have I enjoyed my trip? No, it has not been easy and I would rather have never had to take it in the first place. But I can say that if I could change anything, I would not. This has been a remarkable journey. And it all started with a simple phone call from a scared woman who no longer knew what to do.

In May of 1998, I, and the system that I was a part of, were ready to die. We were not sure if we could be helped, or if we even wanted help. We were not sure that there was anyone in the world that could help us or would stick it out to the very end. We found that person in Rachel Gunner. I do want to say that therapy is really a journey; the patient is the driver, and the therapist is a passenger/guide. When the therapy is "good," it can set a person free. When the therapy is "bad," it can be a trap. And we have now had both experiences. The simple fact of the matter is that not only did Rachel have to work at undoing years of damage caused by the abusers in our life, but she also had to undo the damage caused by pervious therapists and other mental health professionals. I feel that there are some therapists and mental health professionals that do not know what they are doing and should not be in the field. I also feel that there is too much importance placed on hospitalization and medication in the treatment of DID. I know that for me, this did not work, and I question if it really works for other people with this devastating disorder. I also feel that more research and questioning on the part of the mental health community needs to be undertaken, and hope that this book has raised questions about these practices, and that mental health professionals will start to look for better solutions for treating this disorder so that their patients can truly heal.

Throughout our therapy with Rachel, she has shown tenacity, imagination, and a willingness to do whatever was needed to help us heal, all the while maintaining her integrity and professionalism, traits that are rare in a professional, in my biased opinion.

Rachel has given us many gifts that we are thankful for. She showed us that we could heal and that we could live, not just survive. She showed me, Hanna, that I can have hopes and dreams. She taught me that I can be respected and loved as a human being, that I could be vulnerable and not be harmed for it, and could instead be comforted and protected while still being given the room I needed to grow. She taught me that it is okay to feel and just be, even when it is painful, and it is the last thing that a person wants to do. You don't have to die because of how you feel, or because you have emotions and express them. Rachel showed me another world where parents don't harm their children and God does not want the death of sinners. And when I had no hope and felt totally alone, she was willing to share hope, and constantly reminded me that I no longer had to endure my pain by myself. Rachel showed all of us what life really is all about. And we will forever remember that most special of gifts.

I am not sure what we have given her in return. Yes, I taught her how to play cribbage, but that was part of the deal to write this book with her. She has told me that she is a better person, a better mother and wife, and a better therapist, and that we have all taught her patience. I believe that she always had those qualities and abilities, maybe her experience with us brought them out more. All I know is that I am a better person because of everything that she has done for me, and for all that she taught me.

So, thank you Rachel. And, *L'Chaim!* To Life!

Appendix— "Randyisms"

Randy, the eight-year-old little boy, who first introduced me to all the personalities of this "system," became my helper, my ally, and often my teacher. Sometimes, I forgot he was just a little boy who hated using soap, who still needed my help, my support, my nurturing and above all, my love. Of course being Randy, he would remind me of that, and of how I wasn't making sense or understanding him and the others when I thought like a "big person." He was probably one of the wisest "little persons" I had ever met. He would observe people with the keenest of eyes, and then reflect on what he had seen with great clarity and innocence. I know we adults still have a lot yet to learn about human nature. We all need to open our eyes and see the world as a child does. Perhaps then, the world would be a better place—especially if we believed what Randy always knew: "Being nice is so much easier than being mean."

Let me share with you some of Randy's perceptions and wonderings. They are indeed gems.

1) **Anyway**: when people get off a subject and they want to get back to the original subject, they say, "Anyway…" and everyone knows that they are going to go back. They always say it in this high voice and

they draw it out real long, then everybody knows what they are about to do. People will even get quiet sometimes, because it seems that "anyway" is a very important word. It means that the person that is saying it is going to say something really important, or if someone else has interrupted them, then they are going to take back what they were talking about (control of the conversation) and everyone needs to listen to them again.

2) **Snorting**: (Randy's Favorite) If someone doesn't like what someone else has said, and he thinks that they are wrong and what they just said is "garbage," he makes a snorting sound just like a pig. I think that is because everyone knows that pigs snort and they (the pigs) eat garbage, and since lots of people don't like pigs, they make their sounds. It does not make sense to me, because I like pigs. They are very smart and they can be nice if you are nice to them. That is why I do not eat them. If I did not like them, I would not make their sound. If people don't snort, then they sigh like they are trying to blow what the other person said away. People also snort when they think that they have been told a lie, such as, "I didn't eat the last cookie" The other person always snorts and says, "Yea right," because they know that he/she is a cookie-monster. Why do people snort or sigh? Why not just say they don't like what the other person had to say?

3) **Gritting your teeth:** When people are very angry, but they are trying not to yell, they grit their teeth. I think it is because they are trying to hold onto their temper and not lose it. When you don't want to lose something, you hold onto it real tight. They also do not want to say the really bad things that they are thinking, so by gritting their teeth, they think that they can hold the words back. And the madder that they get, the more they grit their teeth.

4) **Big People vs. Little People:** Little people are supposed to ask questions, because they don't know everything, and big people know this. But big people think that others will think they are stupid if they ask questions or say that they don't know (even when a little person is the one asking them the question), so the big people make things up, thinking that no one else will know. However, when people find out, they know that he/she is making it up, and they think that they are, in fact, stupid. Sometimes they also make assumptions when they do not know what is really going on, and then they just make things worse. Why don't big people just follow the rule that there are no stupid questions and it is better to find out the truth than not to know? I think that a big person who can say that they do not know is a smart, big person, not a stupid one.

5) **Pulling your hair out:** "I don't understand this at all!" Why do people want to pull their own hair out when the person that they are really angry with is someone else? Why hurt yourself when you are mad at someone else? Why not just yell at them and tell them how mad you really are? It is so much better if you can just tell someone when you are mad. Then you can get over it and move on, and still be friends.

6) If big people hurt (abuse) little people and they say later that they are sorry, that is not enough. It is too late. The hurt has already been made. The best thing is for big people not to hurt little people in the first place.

Randy also had a lot of questions:
Why do people use colors to describe their feelings?
Green with envy; Blue for sad; Red for mad.
"Feelings are just feelings. Why make them into colors?"

If we adults all listened to our own inner children, I believe we would become more sensitive and compassionate to the children out there in the external world. Let Randy be our guide!

Rachel's Acknowledgments

I want to first and foremost, thank my husband and best friend, Morrie, whose love and support for this project and me has meant so much. His constant encouragement for Hanna and myself, as her healing process unfolded; his acceptance of those late hours and early morning phone calls; and above all, his belief in me, has been invaluable.

I want to thank my parents who gave me unconditional love and respect during my growing years and helped me have a solid foundation to become a caring, empathic person.

My daughter Sarah has been an inspiration to me. Her drive, determination and energy have kept me motivated and focused. My love and respect for her as my child helped me give to all the children in the system of Gabriele.

Thank you Randy, a wise young fellow whose own passion to live, his tenacity, and his will, helped guide this "big person" on the right path—when my own adult thoughts were faltering.

I owe deep gratitude to Dr. Rosa Eberly, former Assistant Professor of Rhetoric and Composition at the University of Texas at Austin, whose excitement and support for this book gave me great hope that it could be published. Her editing of the original manuscript taught me valuable lessons in how to write narrative clearly and distinctly, using the active rather than passive voice, as I tended to do.

I want to thank readers Professor Dana Cloud and Dawn Spinozza who offered their own editing and enthusiasm for this project.

Thank you Mindy Reed for your professional editing of the entire manuscript. Your positive critique encouraged me to finally get this book published.

Above all, thank you Hanna, for you courage to write your story with me, your amazing ability to overcome pain and suffering, your trust in me, your great gifts of humor, for those long hours typing our manuscript over and over again on the computer, and for becoming the woman I knew you would be when we crossed beyond those walls.

Hanna's Acknowledgments

Writing a book takes time and energy. It can also make you feel insane and sometimes, just plain stupid. At some point you find yourself looking at a paragraph and yelling, "This does not make any sense. What was I thinking? I'm no writer!" Then you see friends and have to tell them all about your writer's block and how you just know that this book is never going to be published, much less finished. They look at you and (if you're lucky), tell you that it is going to be okay. So without the support and understanding of the people around you, there is no way that anyone can ever write—or keep their sanity while trying. Because I know all of this, there are many people that I would like to thank. Most of them know who they are, but some of them are very special and without their time and patience, I could not have written this book:

I would like to thank Morrie Schulman for his encouragement, humor and understanding. I want to thank him for the time that he gave up with his wife so that she could work with me, first in therapy and later on this book. Thank you for being willing to read so many drafts of the various chapters, give feedback and praise, and for telling me over and over that I could write this book. Oh, and thanks for helping me fix the computer so many times—it kept me from throwing it in Town Lake.

Then there is Sarah Schulman, Rachel's daughter. She shared her mother—something that most teenagers do not do willingly, with grace, or with much understanding. You did both. Then you showed me what it means to be healthy, happy, frustrated, and sad, while not being scared to show it. You also showed me what tenacity and determination are all about. Thank you Sarah, you don't know what these gifts meant to me—I will always treasure them.

I would like to thank my foster mom—she has always been there in one way or another, and long after her job was "done." She really does have a heart of gold.

Congregation Beth Israel gave me a safe place to grow spiritually, and showed me what Judaism is all about in the process. You all have my undying gratitude.

Rabbi Elizabeth Dunsker, formerly of Congregation Beth Israel, gave me her time, ear, and knowledge. Thank you for giving me patience and acceptance. This meant the world to me, and you helped open up another world to me as well

To my roommates: thank you for putting up with my not doing my part of the housework, my insomnia, my moodiness, and for listening to me bitch, and for not taking it personally. Thanks also for just being great guys.

Finally to my therapist, co-author and friend, Rachel Gunner, I would like to thank you for being willing to learn from your mistakes, help me learn from mine, and for repeating yourself over and over when I refused to listen. Thank you for being there and for showing me what life is all about. Thanks also for understanding my writer's block; it really can be a brick wall. But one little question: Can we wait a little while before we write the next book?

Bibliography

Annadale's English Dictionary; London: Blackie and Son, 1951.

Apisdorf, Shimon. *Passover Survival Kit*; Baltimore: Leviathan Press, 1994.

Borysenko, Joan. *Guilt is the Teacher, Love is the Lesson*; New York: Warner Books, 1990.

Branden, Nathaniel. *The Psychology of Self Esteem*; New York: Bantam Books, 1980.

"Child Abuse." *Microsoft Encarta 1998 Encyclopedia*; Microsoft Corp., 1997.

Evans, Rose Mary. *Childhood's Thief, One Woman's Journey of Healing*; New York: Cosa Drew Books/Macmillan, 1994.

Everstine, Diana Sulliavan and L. Everstein; *Sexual Trauma in Children and Adolescents*; New York: Brunner/Mazel Inc., 1989.

Fromm, Eric. *The Art of Loving*; New York: Bantam Books, 1967.

Harper, James and Margaret H. Hoopes; *Uncovering Shame*; London: W.W. Norton & Co., 1990.

Janov, Arthur. *The Primal Scream*; New York: Dell Publishing, 1970.

Lynn, Steven Jay and Judith W. Rhue. *Dissociation*; London: Guilford Press, 1994.

Olsen, Sarah. *Becoming One*; Pasadena, CA: Trilogy Books, 1997.

Scheiber, Flora Rheta. *Sybil*; New York: Warner Books, 1973.

Schwartz, Ted. *Satanism: is your family safe?*; Grand Rapids, MI: Zondervan Publishing, 1988.

Shakespeare, William. *As You Like It*; Act II, Scene 7: New York: Oxford University Press, 1968.

Watkins, Helen. *Handbook of Hypnotic Suggestions and Metaphors*; "Suggestions for Raising Self Esteem": D. Corydon Hammond, 1990.

Rachel Gunner has a private practice in psychotherapy, life coaching and mediation in Austin, Texas. She has publically addressed audiences in radio and other public forums on issues such as relationships, intimacy, disability, mental health and women in the workplace. Ms. Gunner received her Masters in Social Work from McGill University. She has received awards and praise for her clinical skills. She is married and the mother of a Rhodes Scholar.

Printed in Great Britain
by Amazon